Jean Baudrillard

Selected Writings

Jean Baudrillard

Selected Writings

Second edition, revised and expanded

Edited and introduced by

Mark Poster

Stanford University Press
Stanford, California

Stanford University Press
Stanford, California
© 2001 by the Board of Trustees of the Leland Stanford Junior University

Originating publisher of the English edition:
Polity Press in association with Blackwell Publishers Ltd.

Cloth ISBN 0–8047–4272–3
Paper ISBN 0–8047–4273–1
A catalog record for this book has been applied for from the Library of Congress.

First edition published 1988

Last figure below indicates the year of this printing:
10 09 08 07 06 05 04

Typeset in 10.5 on 12 pt Sabon
by Kolam Information Services Pvt. Ltd, Pondicherry, India.

This book is printed on acid-free paper.

Contents

Acknowledgments

Permission has been granted for the reprinting or translation of the following works of Baudrillard.

Le Système des objets (Paris: Gallimard, 1968), pp. 255–83.

La Société de consommation (Paris: Gallimard, 1970), pp. 17–26, 93–123.

For a Critique of the Political Economy of the Sign, trans. Charles Levin (St Louis: Telos Press, 1981, original publication, 1972), pp. 130–63.

The Mirror of Production, trans. Mark Poster (St Louis: Telos Press, 1975, original publication, 1973), pp. 21–51, 111–29.

L'Échange symbolique et la mort (Paris: Gallimard, 1976), pp. 19–29, and "Symbolic Exchange and Death," trans. Charles Levin in *The Structural Allegory*, ed. John Fekete, *Theory and History of Literature*, vol. 11 (Minneapolis: University of Minnesota Press, 1984), pp. 54–73.

De la séduction (Paris: Editions Galilée, 1979), pp. 75–92, 107–15, 241–3.

Simulacra and Simulations, trans. Paul Foss, Paul Patton and Philip Beitchman (New York: Semiotext(e), 1983, original publication, 1981), pp. 1–13, 23–49.

*Designates new translation from the French, by Jacques Mourrain.

Les Stratégies fatales (Paris: Bernard Grasset, 1983), pp. 9–33, 259–73.

"The Masses: The Implosion of the Social in the Media," trans. Marie Maclean, *New Literary History*, vol. 16, no. 3 (Spring 1985), pp. 577–89.

Cool Memories, trans. Chris Turner (London: Verso, 1990) pp. 113–23.

The Gulf War Did Not Take Place, trans. Paul Patton (Bloomington: Indiana University Press, 1995) pp. 23–8, 41–50.

The Illusion of the End, trans. Chris Turner (Cambridge: Polity and Stanford: Stanford University Press, 1994) pp. 14–27.

The Perfect Crime, trans. Chris Turner (London: Verso, 1996) pp. 94–105.

Paroxysm: Interviews with Philippe Petit, trans. Chris Turner (London: Verso, 1998) pp. 7–25.

Douglas Kellner kindly reviewed my selections and made valuable suggestions. His book, *Jean Baudrillard: From Marxism to Postmodernism and Beyond* (1989) has a good bibliography of works by and on Baudrillard. Helen Tartar, my editor at Stanford, initiated this project, took on some of the duties often done by the volume editor, and encouraged me through its completion.

*Designates new translation from the French, by Jacques Mourrain.

Notes on the Translation

Words that appear in English in Baudrillard's original text, a practice that becomes increasingly prevalent in his writings, have been noted as such. Baudrillard rarely provides full citations in his own notes. The editor and translators have attempted to complete the citation, but in some cases this has proven impossible. At times Baudrillard cites French translations of English or American works which are unavailable in the United States. At other times Baudrillard's quotations have not been located anywhere in the text he cites. [Trans.] indicates a translator's addition to the notes.

EDITOR'S NOTE

We have preserved the spelling and punctuation practices of the translations we have taken from elsewhere. Our own translations use American spelling and punctuation practices.

Introduction

Mark Poster

Baudrillard has developed a theory to make intelligible one of the fascinating and perplexing aspects of advanced industrial society: the proliferation of communications through the media. This new language practice differs from both face to face symbolic exchange and print. The new media employ the montage principle of film (unlike print) and time-space distancing[1] (unlike face to face conversation) to structure a unique linguistic reality. Baudrillard theorizes from the vantage point of the new media to argue that a new culture has emerged, one that is impervious to the old forms of resistance and impenetrable by theories rooted in traditional metaphysical assumptions. Culture is now dominated by simulations, Baudrillard contends, objects and discourses that have no firm origin, no referent, no ground or foundation. In this sense, what Walter Benjamin wrote about "the age of mechanical reproduction,"[2] Baudrillard applied to all reaches of everyday life.

Baudrillard began his writing with *The System of Objects* (1968) and *Consumer Society* (1970) as an effort to extend the Marxist critique of capitalism to areas that were beyond the scope of the theory of the mode of production. He gradually abandoned Marxism, a process that is traced in the pages of this volume, developing his position along lines that have affinities with poststructuralists like Foucault and Derrida. Baudrillard found that the productivist metaphor in Marxism was inappropriate for comprehending the status of commodities in the post-World War II era. Only a semiological model, he argues, can decipher the meaning structure of the modern commodity. But the commodity embodies a communication structure that is a departure from the traditional understanding of the sign. In a commodity the relation of word, image or meaning and referent is broken and restructured so that its force is directed, not to the referent of use value or utility, but to desire.

Like the poststructuralists, Baudrillard rejects traditional assumptions about referentiality. As Lyotard put it, the metanarratives of the past have collapsed, creating a new theoretical situation in which the concept can no longer pretend to control or grasp its object.[3] In Baudrillard's terms, "hyperreality" is the new linguistic condition of society, rendering impotent theories that still rely on materialist reductionism or rationalist referentiality. In these respects, Baudrillard's work is important to the reconstitution of critical theory, and, more generally, appeals to those who would attempt to grasp the strange mixture of fantasy and desire that is unique to late-twentieth-century and early-twenty-first-century culture.

The selections in this volume represent a cross section of Baudrillard's writings from 1968 to 1997 and are drawn mostly from his major books. Most of the selections have previously been translated but are reprinted here because they are out of print, inaccessible, or are necessary to present the full range of Baudrillard's works. In the first edition of *Jean Baudrillard: Selected Writings* (1988), my intention was to make Baudrillard's writings available to non-French readers and thus stimulate the critical reception of his work. That has certainly been accomplished by now. The purpose of the second edition is to provide new readers of Baudrillard with an overview of his thought. Since Baudrillard's position shifted in the course of his career, the selections are presented in chronological order. The following brief introduction to the trajectory of his thought, with indications of his relation to other currents of French and German intellectual movements, might assist the reader unfamiliar with this often difficult material.

In *The System of Objects* (1968) Baudrillard initiated a comprehensive rethinking of the thesis of consumer society from a neo-Marxist perspective, one that relied on both Freudian and Saussurean themes. He explores the possibility that consumption has become the chief basis of the social order and of its internal classifications. He argues that consumer objects constitute a classification system that codes behavior and groups. As such, consumer objects must be analyzed by use of linguistic categories rather than those of Marxian or liberal economics, Freudian or behaviorist psychology, anthropological or sociological theories of needs. Consumer objects have their effect in structuring behavior through a linguistic sign function. Advertising codes products through symbols that differentiate them from other products, thereby fitting the object into a series. The object has its effect when it is consumed by transferring its "meaning" to the individual consumer. A potentially infinite play of signs is thus instituted which orders society while providing the individual with an illusory sense of freedom and self-determination. *The System of Objects* went beyond earlier discussions of consumer society by systematically imposing linguistic categories to reveal the force of the code.

In *Consumer Society* (1970) Baudrillard provided numerous concrete examples of his analysis of consumer objects as a code. He also undertook a critique of discussions of consumer society in the fields of economics and sociology. These disciplines were unable to capture the novelty of consumerism because economics was burdened by a doctrine of *homo economicus*, the free individual acting in the marketplace and sociology was hampered by a notion of individual taste and a determinist concept of society. Against these positions Baudrillard effectively shows that a semiological analysis reveals that consumer objects constitute a system of signs that differentiate the population. This system of signs cannot become intelligible if each sign is related to each object, but only through the play of difference between the signs. In some of the most remarkable pages he has written, he indicates how consumer objects are like hysterical symptoms; they are best understood not as a response to a specific need or problem but as a network of floating signifiers that are inexhaustible in their ability to incite desire. Still a Marxist, Baudrillard goes on to argue that the reproduction of the mode of production has become dependent upon the expansion of consumption, on the reproduction of the act of consumption, thus inaugurating a new epoch in the history of capitalism.

For a Critique of the Political Economy of the Sign (1972) was a unique attempt to develop a radical theory of language as a supplement to Marxism. The title essay is a brilliant "deconstruction" of structuralism. In Ferdinand de Saussure's theory of the sign, the signifier or word is distinguished from both the signified or mental image and the referent. Saussure then marvels at the arbitrariness of the signifier and shows how it is constituted by structural relations with other signifiers. Baudrillard reverses this strategy: Saussure's problem only arises because he has *separated* the elements of the sign in the first place, using the signified and the referent as "alibis." Political economy has a similar strategy: it separates the commodity into exchange value (price) and use value only then to have use value as the alibi for exchange value. Just as Marx exposed the strategy behind the theory of the commodity in political economy, Baudrillard does the same for the theory of the sign by undermining the formalism of the theory of the sign. He has thus prepared the way for a historical analysis of the sign as the mode of signification within capitalism, a task accomplished in *The Mirror of Production* (1973). *For a Critique of the Political Economy of the Sign* goes further than Henri Lefebvre, Roland Barthes, the *Tel Quel* group or Mikhail Bakhtin in opening the path to a social critique of language because it historicizes both the structural and the social aspects of the sign.

The Mirror of Production marks Baudrillard's parting of the ways with Marxism. Henceforth the critique of the political economy of the sign is presented not as a supplement to the critique of political economy, but as its successor, as the new basis for critical social theory. The book was written with a force and systematicity that was not equaled again by Baudrillard. Each of Marx's major positions (the concept of labor, the dialectic, the theory of the mode of production, the critique of capital) are in turn revealed as mirror images of capitalist society. Marxism emerges in Baudrillard's pages not as a radical critique of capitalism but as its highest form of justification or ideology. For example, the anthropology of capitalism is *homo economicus*; the anthropology of Marxism is man as self-producer. In both cases humanity is equated with labor. Marxism does not have enough conceptual distance from political economy, Baudrillard contends, to serve as its theoretical gravedigger.

Baudrillard does not rest with a critique of Marxism: he goes on to develop what is perhaps the pinnacle of his early writings, i.e., a historical theory of sign structures. The weakness of Saussure's structural linguistics and Barthes's semiology was their ahistoricity, the formalism of their categories. Baudrillard remedies this deficiency by outlining the structural stages of the formation of contemporary language usage. He argues, somewhat nostalgically, that pre-industrial societies maintained a "symbolic" structure to communications: signs included words that were attached to referents and were uttered in a context that held open their possible reversal by others. During the Renaissance language began to lose its reciprocity when an abstract code, analogous to money, slowly transformed them.[4] Hence the era of the sign emerged. Baudrillard now theorizes capitalism as a reflection of this change at the level of the economy, a subordinate aspect of the history of modes of signification. In the late twentieth century, signs become completely separated from their referents, resulting in a structure that resembles the signal: signifiers act like traffic lights, emitting meanings to which there is no linguistic response. The composite organization of such signifiers is termed the code by Baudrillard, a concept which he never adequately defines. The code operates by extracting signifieds from the social, redeploying them in the media as "floating signifiers." TV ads especially but not exclusively constitute a new language form in which the code transmits signifiers to the population who are subject to this "terrorist" mode of signification.

Symbolic Exchange and Death (1976) draws out the pessimistic implications of the theory of the code, marking a change in Baudrillard's political stance.[5] As the politics of the 1960s receded so did Baudrillard's radicalism: from a position of firm leftism he gradually moved to one of bleak fatalism. In *Symbolic Exchange and Death* he searches desperately for a source of radicalism that challenges the absorptive capacities of a system with no fixed determinations, a world where anything can be anything else, where everything is both equivalent to and indifferent to everything else, a society, in short, dominated by the digital logic of the code. Baudrillard's morose conclusion is that only death escapes the code, only death is an act without an equivalent return, an exchange of values. Death signifies the reversibility of signs in the gift, a truly symbolic act that defies the world of simulacra, models and codes.[6]

Symbolic Exchange and Death is flawed by the totalizing quality of Baudrillard's writing. Still, the value of the book lies in the refinements it provides of many of the themes of Baudrillard's earlier works. In it Baudrillard grapples, as nowhere before, with the problem of characterizing the structure of communication in a world dominated by the media. This important issue, too much neglected by critical theory, becomes the mainstay of his writing after 1976. Although Baudrillard treats this theme with hyperbole and vague formulations, he has initiated a line of thought that is fundamental to a reconstitution of critical theory. While this project is somewhat akin to the recent work of Jürgen Habermas, Baudrillard wrestles with the communication structure of the media, whereas his German counterpart pursues the quixotic end of defining the "ideal speech situation," a theoretical task that is grounded in the metaphysics of the Enlightenment and is unlikely to prove fruitful for a critical theory of contemporary society.[7]

In *On Seduction* (1979) Baudrillard makes a turn toward a post-structuralist critique of the hermeneutics of suspicion. Theories that deny the surface "appearance" of things in favor of a hidden structure or essence, theories like Marxism, psychoanalysis, and structuralism, come under renewed attack. These interpretive strategies all privilege forms of rationality. Against them Baudrillard celebrates the Nietzschean critique of the "truth" and favors a model based on what he calls "seduction." Seduction plays on the surface thereby challenging theories that "go beyond" the manifest to the latent. Although *On Seduction* elicited a barrage of criticism by feminist theorists (Jane Gallop, Luce Irigaray, and others) for its seeming masculinist and heterosexist formulations, Victoria Grace defends Baudrillard's book on feminist grounds by pointing to his model of symbolic exchange as a basis for a nonessentialist feminism.[8] The model of seduction also prefigures Baudrillard's later term, the hyper-real, with all of its postmodernist implications. At the close of the book, Baudrillard tentatively suggests that seduction might be a mode to replace the model of production.

In *Simulacra and Simulations* (1981) Baudrillard extends, some would say hyperbolically extends, his theory of commodity culture. No longer does the code take priority over, or even precede, the consumer object. The distinctions between object and representation, thing and idea are no longer valid. In their place Baudrillard fathoms a strange new world constructed out of models or simulacra which have no referent or ground in any "reality" except their own. Simulations are different from fictions or lies in that the former not only present an absence as a presence, the imaginary as the real. They also undermine any contrast to the real, absorbing the real within itself. Instead of a "real" economy of commodities that is somehow bypassed by an "unreal" myriad of advertising images, Baudrillard now discerns only a hyperreality, a world of self-referential signs. He has moved from the TV ad which, however, never completely erases the commodity it solicits, to the TV newscast which creates the news if only to be able to narrate it, or the soap opera whose daily events are both referent and reality for many viewers.

If Baudrillard's argument of hyperreality has a modicum of validity, the position of the New Critics and deconstructionists must be taken seriously. The self-referentiality of language, which they promote against materialists, phenomenologists, realists, and historicists as the key to textual analysis, now, in Baudrillard's hands, becomes the first principle of social existence in the era of high-tech capitalism. Critical theory faces the formidable task of unveiling structures of domination when no one is dominating, nothing is being dominated and no ground exists for a principle of liberation from domination. If Auschwitz is the sign of total tyranny and the industrial production of death, the world of "hyperreality" bypasses the distinction between death and life.[9]

The pessimistic implications of *Simulacra and Simulations* are brought home in *Fatal Strategies* (1983). Here Baudrillard attempts to think the social world from the point of view of the object, a seeming oxymoron. Like the poststructuralists, Baudrillard assumes that the era of the representational subject is past. One can no longer comprehend the world as if the Kantian categories of time, space, causality, etc. are necessary, universal paths to truth. Baudrillard takes this to imply that the subject no longer provides a vantage point on reality. The privileged position has shifted to the object, specifically to the hyperreal object, the simulated object. In place of a logic of the subject, Baudrillard proposes a logic of the object, and this is his "fatal strategy." As the reader will discover, the world unveiled by Baudrillard, the world from within the object, looks remarkably like the world as seen from the position of postmodernists.[10]

Baudrillard is not disputing the trivial issue that reason remains operative in some actions, that if I want to arrive at the next block, for example, I can assume a Newtonian universe (common sense), plan a course of action (to walk straight for x meters), carry out the action, and finally fulfill my goal by arriving at the point in question. What is in doubt is that this sort of thinking enables a historically informed grasp of the present in general. According to Baudrillard, it does not. The concurrent spread of the hyperreal through the media and the collapse of liberal and Marxist politics as master narratives, deprives the rational subject of its privileged access to truth. In an important sense individuals are no longer citizens, eager to maximize their civil rights, nor proletarians, anticipating the onset of communism. They are rather consumers, and hence the prey of objects as defined by the code. In this sense, only the "fatal strategy" of the point of view of the object provides any understanding of the present situation.

In a more recent essay "The Masses: The Implosion of the Social in the Media" (1985), Baudrillard recapitulates the theme of his work in the 1980s: the media generate a world of simulations which is immune to rationalist critique, be it Marxist or liberal. The media present an excess of information and they do so in a manner that precludes response by the recipient. This simulated reality has no referent, no ground, no source. It operates outside the logic of representation. But the masses have found a way of subverting it: the strategy of silence or passivity.[11] Baudrillard thinks that by absorbing the simulations of the media, by failing to respond, the masses undermine the code.[12] Whatever the value of this position, it represents a new way of understanding the impact of the media. Instead of complaining about the alienation of the media or the terrorism of the code, Baudrillard proposes a way out: silence. Critical theorists will certainly not remain silent about Baudrillard's paradoxical revolutionary strategy. In fact, more suggestive approaches to the question of resistance have been offered by Pierre Bourdieu and Michel de Certeau in France and cultural studies theorists in the English-speaking world. In *The Practice of Everyday Life* (1984), for example, de Certeau argues that the masses resignify meanings that are presented to them in the media, in consumer objects, in the layout of city streets.[13] To many, de Certeau's position on resistance seems more heuristic and more sensible than Baudrillard's.

Baudrillard's writing up to the mid-1980s is open to several criticisms. He fails to define his major terms, such as the code; his writing style is hyperbolic and declarative, often lacking sustained, systematic analysis when it is appropriate; he totalizes his insights, refusing to qualify or delimit his claims. He writes about particular experiences, television images, as if nothing else in society mattered, extrapolating a bleak view of the world from that limited base. He ignores contradictory evidence such as the many benefits afforded by the new media, for example, by providing vital information to the populace (as in the Vietnam War) and counteracting parochialism with humanizing images of foreigners. The instant, worldwide availability of information has changed the human society forever, probably for the good.

Nevertheless Baudrillard's work is an invaluable beginning for the comprehension of the impact of new communication forms on society. He has introduced a language-based analysis of new kinds of social experience, experience that is sure to become increasingly characterstic of advanced societies. His work shatters the existing foundations for critical social theory, showing how the privilege they give to labor and their rationalist epistemologies are inadequate for the analysis of the media and other new social activities. In these regards he joins with Derrida's critique of logocentrism and Foucault's critique of the human sciences. Unlike these poststructuralist thinkers, Baudrillard fails to reflect on the epistemological novelties he introduces, rendering his work open to the changes outlined above. For the critical theorist, Baudrillard represents the beginning of a line of thought, one that is open to development and refinement by others.

In the 1990s Baudrillard's important concept of simulation becomes entwined with another category, that of the virtual. If simulation captures the culture of television, the virtual points to a further imbrication of the human with information machines, that is, the Internet. The selections added to the second edition of this volume explore this theme.

Before turning to the question of the virtual, another, more autobiographical side of Baudrillard's more recent writing requires some attention. In 1987 Baudrillard published the first volume of *Cool Memories*, offering reflections on his life from 1980 to 1985. Since then he has added two more volumes covering the years until 1995. In 1987 another small book appeared by him, *L'autre par lui-même*, sarcastically subtitled "Habilitation," which also put his life and work into review. The volumes of *Cool Memories* are written in aphoristic style, reminiscent of Nietzsche's writing and of Theodor Adorno's

Minima Moralia (1974).[14] The selection included here gives the reader a sense of this unusual aspect of Baudrillard's work.

Baudrillard's writing begins to be sprinkled with the term "virtual" and "virtual reality" as early as 1991. But he uses these terms interchangeably with "simulation," and without designating anything different from the earlier usage. Concerning the Gulf War of 1991, for example, he writes in his controversial book *The Gulf War Did Not Take Place* (1995): "In our fear of the real, of anything that is too real, we have created a gigantic simulator. We prefer the virtual to the catastrophe of the real, of which television is the universal mirror."[15] The virtual is equivalent to the hyperreal or to simulation. In all cases the electronically mediated communication stands in a double relation to "reality." Mediated communication both reflects reality by first delivering signals from a sender to a receiver that are somehow about it; and, second, it substitutes for reality in the sense that it never simply represents reality but puts forth its own reality. Simulations and the virtual, for Baudrillard, are different from reality but always stand in a certain relation to it.

In *The Illusion of the End* (1994) Baudrillard continues to question the validity of humanist perspectives in an age of the hyperreal. A telos or an end, both in the sense of a purpose and a terminus, no longer, he charges, orient the contemporary traveler. Metanarratives that provide coherence for the individual and disciplines like history which fix societies firmly in a temporal continuum have lost their verisimilitude. In the selection included in this volume, Baudrillard indicates how events, the building blocks of historicizing narratives, have lost their ground in the culture of simulation. *The Illusion of the End* is the centerpiece of Baudrillard's writing on the new millennium, a theme to which he returns several times to show how a chronology of new beginnings and final apocalypses provides only a sham alibi for cultural exposition.

With *The Perfect Crime* (1996), Baudrillard begins to reflect upon the role of his own thought in relation to the culture he has so relentlessly dissected. To paraphrase Marx speaking of communism as the solution to the riddle of history, Baudrillard has become virtual and knows himself to be such: he argues that his critical theory of simulation has become nothing less than the principle of reality.[16] The world has become virtual; Baudrillard's theory is no longer true, but real. What use then for Baudrillard's writings in the age of virtual reality machines? He explains:

The idea of simulacrum was a conceptual weapon against reality, but it has been stolen. Not that it has been pillaged, vulgarized, or has become commonplace (which is true but has no consequence), but because simulacra have been absorbed by reality which has swallowed them and which, from now on, is clad with all the rhetoric of simulation. And to cap it all, simulacra have become reality! Today, simulacra guarantee the continuation of the real. The simulacrum now hides, not the truth, but the fact that there is none, that is to say, the continuation of Nothingness.[17]

Since simulation is now the dominant form of culture, Baudrillard's concept of simulation, he thinks, no longer functions as a concept. Somewhat immodestly he suggests that "theory [his own] that realizes itself is no longer a theory."[18] Eschewing critical theory, he now proposed "radical thought" as an alternative. If nothing else, the notion of radical thought refutes those who find nothing but bleakness in his writing. Baudrillard's engagement with the present emerges as vital and committed.

In the interviews collected as *Paroxysm* (1998), Baudrillard reviews his work of the 1990s, reflecting upon new concerns with globalization and technology. New media in particular draw his attention. He explores the Internet, communications satellites, cryogenics, biotechnology, nanotechnology, robotics, and other phenomena that appear to him to intensify the culture of the hyperreal that he exposed long ago. In his Wellek Library Lectures at the University of California, Irvine, in 1999, he addressed the question of reproductive technologies in relation to the problem of the virtual, confirming his attentiveness to the issue of gender.[19] The selection from *Paroxysm* included here also finds him renewing his critique of history and temporal orientation from *The Illusion of the End*.

NOTES

1   Anthony Giddens has developed this concept especially in *The Constitution of Society* (Cambridge: Polity, 1984).

2   Walter Benjamin, "The Work of Art in the Age of Mechanical Reproduction," *Illuminations*, ed. Hannah Arendt and trans. Harry Zohn (New York: Schocken, 1969) pp. 217–52.

3   Jean François Lyotard, *The Postmodern Condition: A Report on Knowledge*, trans. G. Bennington and B. Massumi (Minneapolis: University of Minnesota Press, 1984) p. xxiv.

4   This idea is developed further by Jean-Joseph Goux in *Économie et symbolique* (Paris: Seuil, 1973) and later by Marc Shell in *The Economy of Literature* (Baltimore: Johns Hopkins, 1978).

5 See the interview with Baudrillard by Maria Shevtsova, "Intellectuals [sic] Commitment and Political Power," in *Thesis Eleven* (1984–5) nos 10–11, pp. 166–75. Baudrillard presents his current views on politics. Also interesting in this regard is Robert Maniquis, "Une Conversation avec Jean Baudrillard," *UCLA French Studies* (1984–5) vols. 2–3, pp. 1–22.

6 It might be noted that Baudrillard defends the notion of the symbolic against psychological theories. See his critique of psychoanalysis in "Beyond the Unconscious: the Symbolic," *Discourse* (1981) vol. 3, pp. 60–87.

7 See Jürgen Habermas, *The Theory of Communicative Action: Volume 1, Reason and the Rationalization of Society*, trans. Thomas McCarthy (Boston: Beacon and Cambridge: Polity, 1984), originally published in 1981.

8 Victoria Grace, *Baudrillard's Challenge: A Feminist Reading* (New York: Routledge, 2000).

9 See Baudrillard, "Fatality or Reversible Imminence: Beyond the Uncertainty Principle," *Social Research* (Summer, 1982) vol. 49, no. 2, pp. 272–93 for a discussion of the chance/necessity distinction in relation to the world of hyperreality.

10 See Hal Foster, ed., *The Anti-Aesthetic: Essays on Postmodern Culture* (Port Townsend, Washington: Bay Press, 1983), especially the brilliant piece by Fredric Jameson. It might be noted that Baudrillard himself is a contributor to this collection.

11 See also Jean Baudrillard, *A l'ombre des majorités silencieuses . . .* (Paris: Utopie, 1978), available in English as *In the Shadow of the Silent Majority* (New York: Semiotext(e), 1983).

12 See Baudrillard's essays "What Are You Doing After the Orgy?," *Artforum* (October, 1983) pp. 42–6; "Astral America," *Artforum* (September, 1984) pp. 70–4, and *L'Amérique* (Paris: Grasset, 1985) for descriptions of life in the new world of the media, especially in the United States where the tendencies Baudrillard discusses are most advanced.

13 Michel de Certeau, *The Practice of Everyday Life*, trans. Steven Rendell (Berkeley: University of California Press, 1984). See also, Pierre Bourdieu, *La Distinction: critique sociale du jugement* (Paris: de Minuit, 1979) or in the English translation by Richard Nice (Cambridge: Harvard University Press, 1984).

14 Theodor Adorno, *Minima Moralia*, trans. E. Jephcott (London: New Left Books, 1974).

15 Jean Baudrillard, "The Reality Gulf," *The Guardian* (January 11, 1991) p. 25. See also the discussion of Baudrillard's political analysis in James Der Derian, "Simulation: The Highest Stage of Capitalism?," in Douglas Kellner, ed., *Baudrillard: A Critical Reader* (Oxford: Blackwell, 1994) pp. 189–208.

16 This Hegelian gesture of identifying one's thought with reality is also made by Derrida, albeit more modestly, when he reports that, on a trip

to Moscow, his then Soviet hosts defined Perestroika as deconstruction: "...a Soviet colleague said to me, scarcely laughing, 'But deconstruction, that's the USSR today.'" Jacques Derrida, "Back from Moscow, in the USSR," in Mark Poster, ed., *Politics, Theory and Contemporary Culture* (New York: Columbia University Press, 1993) p. 222. Derrida relates this incident anew in *Specters of Marx,* trans. Peggy Kamuf (New York: Routledge, 1994) p. 89. One is tempted to make a comment about the role of intellectuals in the age of mass media as a condition for this new insistence on the inscription of theory in history.

17   Jean Baudrillard, *Le Crime parfait* (Paris: Galilée, 1995) p. 146. This translation by François Debrix appeared in "Radical Thought," *Ctheory,* (April 19, 1995) vol. 18, pp. 1–2 and is taken from a pamphlet Baudrillard published as *La Pensée radicale* (Paris: Sens & Tonka, 1994) which appears in revised form in *Le Crime parfait.* It has been published in print as "Radical Thought," trans. David Macey and Mike Gane in *Parallax* (September 1995) vol. 1, pp. 53–62.

18   "Radical Thought," p. 19.

19   These lectures will be published as *The Vital Illusion* by Columbia University Press in January 2001.

1

The System of Objects

Garap

If we consume the product as product, we consume its meaning through advertising. Let us imagine for the moment modern cities stripped of all their signs, with walls bare like a guiltless conscience [*conscience vide*]. And then GARAP appears. This single expression, GARAP, is inscribed on all the walls: pure signifier, without a signified, signifying itself. It is read, discussed, and interpreted to no end. Signified despite itself, it is consumed as sign. Then what does it signify, if not a society capable of generating such a sign? And yet despite its lack of significance it has mobilized a complete imaginary collectivity; it has become characteristic of the (w)hole of society. To some extent, people have come to "believe" in GARAP. We have seen in it the sign (*indice*) of the omnipotence of advertising. And one might think that it would suffice to associate the sign GARAP with a product for it to impose itself immediately. Yet, nothing is less certain, and the trick of advertisers has been, in effect, to conceal this, since individual resistances could express themselves on an explicit signified. Whereas consensus, even when ironic, establishes itself on faith in a pure sign. All of a sudden, the real signified of advertising appears in all its purity. Advertising, like GARAP, is mass society, which, with the aid of an arbitrary and systematic sign, induces receptivity, mobilizes consciousness, and reconstitutes itself in the very process as the collective.[1] Through advertising mass society and consumer society continuously ratify themselves.[2]

A new humanism?

Serial conditioning

In the themes of competition and "personalization" we are better able to see the underlying system of conditioning at work. In fact, the ideology of competition, which under the sign of "freedom" was previously the golden rule of production, has now been transferred entirely to the domain of consumption. Thousands of marginal differences and an often formal differentiation of a single product through conditioning have, at all levels, intensified competition and created an enormous range of precarious freedoms. The latest such freedom is the random selection of objects that will distinguish any individual from others.[3] In fact, one would think that the ideology of competition is here dedicated to the same process, and consequently to the same end, as it is in the field of production. If we can still view consumption as an independent activity (*profession libérale*), allowing the expression of personal preferences, while on the contrary production appears to be quite definitively planned, this is simply because the techniques of psychological conditioning (*planification*) are not as developed as those of economic planning.

We still want what others do not have. We are still at the competitive and heroic stage of product selection and use, at least in Western European societies (in the East the problem is deferred) where the systematic replacement and cyclical synchronization of models has not yet been established as it has in the United States.[4] Psychological resistance? The force of tradition? More simply, the majority of people are still far from achieving the economic status where only one repertoire of models would be available as all commodities would comply with the same maximum standard; where diversity would matter less than possessing the "latest" model – the imperative fetish of social valorization. In the United States 90 per cent of the population experience no other desire than to possess what others possess. From year to year, consumer choices are focused *en masse* on the latest model which is uniformly the best. A fixed class of "normal" consumers has been created that coincides with the whole population. If we have not yet reached this stage in Europe, we can already clearly detect, according to the irreversible trend towards the American model, the ambiguity of advertising: it *provokes us to compete*; yet, through this imaginary competition, *it already invokes a profound monotony*, a uniformula (*postulation uniforme*), a devolution in the bliss of the consuming masses.[5] Advertising tells us, at the same time: "Buy this, for it is like nothing else!" ("The meat of the elite, the cigarette of the *happy few!*"[6] etc.); but also: "Buy this because everyone else is using it!"[7] And this is in no way contradictory. We can imagine that each individual feels unique while resembling everyone else: all we need is a schema of collective and mythological projection – a model.[8]

Hence, one could think that the ultimate goal of consumer society (not through any technocratic Machiavellianism, but through the ordinary structural play of competition) is the functionalization of the consumer and the psychological monopolization of all needs – a unanimity in consumption which at last would harmoniously conform to the complete consolidation and control of production.

Freedom by default

Everywhere today, in fact, the ideology of competition gives way to a "philosophy" of self-fulfillment. In a more integrated society individuals no longer compete for the possession of goods, they actualize themselves in consumption, each on his own. The leitmotiv is no longer one of selective competition, it is personalization for all. At the same time, advertising has changed from a commercial practice to a theory of the praxis of consumption, a theory that crowns the whole edifice of society. We find this illustrated by American advertisers (Dichter, Martineau, etc.)[9] The reasoning is simple:

1 Consumer society (objects, products, advertising), for the first time in history, offers the individual the opportunity for total fulfillment and liberation;
2 The system of consumption constitutes an authentic language, a new culture, when pure and simple consumption is transformed into a means of individual and collective expression. Thus, a "new humanism" of consumption is opposed to the "nihilism" of consumption.

The first issue: self-fulfillment. Dr Dichter, director of the Institute for Motivational Research, defines at once the problematics of this new man:

We are now confronted with the problem of permitting the average American to feel moral even as he flirts, even when he spends, or when he buys a second or third car. One of the fundamental problems of prosperity is to sanction and to justify its enjoyment, to convince people that making their life enjoyable is moral, and not immoral. One of the fundamental tasks of all advertising, and of every project destined to promote sales, should be to permit the consumer freely to enjoy life and confirm his right to surround himself with products that enrich his existence and make him happy.[10]

Hence, through planned (*dirigée*) motivation we find ourselves in an era where advertising takes over the moral responsibility for all of society and replaces a puritan morality with a hedonistic morality of pure satisfaction, like a new state of nature at the heart of hypercivilization. Dichter's last sentence is ambiguous, however. Is the goal of advertising to liberate man's resistance to happiness or to promote sales? Do advertisers wish to reorganize society in relation to satisfaction, or in relation to profit? "No," answers Bleustein-Blanchet (Preface to Packard's *The Hidden Persuaders*), "motivation research does not threaten the freedom of individuals and in no way impinges on the individual's right to be rational or irrational."[11] There is too much honesty in these words, or perhaps too much cunning. Dichter is more clear. What we have are *conceded* freedoms: "To permit the consumer..." we must allow men to be children without being ashamed of it. "Free to be oneself" in fact means: free to project one's desires onto produced goods. "Free to enjoy life" means: free to regress and be irrational, and thus adapt to a certain social organization of production.[12] This sales "philosophy" is in no way encumbered by paradox. It advertises a rational goal (to enlighten people about their wants) and scientific methods, in order to promote irrational behavior in man (to accept being only a complex of immediate drives and to be satisfied with their satisfaction). Even drives are dangerous however, and the neo-sorcerers of consumption are careful not to liberate people in accordance with some explosive end state of happiness. They only offer the resolution of tensions, that is to say, a freedom *by default*: "Every time a tension differential is created, which leads to frustration and action, we can expect a product to overcome this tension by responding to the aspirations of the group. Then the product has a chance of success."[13] The goal is to allow the drives that were previously blocked by mental determinants (*instances*) (taboo, superego, guilt) to crystallize on objects, concrete determinants where the explosive force of desire is annulled and the ritual repressive function of social organization is materialized. The freedom of existence that pits the individual against society is dangerous. But the freedom to possess is harmless, since it enters the game without knowing it. As Dr Dichter claims, this freedom is a moral one. It is even the ultimate in morality, since the consumer is simultaneously reconciled with himself and with the group. He becomes the perfect social being. Traditional morality only required that the individual conform to the group; advertising "philosophy" requires that they now conform to themselves, and that they resolve their own conflicts. In this way it invests him morally as never before. Taboos, anxieties, and neuroses, which made the individual a deviant and an outlaw, are lifted at the cost of a regression in the security of objects, thus reinforcing the images of the Father and the Mother. The irrationality of drives increasingly more "free" at the base will go hand in hand with control increasingly more restricted at the top.

A new language?

A second issue: does the object/advertising system form a language? The idealist-consumerist philosophy is based on the substitution of lived and conflictual human relations with "personalized" relations to objects. According to Pierre Martineau, "Any buying process is an interaction between the personality of the individual and the so-called 'personality' of the product itself."[14] We make believe that products are so differentiated and multiplied that they have become complex beings, and consequently purchasing and consumption must have the same value as any *human* relation.[15] But precisely: is there an active syntax? Do objects instruct needs and structure them in a new way? Conversely, do needs instruct new social structures through the mediation of objects and their production? If this is the case, we can speak of a language. Otherwise, this is nothing more than a manager's cunning idealism.

Structure and demarcation: the brand

The act of buying is neither a lived nor a free form of exchange. It is a preconditioned activity where two irreducible systems confront each other. At the level of the individual, with his or her needs, conflicts, and negativity, the system is fluid and disconnected. At the level of products, in all of their positivity, the system is codified, classified, discontinuous, and relatively integrated. This is not interaction but rather the forced integration of the system of needs within the system of products. Of course, together they constitute a system of signification, and not merely one of satisfaction. But a syntax is necessary for there to be "language": the objects of mass consumption merely form a repertoire. Let me explain.

At the stage of artisanal production objects reflect the contingent and singular character of needs. While the two systems are adapted to one another they are no better integrated since they depend on the relative coherence of needs, which are fluid and contingent: there is no objective technological (*technique*) progress. Since the beginning of the industrial era, manufactured goods have acquired coherence from technological organization (*l'ordre technique*) and from the economic structure. The system of needs has become less integrated than the system of objects; the latter imposes its own coherence and thus acquires the capacity to fashion an entire society.[16] We could add that "the machine has replaced the unlimited series of variables (objects 'made to measure' in accordance with needs) with a limited number of constants."[17] Certainly we can identify the premises of a language in this transformation: internal structuration, simplification, transition to the limited and discontinuous, constitution of *technemes* and the increasing convergence of these technemes. If the artisanal object is at the level of speech (*parole*), industrial technology institutes a set of expressions (*langue*). But a set of expressions (*langue*) is not language (*langage*):[18] it is not the concrete structure of the automobile engine that is expressed but rather the form, color, shape, the accessories, and the "social standing" of the object. Here we have the tower of Babel: each item speaks its own idiom. Yet at the same time, through calculated differences and combinatorial variations, serial production demarcates significations, establishes a repertoire and creates a lexicon of forms and colors in which recurrent modalities of "speech" can be expressed: nevertheless, is this language? This immense paradigm lacks a true syntax. It neither has the rigorous syntax of the technological level, nor the loose syntax of needs: floating from one to the other like an extensive repertoire, reduced, at the level of the quotidian, to an immense combinatorial matrix of types and models, where incoherent needs are distributed (*ventiler*) without any reciprocal structuration occurring. Needs disappear into products which have a greater degree of coherence. Parceled out and discontinuous, needs are inserted arbitrarily and with difficulty into a matrix of objects. Actually, the world of objects is overwhelmed by the absolute contingency of the system of individual needs. But this contingency is in some way indexed, classified, and demarcated by objects: it can therefore be directed (and this is the system's real objective on the socioeconomic level).

If the industrial technological order is capable of shaping our society it is, in a way that is contradictory, a function of society's coherence and incoherence: through its structural (technological) coherence "at the top;" and through the astructural (yet directed) incoherence of the process of product commercialization and the satisfaction of needs "at the base." We can see that language, because it is actually neither consumed nor possessed by those who speak it, still maintains the possibility of the "essential" and of a syntax of exchange (the structuration of communication). The object/advertising system, however, is overwhelmed by the "inessential" and by a destructured world of needs; it is content to satisfy those needs in their detail, without ever establishing any new structures of collective exchange.

Martineau adds: "There is no simple relationship between kinds of buyers and kinds of cars, however. Any human is a complex of many motives... which may vary in countless combinations. Nevertheless the different makes and models are seen as helping people give expression to their own personality dimensions."[19] He goes on to illustrate this "personalization" with a few examples.

> The conservative, in choosing and using a car, wishes to convey such ideas as dignity, reserve, maturity, seriousness... Another definite series of automotive personalities is selected by the people wanting to make known their middle-of-the-road moderation, their being fashionable... Further along the range of personalities are the innovators and the ultramoderns... "[20]

No doubt Martineau is right: it is in this way that people define themselves in relation to objects. But this also shows that it is not a language, but rather a gamut of distinguishing criteria more or less arbitrarily indexed on a gamut of stereotyped personalities. It is as if the differential system of consumption significantly helped to distinguish:

1 Within the consumer, categories of needs which now have but a distant relation with the person as a lived being;
2 Within society, categories or "status groups," recognizable in a specific collection of objects. The hierarchized gamuts of objects and products play exactly the same role as the set of distinguishing values played in previous times: the foundation of group morality.

On both levels, there is solicitation, coerced grouping and categorization of the social and personal world based on objects, developing into a hierarchal repertoire without syntax; that is, into *a system of classification, and not a language*. It is as if, through the demarcation of the social, and not by a dialectic, an imposed order was created, and through this order, for each group, a kind of objective future (materialized in objects): in short, a grid in which relations become rather impoverished. The euphoric and wily "motivation" philosophers would like to persuade themselves and others that the reign of the object is still the shortest path to freedom. They offer as proof the spectacular mélange of needs and satisfactions, the abundance of choice, and the festival of supply and demand whose effervescence can provide the illusion of culture. But let us not be fooled: objects are *categories of objects* which quite tyrannically induce *categories of persons*. They undertake the policing of social meanings, and the significations they engender are controlled. Their proliferation, simultaneously arbitrary and coherent, is the best vehicle for a social order, equally arbitrary and coherent, to materialize itself effectively under the sign of affluence.

The concept of "brand," the principal concept of advertising, summarizes well the possibilities of a "language" of consumption. All products (except perishable foods) are offered today as a specific acronym: each product "worthy of the name" has a brand name (which at times is substituted for the thing itself: Frigidaire or Xerox). The function of the brand name is to signal the product; its secondary function is to mobilize connotations of affect:

> Actually, in our highly competitive system, few products are able to maintain any technical superiority for long. They must be invested with overtones to individualize them; they must be endowed with richness of associations and imagery; they must have many levels of meaning, if we expect them to be top sellers, if we hope that they will achieve the emotional attachment which shows up as brand loyalty.[21]

The psychological restructuration of the consumer is performed through a single word – Philips, Olida, General Motors – a word capable of summing up both the diversity of objects and a host of diffuse meanings. Words of synthesis summarizing a synthesis of affects: that is the miracle of the "psychological label." In effect this is the only language in which the object speaks to us, the only one it has invented. Yet, this basic lexicon, which covers walls and haunts consciences, is strictly asyntactic: diverse brands follow one another, are juxtaposed and substituted for one another without an articulation or transition. It is an erratic lexicon where one brand devours the other, each living for its own endless repetition. This is undoubtedly the most impoverished of languages: full of signification and empty of meaning. It is a language of signals. And the "loyalty" to a brand name is nothing more than the conditioned reflex of a controlled affect.

But is it not a beneficial thing, our philosophers object, to tap into deep motives (*forces profondes*) (in order to reintegrate them within the impoverished system of labels)? Liberate yourself from censorship! Overcome your superego! Take courage in your desires! Yet, are we actually tapping into these deep motives in order to articulate them in language? Does this system of signification give meaning to presently hidden aspects of the individual, and if so, to which meanings? Let us listen once again to Martineau:

> Naturally it is better to use acceptable, stereotyped terms . . . This is the very essence of metaphor . . . If I ask for a "mild" cigarette or a "beautiful" car, while I can't define these attributes literally, I still know that they indicate something desirable . . . The average motorist isn't sure at all what "octane" in gasoline actually is . . . But he does know vaguely that it is something good. So he orders "high-octane" gasoline, because he desires this essential quality behind the meaningless surface jargon.[22]

In other words, the discourse of advertising only arouses desire in order to generalize it in the most vague terms. "Deep motives," rephrased in their simplest expression, are indexed on an institutionalized code of connotations. And in fact, "choice" only confirms the collusion between this *moral* order and my most profound whims (*velléités*): this is the alchemy of the "psychological label."

The stereotyped evocation of "deep motives" is simply equivalent to *censorship*. The ideology of personal fulfillment, the triumphant illogicality of drives cleansed of guilt (*deculpabilisées*), is nothing more than a tremendous endeavor to materialize the superego. *It is a censor, first of all, that is "personalized" in the object.* The philosophers of consumption may well speak of "deep motives" as the immediate possibilities of happiness which need only be liberated. But the unconscious is conflictual and, in so far as advertising mobilizes it, it is mobilized as conflict. Advertising does not liberate drives. Primarily, it mobilizes phantasms which block these drives. Hence, the ambiguity of the object, in which individuals never have the opportunity to surpass themselves, but can only re-collect themselves in contradiction, in their desires and in the forces that censor their desires. We have here a general schema of gratification/frustration:[23] under the formal resolution of tensions and an incomplete regression, the object serves as a vehicle for the perpetual rechannelling of conflicts. This could possibly be a definition of the specific form of contemporary alienation: in the process of consumption internal conflicts or "deep drives" are mobilized and alienated in the same way as labor power is in the process of production.

Nothing has changed, or rather it has: restrictions in personal fulfillment no longer manifest themselves through repressive laws, or norms of obedience. Censorship operates through "unconstrained" behaviors (purchasing, choice consumption), and through spontaneous investment. In a way, it is internalized in pleasure (*jouissance*).

A *universal code: social standing*

The object/advertising system constitutes a system of signification but not language, for it lacks an active syntax: it has the simplicity and effectiveness of a code. It does not structure the personality; it designates and classifies it. It does not structure social relations: it demarcates them in a hierarchical repertoire. It is formalized in a universal system of recognition of social statuses: a code of "social standing."

Within "consumer society," the notion of status, as the criterion which defines social being, tends increasingly to simplify and to coincide with the notion of "social standing." Yet "social standing" is also measured in relation to power, authority, and responsibility. But in fact: There is no real responsibility without a Rolex watch! Advertising refers explicitly to the object as a necessary criterion: You will be judged on . . . An elegant woman is recognized by . . . etc. Undoubtedly objects have always constituted a system of recognition (*repérage*), but in conjunction with, and often in addition to, other systems (gestural, ritual, ceremonial, language, birth status, code of moral values, etc.). What is specific to our society is that other systems of recognition (*reconnaissance*) are progressively withdrawing, primarily to the advantage of the code of "social standing." Obviously this code is more or less determinant given the social and economic level; nevertheless, the collective function of advertising is to convert us all to the code. Since it is sanctioned by the group the code is moral, and every infraction is more or less charged with guilt. The code is totalitarian; no one escapes it: our individual flights do not negate the fact that each day we participate in its collective elaboration. Not believing in the code requires at least that we believe that others sufficiently believe in it so that we can enter the game, even if only ironically. Even actions that resist the code are carried out in relation to a society that conforms to it. This code has positive aspects, however:

1 It is no more arbitrary than any other code: the manifestation of value, even for ourselves, is the car we periodically trade in, the neighborhood we live in, and the multitude of objects that surround us and distinguish us from others. But that's not all. Have not all codes of values always been partial and arbitrary (moral codes to begin with)?

2 The code is a form of socialization, the total secularization of signs of recognition: it is therefore involved in the – at least formal – emancipation of social relations. Objects do not only facilitate material existence through their proliferation as commodities, but, generalized into signs of recognition, they facilitate the reciprocation of status among people. The system of social standing, at least, has the advantage of rendering obsolete the rituals of caste or of class and, generally, all preceding (and internal) criteria of social discrimination.

3 The code establishes, for the first time in history, a *universal* system of signs and interpretation (*lecture*). One may regret that it supplants all others. But conversely, it could be noted that the progressive decline of all other systems (of birth, of class, of positions) – the extension of competition, the largest social migration in history, the ever-increasing differentiation of social groups, and the instability of languages and their proliferation – necessitated the institution of a clear, unambiguous, and universal code of recognition. In a world where millions of strangers cross each other daily in the streets the code of "social standing" fulfills an essential social function, while it satisfies the vital need of people to be always informed about one another.

Nevertheless:

1 This universalization, this efficiency is obtained at the price of a radical simplification, of an impoverishment, and of an almost irrevocable regression in the "language" of value: "All individuals are described in terms of their objects." Coherence is obtained through the formation of a combinatorial matrix or a repertoire: hence a functional language is established, but one that is symbolically and structurally impoverished.

2 The fact that a system of interpretation (*lecture*) and recognition is today applied by everyone, or that value signs are completely socialized and objectified does not necessarily lead to true "democratization." On the contrary, it appears that the *constraint of a single referent only acts to exacerbate the desire for discrimination*. Within the very framework of this homogeneous system, we can observe the unfolding of an always renewed obsession with hierarchy and

distinction. While the barriers of morality, of stereotypes, and of language collapse, new barriers and new exclusions are erected in the field of objects: a new morality of class, or caste, can now invest itself in the most material and most undeniable of things.

Society is not becoming any more transparent, even if today the code of "social standing" is in the process of constituting an immediately legible, universal structure of signification, one that enables the fluid circulation of social representations within the group hierarchy. The code provides the image of a false transparency, of a false legibility of social relations, behind which the real structures of production and social relations remain illegible. A society would be transparent only if knowledge of the order of signification was also knowledge of the organization (*ordre*) of its structures and of social facts. This is not the case with the object/advertising system, which only offers a code of significations that is always complicit and opaque. In addition, if the code's coherence provides a formal sense of security, that is also the best means for it to extend its immanent and permanent jurisdiction over all individuals in society.

Conclusion: towards a definition of "consumption"

I would like to conclude the analysis of our relation to objects as a systematic process, which was developed on different levels, with a definition of "consumption," since it is here that all the elements of an actual practice in this domain converge.

In fact we can conceive of consumption as a characteristic mode of industrial civilization on the condition that we separate it fundamentally from its current meaning as a process of satisfaction of needs. Consumption is not a passive mode of assimilation (*absorption*) and appropriation which we can oppose to an active mode of production, in order to bring to bear naive concepts of action (and alienation). From the outset, we must clearly state that consumption is an active mode of relations (not only to objects, but to the collectivity and to the world), a systematic mode of activity and a global response on which our whole cultural system is founded.

We must clearly state that material goods are not the objects of consumption: they are merely the objects of need and satisfaction. We have all at times purchased, possessed, enjoyed, and spent, and yet not "consumed." "Primitive" festivities, the prodigality of the feudal lord, or the luxury of the nineteenth-century bourgeois – these are not acts of consumption. And if we are justified in using this term for contemporary society, it is not because we are better fed, or that we assimilate more images and messages, or that we have more appliances and gadgets at our disposal. Neither the quantity of goods, nor the satisfaction of needs is sufficient to define the concept of consumption: they are merely its preconditions.

Consumption is neither a material practice, nor a phenomenology of "affluence." It is not defined by the food we eat, the clothes we wear, the car we drive, nor by the visual and oral substance of images and messages, but in the organization of all this as signifying substance. Consumption is *the virtual totality of all objects and messages presently constituted in a more or less coherent discourse.* Consumption, in so far as it is meaningful, is *a systematic act of the manipulation of signs.*

The traditional object-symbol (tools, furniture, even the house), mediator of a real relation or of a lived (*veçue*) situation, clearly bears the trace, in its substance and in its form, of the conscious and unconscious dynamics of this relation, and is therefore not arbitrary. This object, which is bound, impregnated, and heavy with connotation, yet actualized (*vivant*) through its relation of interiority and transitivity with the human gesture or fact (collective or individual), is not consumed. *In order to become object of consumption, the object must become sign*; that is, in some way it must become external to a relation that it now only signifies, a-signed *arbitrarily* and noncoherently to this concrete relation, yet obtaining its coherence, and consequently its meaning, from an abstract and systematic relation to all other object-signs. It is in this way that it becomes "personalized," and enters in the series, etc.: it is never consumed in its materiality, but in its difference.

The conversion of the object to a systematized status of signs entails a concomitant modification in the human relation, which becomes a relation of consumption. That is to say, human relations tend to be consumed (*consommer*) (in the double sense of the word: to be "fulfilled," and to be "annulled")[24] in and through objects, which become the necessary mediation and, rapidly, the substitutive sign, *the alibi*, of the relation.

We can see that what is consumed are not objects but the relation itself – signified and absent, included and excluded at the same time – it is *the idea of the relation* that is consumed in the series of objects which manifests it.

This is no longer a lived relation: it is abstracted and annulled in an object-sign where it is consumed.

At all levels, the status of the relation/object is orchestrated by the order of production. All of advertising suggests that the lived and contradictory relation must not disturb the "rational" order of production. It is to be consumed like all the rest. In order to be integrated it must be "personalized." We rejoin here, in its conclusions, the formal logic of commodities analyzed by Marx: needs, affects, culture, knowledge – all specifically human capacities are integrated in the order of production as commodities, and materialized as productive forces in order to be sold. Today every desire, plan, need, every passion and relation is abstracted (or materialized) as sign and as object to be purchased and consumed. For example, a couple's ultimate objective becomes the consumption of objects that previously symbolized the relation.[25]

The beginning of Georges Perec's novel *Les Choses: A Story of the Sixties* reads:

> The eye, at first, would glide over the gray rug of a long corridor, high and narrow. The wall would be cabinets, whose copper fittings would gleam. Three engravings...would lead to a leather curtain, hanging from large rings of black-veined wood, that a simple gesture would suffice to slide back...[Then] It would be a living room, about twenty-one feet long and nine feet wide. On the left, in a sort of alcove, a large couch of worn black leather would be flanked by two book cases in pale wild-cherry wood, on which books would be piled helter-skelter. Above the divan a nautical chart would run the whole length of the wall panel. Beyond a little low table, under a silk prayer rug attached to the wall with three copper nails with large heads, and balancing the leather hanging, another divan, perpendicular to the first, upholstered in light brown velvet, would lead to a small piece of furniture on high legs, lacquered in dark red, with three shelves that would hold bric-a-brac; agates and stone eggs, snuffboxes, jade ashtrays, [etc.]...Farther on...small boxes and records, next to a closed phonograph of which only four machine-turned steel knobs would be visible...[26]

Clearly nothing here has any symbolic value, despite the dense and voluptuous nostalgia of the "interior" decor. It only suffices to compare this description with Balzac's description of an interior to see that here human relations are not inscribed in things: everything is sign, pure sign. Not a single object has presence or history, and yet everything is full of reference: Oriental, Scottish, *early American*, etc.[27] All these objects *merely possess a characteristic singularity*: in difference (their mode of referentiality) they are abstract, and are combined precisely by virtue of this abstraction. We are in the domain (*univers*) of consumption.[28]

The rest of the story provides a glimpse of the function of such an object/sign system: far from symbolizing a relationship, these objects are external to it in their continual "reference." They describe the absence of a relationship, which everywhere can be read in the two partners' absence to one another. Jerome and Sylvia do not exist as a couple: their only reality is "Jerome-and-Sylvia," as sign in pure complicity with the system of objects which signifies it. Which is not to say that objects are mechanically substituted for an absent relation, to fill a void, no: they *describe* the void, the locus of the relation, in a development which actually is a way of not experiencing (*vivre*) it, while always referring to the possibility of an experience (except in the case of total regression). The relation is not absorbed in the absolute positivity of objects, it is articulated on objects, as if through so many material points of contact on a chain of signification. In most cases however, this signifying configuration of objects is impoverished, schematic, and bound, where the *idea of a relation*, unavailable to experience, merely repeats itself over and over again. Leather couch, phonograph, bric-a-brac, jade ashtrays: it is the *idea of a relation* that is signified in these objects, "consumed" in them, and consequently annulled as a lived relation.

This defines consumption as a systematic and *total idealist practice*, which far exceeds our relations to objects and relations among individuals, one that extends to all manifestations (*registres*) of history, communication and culture. Thus, the need for culture is alive: but in the collector's book or in the dining room lithograph; only the *idea* is *consumed*. The revolutionary imperative is alive, but unable to realize itself in practice; it is consumed in the idea of Revolution. As idea, Revolution is in fact external, and will be eternally consumable in the same way as any other idea. All ideas, even the most contradictory, can coexist as signs within the idealist logic of consumption. Revolution is signified, then, in a combinatorial terminology, in a lexicon of immediate terms, where it is presented as fulfilled, where it is "consumed."[29]

In the same way, objects of consumption constitute an idealist lexicon of signs, an elusive materiality to which the project of lived existence is referred. This can also be read in Perec:

> It sometimes seemed to them that a whole life could go harmoniously by between these book-lined walls, among these objects so perfectly domesticated that the two of them would end up believing that they had been forever created for their own use alone ... But they would not feel themselves tied down by them; on certain days they would go looking for adventure. Nothing they planned would be impossible.[30]

But it is precisely announced in the conditional, and the book renounces it: there are no longer any projects; there are only objects. Or rather, the project has not disappeared: it is satisfied in its realization as a sign located in the object. The object of consumption quite precisely is *that in which the project is "re-signed."*

This suggests that *there are no limits to consumption*. If it was that which it is natively taken to be, an absorption, a devouring, then we should achieve saturation. If it was a function of the order of needs, we should achieve satisfaction. But we know that this is not the case: we want to consume more and more. This compulsion to consume is not the consequence of some psychological determinant (*"qui a bu boira?"*) etc., nor is it simply the power of emulation. If consumption appears to be irrepressible, this is precisely because it is a total idealist practice which has no longer anything to do (beyond a certain point) with the satisfaction of needs, nor with the reality principle; it becomes energized in the project that is always dissatisfied [*deçu*] and implicit in the object. The project, made immediate in the sign, transfers its essential dynamics onto the systematic and indefinite possession of object-signs of consumption. Consequently, it must transcend itself, or continuously reiterate itself in order to remain what it is: a reason for living. The very project of life, segmented, dissatisfied, and signified, is reclaimed and annulled in successive objects. Hence, the desire to "moderate" consumption or to establish a normalizing network of needs is naive and absurd moralism.

At the heart of the project from which emerges the systematic and indefinite process of consumption is a frustrated desire for totality. Object-signs are equivalent to each other in their ideality and can proliferate indefinitely: and *they must* do so in order continuously to fulfill the absence of reality. It is ultimately because consumption is founded on a *lack* that it is irrepressible.

NOTES

1 In this tautological system of recognition, each advertising sign is already testimony in itself, since it always refers to itself at the same time as an advertisement.

2 Is this not to some extent the function of the totemic system according to Lévi-Strauss? The social order offers itself the vision of its own lasting immanence in the arbitrary totemic sign. Advertising would thus be the result of a cultural system which has reverted (in the gamut of "brand names") to a poverty of sign codes and archaic systems.

3 The term competition (*concurrence*) is ambiguous: that which "competes" (*concourt*) at the same time rivals and converges. It is

through relentless rivalry that one "concurs" (*concourt*) most assuredly towards the same point. At a certain level of technological development (particularly in the United States) all objects of one category become equivalent. The imposition of creating distinctions only forces them every year to change as a group, and according to the same norms. In addition, the extreme freedom of choice imposes on everyone the ritual constraint of owning the same things.

4 In the United States, the essentials – automobiles, refrigerators – have a tendency to last a predictable and mandatory period of one year (three for the TV, a little longer for the apartment). The norms of social standing eventually metabolize the object. They impose a metabolism of an increasingly rapid cycle, which is far from nature's cycles, and yet at times curiously coincides with ancient seasonal ones. It is this new cycle, and the need to observe it, which today establishes the genuine morality of the American citizen.

5 The phrase, *"une involution dans le sens bienheureux de la masse con-somatrice,"* has a dynamics created by the imagery of the word "involu-tion" (movement from heterogeneity to homogeneity) and by the duality of the word "sens" (both "meaning" and "direction"). [Trans.]

6 Original in English.

7 This is perfectly summarized in the ambiguity of the word "you" (*vous*) in advertising, for example in: "Guinness is good for you." Is this a particular form of politeness (hence personalizing) or an address to the collectivity? "You" singular or "you" plural? Both. It is each individual to the extent that he or she resembles all others: in fact, the gnomic you (*vous*) = they (*on*). (Cf. Leo Spitzer, *Sprache im technischen Zeitalter*, 1964, p. 961).

8 When it was fashionable to wear one's hair *à la Bardot*, each girl in style was unique in her own eyes, since she never compared herself to the thousand other similar girls, but each to Bardot herself, the sublime archetype from whom originality flowed. To a certain extent, this is not stranger than having four or five Napoleons in the same asylum. Con-sciousness here is qualified, not in the Real relation, but in the Imaginary.

9 Ernest Dichter is the author of *The Strategy of Desire* (Garden City, NY: Doubleday, 1960). Pierre Martineau is the author of *Motivation in Advertising: Motives that make People Buy* (New York: McGraw Hill, 1957). Baudrillard is not consistent or logical in his supply of references. Since we demand this of him in an English translation I have imposed coherence by inserting and extracting the reference from the text. [Trans.]

10 *The Strategy of Desire.* This quotation appears to be from the French edition. Unless otherwise noted quotations from original English texts or existing translations of French texts have been used. [Trans.]

11 Bleustein-Blanchet's Preface to the French edition of Vance Packard's *The Hidden Persuaders* (New York: D. McKay, 1957). (*La persuasion clandestine*). [Trans.]

12 Taking up the Marxian schema of "On the Jewish Question," the individual in consumer society is free as consumer and is only free as such – this is only a formal emancipation.

13 Dichter's English version reads as follows:

> Whenever a person in one socioeconomic category aspires to a different category, a *'tension differential'* is developed within him and this leads to frustration and action. Where a product promises to help a group overcome this tension, achieve its level of aspiration in whatever area it may fall, that product has a chance of success. (*The Strategy of Desire*, p. 84) [Trans.]

14 Martineau, *Motivation in Advertising*, p. 73.

15 Other more archaic methods exist which personalize the purchase: bartering, buying second-hand, [shopping] (patience and play), etc. These are archaic for they assume a passive product and an active consumer. In our day the whole initiative of personalization is transferred to advertising.

16 Gilbert Simondon *Du mode d'existence des objects techniques* (Paris: Aubier, 1958) p. 24.

17 L. Mumford, *Technique et Civilisation* (Paris: Seuil, 1950) p. 246. English edition: Lewis Mumford, *Technics and Civilization* (New York: Harcourt, Brace, 1934).

18 The tri-logy *parole/langue/langage* finds no unmediated (immediate) articulation in English: *Parole* as speech/word; *langue* as specific language (e.g. Serbo-Croatian); and *langage* as language (e.g. the structure of language). I have translated *langue* in this sentence ("*Mais langue n'est pas language*") as "set of expressions" to keep in line with Baudrillard's argumentation. [Trans.]

19 *Motivation in Advertising*, p. 75.

20 Ibid.

21 Ibid., p. 50.

22 Ibid., p. 100.

23 In fact, we are giving too much credit to advertising by comparing it with *magic*: the nominalist lexicon of alchemy has already in itself something of an actual language, structured by a research and interpretive (*déchiffrement*) praxis. The nominalism of the "brand name," however, is purely immanent and fixated (*figé*) by an economic imperative.

24 The word *consommer* means consumed (therefore annulled) and consummated (therefore fulfilled) as Baudrillard is pointing out. I was tempted to present it hyphenated, consume-consummate, to maintain the duality but found it awkward. In the argument that follows the reader will supplement a reading with this in memory/mind. [Trans.]

25 Thus, in the United States couples are encouraged to exchange wedding rings every year [sic], and to "signify" their relation through gifts and purchases made "together."

26 George Perec, *Les Choses: A Story of the Sixties* (New York: Grove Press, 1967) pp. 11–12.

27 Original in English. [Trans.]

28 In G. Perec's description of the "interior," the objects are, through fashion, transcendent, and not objects of a "series." A total cultural constraint, a cultural terrorism, dominates this interior. But this has little effect on the system of consumption itself.

29 The etymology is rather illuminating: "Everything is consumed" = "everything is accomplished" and of course "everything is destroyed." The Revolution is consumed in the idea of Revolution means that the Revolution is (formally) accomplished and abolished: what is given as realized is, henceforth, im-mediately consumable.

30 Perec, *Les Choses*, pp. 15–16.

2

Consumer Society

Today, we are everywhere surrounded by the remarkable conspicuousness of consumption and affluence, established by the multiplication of objects, services, and material goods. This now constitutes a
fundamental mutation in the ecology of the human species. Strictly
speaking, men of wealth are no longer surrounded by other human
beings, as they have been in the past, but by *objects*. Their daily
exchange is no longer with their fellows, but rather, statistically as a
function of some ascending curve, with the acquisition and manipulation of goods and messages: from the rather complex domestic organization with its dozens of technical slaves to the "urban estate" with
all the material machinery of communication and professional activity, and the permanent festive celebration of objects in advertising
with the hundreds of daily mass media messages; from the proliferation of somewhat obsessional objects to the symbolic psychodrama
which fuels the nocturnal objects that come to haunt us even in our
dreams. The concepts of "environment" and "ambiance" have
undoubtedly become fashionable only since we have come to live in
less proximity to other human beings, in their presence and discourse,
and more under the silent gaze of deceptive and obedient objects
which continuously repeat the same discourse, that of our stupefied
(*medusée*) power, of our potential affluence and of our absence from
one another.

As the wolf-child becomes wolf by living among them, so are we
becoming functional. We are living the period of the objects: that is,
we live by their rhythm, according to their incessant cycles. Today, it
is we who are observing their birth, fulfillment, and death; whereas in
all previous civilizations, it was the object, instrument, and perennial
monument that survived the generations of men.

While objects are neither flora nor fauna, they give the impression of being a proliferating vegetation; a jungle where the new savage of modern times has trouble finding the reflexes of civilization. These fauna and flora, which people have produced, have come to encircle and invest them, like a bad science fiction novel. We must quickly describe them as we see and experience them, while not forgetting, even in periods of scarcity or profusion, that they are in actuality the *products of human activity*, and are controlled, not by natural ecological laws, but by the law of exchange value.

The busiest streets of London are crowded with shops whose show cases display all the riches of the world: Indian shawls, American revolvers, Chinese porcelain, Parisian corsets, furs from Russia and spices from the tropics; but all of these worldly things bear odious white paper labels with Arabic numerals and then laconic symbols £SD. This is how commodities are presented in circulation.[1]

Profusion and displays

Accumulation, or *profusion*, is evidently the most striking descriptive feature. Large department stores, with their luxuriant abundance of canned goods, foods, and clothing, are like the primary landscape and the geometrical locus of affluence. Streets with overcrowded and glittering store windows (lighting being the least rare commodity, without which merchandise would merely be what it is), the displays of delicacies, and all the scenes of alimentary and vestimentary festivity, stimulate a magical salivation. Accumulation is more than the sum of its products: the conspicuousness of surplus, the final and magical negation of scarcity, and the maternal and luxurious presumptions of the land of milk and honey. Our markets, our shopping avenues and malls mimic a new-found nature of prodigious fecundity. Those are our Valleys of Canaan where flows, instead of milk and honey, streams of neon on ketchup and plastic – but no matter! There exists an anxious anticipation, not that there may not be enough, but that there is too much, and too much for everyone: by purchasing a portion one in effect appropriates a whole crumbling pyramid of oysters, meats, pears or canned asparagus. One purchases the part for the whole. And this repetitive and metonymic discourse of the consumable, and of commodities is represented, through collective metaphor and as a product of its own surplus, in the image of the *gift*, and of the inexhaustible and spectacular prodigality of the *feast*.

In addition to the stack, which is the most rudimentary yet effective form of accumulation, objects are organized in *displays*, or in *collections*. Almost every clothing store or appliance store presents a gamut of differentiated objects, which call upon, respond to, and refute each other. The display window of the antique store is the aristocratic, luxurious version of this model. The display no longer exhibits an overabundance of wealth but a *range* of select and complementary objects which are offered for the choosing. But this arrangement also invokes a psychological chain reaction in the consumer who peruses it, inventories it, and grasps it as a total category. Few objects today are offered *alone*, without a context of objects to speak for them. And the relation of the consumer to the object has consequently changed: the object is no longer referred to in relation to a specific utility, but as a collection of objects in their total meaning. Washing machine, refrigerator, dishwasher, have different meanings when grouped together than each one has alone, as a piece of equipment (*ustensile*). The display window, the advertisement, the manufacturer, and the *brand name* here play an essential role in imposing a coherent and collective vision, like an almost inseparable totality. Like a chain that connects not ordinary objects but *signifieds*, each object can signify the other in a more complex super-object, and lead the consumer to a series of more complex choices. We can observe that objects are never offered for consumption in an absolute disarray. In certain cases they can *mimic* disorder to better seduce, but they are always arranged to trace out directive paths. The arrangement directs the purchasing impulse towards *networks* of objects in order to seduce it and elicit, in accordance with its own logic, a maximal investment, reaching the limits of economic potential. Clothing, appliances, and toiletries thus constitute object *paths*, which establish inertial constraints on the consumer who will proceed *logically* from one object to the next. The consumer will be caught up in a *calculus* of objects, which is quite different from the frenzy of purchasing and possession which arises from the simple profusion of commodities.

The drugstore

The drugstore is the synthesis of profusion and calculation. The drugstore (or the new shopping malls) makes possible the synthesis of all consumer activities, not least of which are shopping, flirting with objects, idle wandering, and all the permutations of these. In this way, the drugstore is more appropriately representative of modern consumption than the large department store where quantitative centralization leaves little margin for idle exploration. The arrangement of departments and products here imposes a more utilitarian approach to consumption. It retains something of the period of the emergence of department stores, when large numbers of people were beginning to get access to *everyday* consumables. The drugstore has an altogether different function. It does not juxtapose categories of commodities, but practices an *amalgamation of signs* where all categories of goods are considered a partial field in a general consumerism of signs. The cultural center becomes, then, an integral part of the shopping mall. This is not to say that culture is here "prostituted"; that is too simple. It is *culturalized*. Consequently, the commodity (clothing, food, restaurant, etc.) is also culturalized, since it is transformed into a distinctive and idle substance, a luxury, and an item, among others, in the general display of consumables.

> A new art of living, a new way of living, claims advertising, (and fashionable magazines): a pleasant shopping experience, in a single air-conditioned location; one is able to purchase food, products for the apartment or summer home, clothing, flowers, the latest novel, or the latest gadget in a single trip, while husband and children watch a film; and then later you can all dine together on the spot.

Cafe, cinema, book store, auditorium, trinkets, clothing, and many other things can be found in these shopping centers. The drugstore recaptures it all in a kaleidoscopic mode. Whereas the large department store provides a marketplace pageantry for merchandise, the drugstore offers the subtle recital of consumption, where, in fact, the "art" consists in playing on the ambiguity of the object's sign, and sublimating their status and utility as commodity in a play of "ambiance."

The drugstore is neo-culture universalized, where there is no longer any difference between a fine gourmet shop and a gallery of paintings, between *Playboy* and a *Treatise on Paleontology*. The drugstore will be modernized to the point of offering a bit of "gray matter":

> Just selling products does not interest us, we would like to supply a little gray matter...Three stories, a bar, a dance floor, and shops;

trinkets, records, paperbacks, intellectual books, a bit of everything. But we are not looking to flatter the customer. We are actually offering them "something": a language lab on the second floor; records and books where you find the great trends that move our society; music for research; works that explain an epoch. Products accompanied by "gray matter", this is the drugstore, but in a new style, with something more, perhaps a bit of intelligence and human warmth.[2]

A drugstore can become a whole city: such as Parly 2,[3] with its giant shopping center, where "art and leisure mingle with everyday life"; where each residential group encircles a pool club (the center of attraction), a circular church, tennis courts ("the least of things"), elegant boutiques, and a library. Even the smallest ski resort is organized on the "universalist" model of the drugstore, one where all activities are summarized, systematically combined and centered around the fundamental concept of "ambiance." Thus Idleness-on-the-Wasteful[4] simultaneously offers you a complete, polymorphic and combinatorial existence:

> Our Mt Blanc, our Norway spruce forest; our Olympic runs, our "park" for children; our architecture, carved, trimmed, and polished like a work of art; the purity of the air we breathe; the refined ambiance of our Forum, modeled after Mediterranean cities where, upon return from the ski slopes, life flourishes. Cafes, restaurants, boutiques, skating rinks, night clubs, cinemas, and centers of culture and amusement are all located in the Forum to offer you a life off the slopes that is particularly rich and varied. There is our closed-circuit TV; and our future on a human scale (soon, we will be classified as a work of art by the department of cultural affairs).

We have reached the point where "consumption" has grasped the whole of life; where all activities are sequenced in the same combinatorial mode; where the schedule of gratification is outlined in advance, one hour at a time; and where the "environment" is complete, completely climatized, furnished, and culturalized. In the phenomenology of consumption, the general climatization of life, of goods, objects, services, behaviors, and social relations represents the perfected, "consummated,"[5] stage of evolution which, through articulated networks of objects, ascends from pure and simple abundance to a complete conditioning of action and time, and finally to the systematic organization of ambiance, which is characteristic of the drugstores, the shopping malls, or the modern airports in our futuristic cities.

Parly 2

"The largest shopping center in Europe."

"Printemps, B.H.V., Dior, Prisunic, Lanvin, Frank et Fils, Hediard, two cinemas, a drugstore, a supermarket, Suma, a hundred other shops, all gathered in a single location!"[6]

In the choice of shops, from groceries to high fashion, there are two requirements: progressive marketing and a sense of aesthetics. The famous slogan "uglyness doesn't sell" is outmoded, and could be replaced by "the beauty of the surroundings is the precondition for a happy life": a two-story structure... organized around a central mall, with a main street and promenades on two levels; the reconciliation of the small and large shop and of the modern pace with the idleness of antiquity.

The mall offers the previously unexperienced luxury of strolling between stores which freely (*plain-pièd*) offer their temptations without so much interference as glare from a display window. The central mall, a combination of rue de la Paix and the Champs-Elysées, is adorned by fountains and artificial trees. Kiosks and benches are completely indifferent to seasonal changes and bad weather. An exceptional system of climate control, requiring eight miles of air conditioning ducts, creates a perpetual springtime.

Not only can anything be purchased, from shoestrings to an airline ticket, or located, such as insurance company, cinema, bank or medical service, bridge club and art exhibition, but one need not be the slave of time. The mall, like every city street, is accessible seven days a week, day or night.

Naturally, the shopping mall has instituted, for those who desire, the most modern form of payment: the "credit card." The card frees us from checks, cash, and even from financial difficulties at the end of the month. Henceforth, to pay you present your card and sign the bill. That's all there is to it. Each month you receive a bill which you can pay in full or in monthly installments.

In the marriage between comfort, beauty, and efficiency, Parlysians discover the material conditions of happiness which the anarchy of older cities refuses them.

Here we are at the heart of consumption as the total organization of everyday life, as a complete homogenization. Everything is appropriated and simplified into the translucence of abstract "happiness," simply defined by the resolution of tensions. Expanded to the dimensions of the shopping mall and the futuristic city, the drugstore is the *sublimation* of real life, of objective social life, where not only work and money are abolished, but the seasons disappear as well – the distant vestige of a cycle finally domesticated! Work, leisure, nature, and culture, all previously dispersed, separate, and more or less irreducible activities that produced anxiety and complexity in our real life, and in our "anarchic and archaic" cities, have finally become mixed, massaged, climate controlled, and domesticated into the simple activity of perpetual shopping. All these activities have finally become desexed into a single hermaphroditic ambiance of style! Everything is finally *digested* and reduced to the same homogeneous fecal matter (this occurs, of course, precisely under the sign of the disappearance of *"liquid" currency*, the still too visible symbol of the *real* excretion (*fecalité*) of real life, and of the economic and social contradictions that previously haunted it). All that is past (passed): a *controlled*, lubricated, and *consumed* excretion (*fecalité*) is henceforth transferred into things, everywhere diffused in the indistinguishability of things and of social relations. Just like the Roman Pantheon, where the gods of all countries coexisted in a syncretism, in an immense "digest," the super shopping center,[7] our new pantheon, our pandemonium, brings together all the gods, or demons, of consumption. That is to say, every activity, labor, conflict and all the seasons are abolished in the same abstraction. The substance of life, unified in this universal digest, can no longer have any *meaning*: that which produced the dream work, the poetic work, the work of meaning, that is to say the grand schemas of displacement and condensation, the great figures of metaphor and contradiction, which are founded on the lived articulation of distinct elements, is no longer possible. The eternal substitution of homogeneous elements alone remains. There is no longer a symbolic function, but an eternal combinatory of "ambiance" in a perpetual Springtime.

Towards a theory of consumption

The autopsy of homo economicus

There is a fable: "There once was a man who lived in Scarcity. After many adventures and a long voyage in the Science of Economics, he encountered the Society of Affluence. They were married and had many needs." "The beauty of *homo economicus*," said A. N. Whitehead, "was that we knew exactly what he was searching for." This human fossil of the Golden Age, born in the modern era out of the fortuitous conjunction of Human Nature and Human Rights, is gifted with a heightened principle of formal rationality which leads him to:

1   Pursue his own happiness without the slightest hesitation;
2   Prefer objects which provide him with the maximum satisfaction.

The whole discourse on consumption, whether learned or lay, is articulated on the mythological sequence of the fable: a man, "endowed" with needs which "direct" him towards objects that "give" him satisfaction. Since man is really never satisfied (for which, by the way, he is reproached), the same history is repeated indefinitely, since the time of the ancient fables.

Some appear to be perplexed: "Among all the unknowns of economic science, needs are the most persistently obscure" (Knight).[8] But this uncertainty does not prevent the advocates of the human sciences, from Marx to Galbraith, and from Robinson Crusoe to Chombart de Lauwe,[9] from faithfully reciting the litany of needs. For the economists, there is the notion of "utility." Utility is the desire to consume a specific commodity, that is to say, to nullify its utility. Need is therefore already embedded in commodities on the market. And preferences are manipulated by the arrangement of products already offered on the market: this is in fact an elastic demand.

For the psychologist there is the theory of "motivation" which is a bit more complex, less "object oriented"[10] and more "instinct oriented,"[11] derived from a sort of ill-defined, preexisting necessity. For the sociologist and psychosociologist, who arrived last on the scene, there is the "sociocultural." The anthropological postulate, of the *individual* endowed with needs and moved by nature to satisfy them, or of a consumer who is free, conscious and aware of his needs, is not put into question by sociologists (although sociologists are suspicious of "deep motivations"). But rather, on the basis of this idealistic postulate, sociologists allow for a "social-dynamics" of needs. They activate models of conformity and competition ("Keeping up with the Joneses")[12] derived from the pressure of peer group, or they elaborate grand "cultural models" which are related to society in general or to history.

Three general positions can be identified: for Marshall, needs are interdependent and rational; for Galbraith, choices are imposed by motivation (we will come back to this); for Gervasi (and others), needs are interdependent, and are the result of learning rather than of rational calculation.

Gervasi: "Choices are not made randomly. They are socially controlled, and reflect the cultural model from which they are produced.

We neither produce nor consume just any product: the product must have some meaning in relation to a system of values."[13] This leads to a perspective on consumption in terms of integration: "The goal of the economy is not the maximization of production *for the purposes of the individual*, but the maximization of production in relation to society's value system" (Parsons).[14] Similarly, Duesenbury will claim that the only choice is, in fact, varying one's possessions according to one's position in the social hierarchy. In effect, the differences in choice from one society to another, and the similarity of choices within a society, compels us to view consumer behavior as a social phenomenon. The economist's notion of "rational" choice has been changed into the model of choice as conformity, which is significantly different. Needs are not so much directed at objects, but at values. And the satisfaction of needs primarily expresses an *adherence to these values*. The fundamental, unconscious, and automatic choice of the consumer is to accept the life-style of a particular society (no longer therefore a real choice: the theory of the autonomy and sovereignty of the consumer is thus refuted).

This kind of sociology culminates in the notion of the "standard package,"[15] defined by Riesman as the collection of products and services which constitutes the basic heritage of the middle-class American. Constantly on the rise and indexed on the national standard of living, the standard package is a minimum ideal of a statistical kind, and a middle-class model of conformity. Surpassed by some, only dreamed of by others, it is an *idea* which encapsulates the American way of life.[16] Here again, the "standard package" does not so much refer to the materiality of goods (TV, bathroom, car, etc.) as to *the ideal of conformity*.

All of this sociology gets us nowhere. Besides the fact that the notion of conformity is nothing more than an immense tautology (in this case the middle-class American defined by the "standard package," itself defined by the statistical mean of consumed goods – or sociologically: a particular individual belongs to a particular group which consumes a particular product, and the individual consumes such a product because he or she belongs to such a group), the postulate of formal rationality, which in economics determined the individual's relation to objects, is simply transferred to the relation of the individual to the group. Conformity and satisfaction are interrelated: the resulting similarity in the subject's relation to objects, or to a group *posited as a distinct entity*, is established according to the logical principle of equivalence. The concepts of "need" and "norm" respectively are the expressions of this miraculous equivalence.

The difference between the economic notion of "utility" and the sociological notion of conformity is identical to the distinction Galbraith establishes between the pursuit of profit and economic motivation, which is characteristic of the "traditional" capitalist system, on the one hand, and the behavior of identification and adaptation, which is specific to the era of organization and of the technostructure, on the other. The *conditioning of needs* becomes the central issue for both the psycho-sociologists of conformity, and for Galbraith. This is never an issue for economists (and for good reasons), for whom consumers, with their ultimate rational calculation, remain ideally free.

Since Packard's *The Hidden Persuaders* and Dichter's *The Strategy of Desire* (and some others as well),[17] the conditioning of needs (particularly through advertising) has become the favorite theme in the discourse on consumer society. The celebration of affluence and the great lament over "artificial" or "alienated needs," together have fueled the same mass culture, and even the intellectual discourse on the issue. Generally this discourse is grounded in the antiquated moral and social philosophy of a humanist tradition. With Galbraith, however, it develops into a more rigorous economic and political theory. We will therefore remain with him, starting from his two books, *The Affluent Society* and *The New Industrial State*.

Briefly summarizing his position, we could say that the fundamental problem of contemporary capitalism is no longer the contradiction between the "maximization of profit" and the "rationalization of production" (from the point of view of the producer), but rather a contradiction between a virtually unlimited productivity (at the level of the technostructure) and the need to dispose of the product. It becomes vital for the system at this stage to control not only the mechanism of production, but also consumer demand; not only prices, but what will be asked for the price. Either prior to production (polls, market studies) or subsequent to it (advertising, marketing, conditioning), the general idea "is to shift the locus of decision in the purchase of goods from the consumer where it is beyond control to the firm where it is subject to control."[18] Even more generally:

> The accommodation of the market behavior of the individual, as well as of social attitudes in general, to the needs of producers and the goals of the technostructure is an inherent feature of the system [it would be more appropriate to say: a *logical* characteristic]. It becomes increasingly important with the growth of the industrial system.[19]

This is what Galbraith calls the "revised sequence," in opposition to the "accepted sequence" whereby the consumer is presumed to have the initiative which will reflect back, through the market, to the manufacturers. Here, on the contrary, the manufacturers control behavior, as well as direct and model social attitudes and needs. In its tendencies at least, this is a total dictatorship by the sector of production.

The "revised sequence," at least, has the critical value of undermining the fundamental myth of the classical relation, which assumes that it is the individual who exercises power in the economic system. This emphasis on the power of the individual largely contributed to the legitimation of the organization; all dysfunctions, all nuisances, the inherent contradictions in the order of production are justified, since they enlarge the consumer's domain of sovereignty. On the contrary, it is clear that the whole economic and psychosociological apparatus of market and motivation research, which pretends to uncover the underlying needs of the consumer and the real demand prevailing in the market, exists only to generate a demand for further market opportunities. And it continuously masks this objective by staging its opposite. "Man has become the object of science for man only since automobiles have become harder to sell than to manufacture."[20]

Thus everywhere Galbraith denounces the boosting of demand by "artificial accelerators," which the technostructure carries out in its imperialist expansion, rendering the stabilization of demand impossible.[21] Income, luxury goods, and surplus labor form a vicious and frantic circle. The infernal round of consumption is based on the celebration of needs that are purported to be "psychological." These are distinguished from "physiological" needs since they are supposedly established through "discretionary income" and the freedom of choice, and consequently manipulable at will. Advertising here of course plays a capital role (another idea which has become conventional) for it appears to be in harmony with commodities and with the needs of the individual. In fact, says Galbraith, advertising is adjusted to the industrial system: "It appears to place a significance on products only in so far as it is important for the system, and it upholds the importance and prestige of the technostructure from the social point of view." Through advertising, the system appropriates social goals for its own gain, and imposes its own objectives as social goals: "What's good for General Motors..."

Again we must agree with Galbraith (and others) in acknowledging that the liberty and sovereignty of the consumer are nothing more than a mystification. The well-preserved mystique of satisfaction and individual choice (primarily supported by economists), whereby a "free" civilization reaches its pinnacle, is the very ideology of the industrial system. It justifies its arbitrariness and all sorts of social problems: filth, pollution, and deculturation – in fact the consumer is sovereign in a jungle of ugliness, where *the freedom of choice is imposed on him.* The revised sequence (that is to say, the *system* of consumption) thus ideologically supplements and connects with the *electoral system.* The drugstore and the polling booth, the geometric spaces of individual freedom, are also the system's two mammary glands.

We have discussed at length the analysis of the "technostructural" conditioning of needs and consumption because it is currently quite prominent. This kind of analysis, thematized in multiple ways in the pseudo-philosophy of "alienation," constitutes a representation of society which is itself part of consumerism. But it is open to fundamental objections that are all related to its idealist anthropological postulates. For Galbraith individual needs can be stabilized. There exists in human *nature* something like an *economic principle* that would lead man, were it not for "artificial accelerators," to impose limits on his own objectives, on his needs and at the same time on his efforts. In short, there is a tendency towards satisfaction, which is not viewed as optimizing, but rather as "harmonious" and balanced at the level of the individual, a tendency that would allow the individual to express himself in a society that is itself a harmony of collective needs, instead of becoming caught up in the vicious circle of infinite gratifications described above. All this sounds perfectly utopian.

1   Galbraith denounces the "specious" reasoning of economists on the issue of "authentic" or "artificial" gratification: "There is no proof that an expensive woman obtains the same satisfaction from yet another gown as does a hungry man from a hamburger. But there is no proof that she does not. Since it cannot be proven that she does not, her desire, it is held, must be accorded equal standing with that of a poor man for meat."[22] "Absurd," says Galbraith. Yet, not at all (and here classical economists are almost correct in their opposition to him: quite simply, they position themselves to establish the equivalency of satiable demands and thereby avoid all the problems). It is nevertheless the case that, from the perspective of the satisfaction of the consumer, there is no basis on which to define what is "artificial" and what is not. The pleasure obtained from a television or a second home is experienced as "real" freedom. No one experiences this as alienation. Only the intellectual can describe it in this way, on the basis of a moralizing idealism, one which at best reveals him as an alienated moralist.

2   On the "economic principle," Galbraith claims: "What is called economic development consists in no small part in devising strategies to overcome the tendency of men to place limits on their objectives as regards income and thus on their efforts."[23] And he cites the example of Filipino workers in California: "The pressure of debt, and the pressure on each to emulate the most extravagant, quickly converted these happy and easygoing people into a modern and reliable work force."[24] In addition, in underdeveloped countries the introduction of Western gadgets is the best form of economic stimulation. This theory, which we could call economic "pressure," or disciplined consumption, and which is connected to forced economic growth, is seductive. It makes it appear that the forced acculturation to the processes of consumption is a *logical development* in the evolution of the industrial system. An evolution which progresses from the discipline of timetables and everyday behavior (to which workers have been subjected since the nineteenth century) to the processes of industrial production. Once having asserted this, we need to explain *why* consumers "take the bait," why they are vulnerable to this strategy. It is much too easy to appeal to "a happy and carefree" disposition, and mechanically to assign responsibility to the system. There is no "natural" inclination to a carefree disposition any more than there is to the work ethic. Galbraith does not take into consideration the logic of social differentiation. Hence he is forced to represent the individual as a completely passive victim of the system. These processes of class and caste distinctions are basic to the social structure, and are fully operational in "democratic" society. In short, what is lacking is a socio-logic of difference, of status, etc., upon which needs are reorganized in accordance to the *objective* social demand of signs and differences. Thus consumption becomes, not a function of "harmonious" individual satisfaction (hence limited according to the ideal rules of "nature"), but rather an infinite social *activity*. We will eventually come back to this issue.

3   "Needs are in reality the fruits of production," says Galbraith, pleased with himself for having put it so well. Expressed in a clear and demystified tone, this thesis, as he understood it, is nothing more than a subtle version of the natural "authenticity" of certain needs and of the bewitching character of the "artificial." What Galbraith means is that without the system of production a large proportion of needs would not exist. He contends that, in the production of specific goods and services, manufacturers simultaneously produce all the powers of suggestion necessary for the products to be accepted. In fact, they "produce" the need which corresponds to the product. There is here a serious psychological lacuna. Needs are strictly specified in advance in

relation to *finite objects*. There is only need for *this or that* object. In effect, the psyche of the consumer is merely a display window or a catalog. Certainly once we have adopted this simplistic view of man we cannot avoid the psychological reduction: empirical needs are the specular reflections of empirical objects. At this level, however, the thesis of conditioning is false. We are well aware of how consumers resist such a precise injunction, and of how they play with "needs" on a keyboard of objects. We know that advertising is not omnipotent and at times produces opposite reactions; and, we know that in reference to a single "need," objects can be substituted for one another. Hence, at the empirical level, a rather complicated strategy having a psychological and sociological nature intersects with the strategy of production.

The truth is not that "needs are the fruits of production," but that *the system of needs is the product of the system of production*, which is a quite different matter. By a system of needs we mean to imply that needs are not produced one at a time, in relation to their respective objects. Needs are produced as a *force of consumption*, and as a general potential reserve (*disponibilité globale*) within the larger framework of productive forces. It is in this sense that we can say that the technostructure is extending its empire. The system of production does not "shackle" the system of pleasure (*jouissance*) to its own ends (strictly speaking, this is meaningless). This hypothesis *denies* autonomy to the system of pleasure and substitutes itself in its place by reorganizing everything into a system of productive forces. We can trace this *genealogy of consumption* in the course of the history of the industrial system:

1   The order of production produces the productive machine/force, a technical system that is radically different from traditional tools.
2   It produces the rationalized productive capital/force, a rational system of investment and circulation that is radically different from previous forms of "wealth" and modes of exchange.
3   It produces the wage-labor force, an abstract and systematized productive force that is radically different from concrete labor and traditional "workmanship."
4   In this way it produces needs, the *system* of needs, the productive demand/force as a rationalized, controlled and integrated whole, complementary to the three others in a process of the total control of productive forces and production processes. As a system, needs are also radically different from pleasure and satisfaction. They are produced *as elements of a system* and not *as a relation*

between an individual and an object. In the same sense that labor power is no longer connected to, and even denies, the relation of the worker to the product of his labor, so exchange value is no longer related to concrete and personal exchange, nor the commodity form to actual goods, etc.)

This is what Galbraith does not see and along with him all of the "alienists" of consumption, who persist in their attempts to demonstrate that *people's relation to objects, and their relation to themselves is falsified*, mystified, and manipulated, consuming this myth at the same time as the object. Once having stated the universal postulate of the free and conscious subject (in order to make it reemerge at the end of history as a happy end[ing]),[25] they are forced to attribute all the "dysfunctions" they have uncovered to a diabolic power – in this case to the technostructure, armed with advertising, public relations, and motivation research. This is magical thinking if there is such a thing. They do not see that, taken one at a time, needs are *nothing*; that there is only the system of needs; or rather, that needs are nothing but *the most advanced form of the rational systematization of productive forces at the individual level*, one in which "consumption" takes up the *logical* and necessary relay from production.

This can clear up a certain number of unexplained mysteries for our pious "alienists." They deplore, for example, the fact that puritan ethics are not abandoned in periods of affluence, and that an outdated moral and self-denying Malthusianism has not been replaced by a modern ethos of pleasure. Dichter's *Strategy of Desire* is determined to twist and subvert these old mental structures "from below." And it is true: there has not been a revolution in morals; puritan ideology is still in place. In the analysis of leisure, we will see how it permeates what appear to be hedonistic practices. We can affirm that puritan ethics, and what it implies about sublimation, transcendence, and repression (in a word, morality), *haunts* consumption and needs. It is what motivates it from within and that which gives needs and consumption its compulsive and boundless character. And puritan ideology is itself reactivated by the process of consumption; this is what makes consumption the powerful factor of integration and social control we know it to be. Whereas from the perspective of consumption/pleasure, this remains paradoxical and inexplicable. It can all be explained only if we acknowledge that needs and consumption are in fact an *organized extension of productive forces*. This is not surprising since they both emerged from the productivist and puritan ethics which was the dominant morality of the industrial era. The generalized integration of the "private" individual ("needs," feelings, aspirations, drives) as a productive force can only be accompanied by a generalized extension, at this level, of the schemas of repression, of sublimation, of concentration, of systematization, of rationalization (and of "alienation" of course!), which, for centuries, but especially since the nineteenth century, have governed the structuration (*edification*) of the industrial system.

The fluidity of objects and needs

Until now, the analysis of consumption has been founded on the naive anthropology of *homo economicus*, or at best *homo psychoeconomicus*. It is a theory of needs, of objects (in the fullest sense), and of satisfactions within the ideological extension of classical political economy. This is really not a theory. It is an immense tautology: "I buy this because I need it" is equivalent to the claim that fire burns because of its phlogistic essence. I have shown elsewhere[26] how this empiricist/teleologist position (the individual taken as an end in itself and his or her conscious representations as the logic of events) is identical to the magical speculation of primitive peoples (and of ethnologists) concerning the notion of mana. No theory of consumption is possible at this level: the immediately self-evident, such as an analysis in terms of needs, will never produce anything more than a consumed reflection on consumption.

The rationalist mythology of needs and satisfactions is as naive and "disabled" as is traditional medicine when confronted with psychosomatic or hysterical symptoms. Let us explain: within the field of their objective function objects are not interchangeable, but outside the field of its denotation, an object becomes substitutable in a more or less unlimited fashion. In this field of connotations the object takes on the value of a sign. In this way a washing machine *serves* as equipment and *plays* as an element of comfort, or of prestige, etc. It is the field of play that is specifically the field of consumption. Here all sorts of objects can be substituted for the washing machine as a signifying element. In the logic of signs, as in the logic of symbols, objects are no longer tied to a function or to a *defined* need. This is precisely because objects respond to something different, either to a social logic, or to a logic of desire, where they serve as a fluid and unconscious field of signification.

Relatively speaking, objects and needs are here interchangeable just like the symptoms of hysterical or psychosomatic conversion. They obey the same logic of shifts, transferals, and of apparently arbitrary and infinite convertibility. When an illness is *organic*, there is a necessary relation between the symptom and the organ (in the same way that in its role as equipment there is a necessary relation between the object and its function). In the hysterical or psychosomatic conversion the symptom, like the sign, is (relatively) arbitrary. Migraine, colitis, lumbago, angina, or general fatigue form a chain of somatic signifiers along which the symptom "parades." This is just like the interconnection of object/signs, or of object/ symbols, along which parades, not needs (which remain tied to the object's rational goal), but desire, and some other determination, derived from an unconscious social logic.

If we trace a need to a particular locus, that is, if we satisfy it by taking it literally, as it presents itself, as a need for a *specific* object, we would make the same error as if we performed traditional therapy on an organ where the symptom is localized. Once healed it would reappear elsewhere.

The world of objects and of needs would thus be a world of *general hysteria*. Just as the organs and the functions of the body in hysterical conversion become a gigantic paradigm which the symptom replaces and refers to, in consumption objects become a vast paradigm designating another language through which something else speaks. We could add that this evanescence and continual mobility reaches a point where it becomes impossible to determine the specific objectivity of needs, just as it is impossible in hysteria to define the specific objectivity of an illness, for the simple reason that it does not exist. The flight from one signifier to another is no more than the surface reality of a *desire*, which is insatiable because it is founded on a lack. And this desire, which can never be satisfied, signifies itself locally in a succession of objects and needs.

In view of the repeated and naive confusion one finds when faced with the continual forward flight and unlimited renewal of needs – which in fact is irreconcilable with a rationalist theory claiming that a satisfied need produces a state of equilibrium and a resolution of tensions – we can advance the following sociological hypothesis (although it would be interesting and essential to articulate both desire and the social): if we acknowledge that a need is not a need for a particular object as much as it is a "need" for difference (the *desire for social meaning*), only then will we understand that satisfaction can never be *fulfilled*, and consequently that there can never be a *definition* of needs.

The fluidity of desire is supplemented by the fluidity of differential meanings (is there a metaphoric relation between the two?). Between them specific and finite needs only become meaningful as the focus of successive conversions. In their substitutions they signify, yet simultaneously veil, the true domain of signification – that of lack and difference – which overwhelms them from all sides.

The denial of pleasure

The acquisition of objects is *without an object* ("objectless craving,"[27] for David Riesman). Consumer behavior, which appears to be focused and directed at the object and at pleasure, in fact responds to quite different objectives: the metaphoric or displaced expression of desire, and the production of a code of social values through the use of differentiating signs. That which is determinant is not the function of individual interest within a corpus of objects, but rather the specifically social function of exchange, communication and distribution of values within a corpus of signs.

The truth about consumption is that it is *a function of production* and not a function of pleasure, and therefore, like material production, is not an individual function but one that is *directly and totally* collective. No theoretical analysis is possible without the reversal of the traditional givens: otherwise, no matter how we approach it, we revert to a phenomenology of pleasure.

Consumption is a system which assures the regulation of signs and the integration of the group: it is simultaneously a morality (a system of ideological values) and a system of communication, a structure of exchange. On this basis, and on the fact that this social function and this structural organization by far transcend individuals and are imposed on them according to an unconscious social constraint, we can formulate a theoretical hypothesis which is neither a recital of statistics nor a descriptive metaphysics.

According to this hypothesis, paradoxical though it may appear, consumption is defined as *exclusive of pleasure*. As a social logic, the system of consumption is established on the basis of the denial of pleasure. Pleasure no longer appears as an objective, as a rational end, but as the individual rationalization of a process whose objectives lie elsewhere. Pleasure would define consumption *for itself*, as autonomous and final. But consumption is never thus. Although we experience pleasure for ourselves, when we consume we never do it on our own (the isolated consumer is the carefully maintained illusion of the *ideological* discourse on consumption). Consumers are mutually implicated, despite themselves, in a general system of exchange and in the production of coded values.

In this sense, consumption is a system of meaning, like language, or like the kinship system in primitive societies.

A structural analysis?

In the language of Lévi-Strauss we can say that the social aspect of consumption is not derived from what appears to be of the realm of nature (satisfaction or pleasure), but rather from the essential processes by which it separates itself from nature (what defines it as a code, an institution, or a system of organization). Consumption can be compared with the kinship system, which is not determined in the final analysis by consanguinity and filiation, by a natural given, but rather by the arbitrary regulation of classification. In the final analysis, the system of consumption is based on a code of signs (object/signs) and differences, and not on need and pleasure.

Rules of marriage represent the multiple ways of assuring the circulation of women within the social group. It is the replacement of a consanguineous system of relations of biological origin by a sociological system of alliance. Thus, rules of marriage and kinship systems can be seen as a kind of language, that is, a set of operations intended to assure, between individuals and groups, a certain kind of communication. The same is true for consumption: a sociological system of signs (the level characteristic of consumption) is substituted for a bio-functional and bio-economic system of commodities and products (the biological level of needs and subsistence). And the essential function of the regulated circulation of objects and commodities is the same as that of women and words. It is designed to assure a certain type of communication.

We will come back to the differences between these various types of "languages": they are essentially related to the mode of production of the values exchanged and to the type of division of labor associated with it. Commodities obviously are produced, whereas women are not, and they are produced differently from words. Nevertheless, at the level of distribution, commodities and objects, like words and once like women, constitute a global, arbitrary, and coherent system of signs, a *cultural* system which substitutes a social order of values and classifications for a contingent world of needs and pleasures, the natural and biological order.

This is not to claim that there are no needs, or natural utilities, etc. The point is to see that consumption, as a concept specific to contemporary society, is not organized along these lines. For this is true of all societies. What is sociologically significant for us, and what marks our era under the sign of consumption, is precisely the generalized reorganization of this primary level in a system of signs which appears to be a particular mode of transition from nature to culture, perhaps *the* specific mode of our era.

Marketing, purchasing, sales, the acquisition of differentiated commodities and object/signs – all of these presently constitute our language, a code with which our entire society *communicates* and speaks of and to itself. Such is the present day structure of communication: a language (*langue*) in opposition to which individual needs and pleasures are but the *effects of speech* (*parole*).

The fun-system, or the constraint of pleasure[28]

The best evidence that pleasure is not the basis or the objective of consumption is that nowadays pleasure is constrained and institutionalized, not as a right or enjoyment, but as the citizen's *duty*.

The puritans considered themselves, considered their actual being, to be an enterprise to make profit for the greater glory of God. Their "personal" qualities, and their "character," which they spent their lives producing, were capital to be invested wisely, and managed without speculation or waste. Conversely, yet in the same way, man-as-consumer considers the *experience of pleasure an obligation*, like an *enterprise of pleasure and satisfaction*; one is obliged to be happy, to be in love, to be adulating/adulated, seducing/seduced, participating, euphoric, and dynamic. This is the principle of the maximization of existence by the multiplication of contacts and relations, by the intensive use of signs and objects, and by the systematic exploitation of all the possibilities of pleasure.

The consumer, the modern citizen, cannot evade the constraint of happiness and pleasure, which in the new ethics is equivalent to the traditional constraint of labor and production. Modern man spends less and less of life in production, and more and more in the continuous production and creation of personal needs and of personal well-being. He must constantly be ready to actualize all of his potential, all of his capacity for consumption. If he forgets, he will be gently and instantly reminded that he has no right not to be happy. He is therefore not passive: he is engaged, and must be engaged, in continuous activity. Otherwise he runs the risk of being satisfied with what he has and of becoming asocial.

A *universal curiosity* (a concept to be exploited) has as a consequence been reawakened in the areas of cuisine, culture, science, religion, sexuality, etc. "Try Jesus!" says an American slogan. *Everything* must be tried: since man as consumer is haunted by the fear of "missing" something, any kind of pleasure. One never knows if such and such a contact, or experience (Christmas in the Canaries, eel in whisky, the Prado, LSD, love Japanese style) will not elicit a "sensation." It is no longer desire, nor even "taste" nor a specific preference which are at issue, but a generalized curiosity driven by a diffuse obsession, a *fun morality*,[29] whose imperative is enjoyment and the complete exploitation of all the possibilities of being thrilled, experiencing pleasure, and being gratified.

Consumption as the rise and control of new productive forces

Consumption is a sector that only *appears* anomic, since, following the Durkheimian definition, it is not governed by formal rules. It appears to surrender to the individualistic immoderation and contingency of needs. Consumption is not, as one might generally imagine (which is why economic "science" is fundamentally averse to discussing it), an indeterminate marginal sector where an individual, elsewhere constrained by social rules, would finally recover, in the "private" sphere, a margin of freedom and personal play when left on his own. Consumption is a collective and active behavior, a constraint, a morality, and an institution. It is a complete system of values, with all that the term implies concerning group integration and social control.

Consumer society is also the society for the apprenticeship of consumption, for the social indoctrination of consumption. In other words, this is a new and specific mode of *socialization* related to the rise of new productive forces and the monopolistic restructuration of a high output economic system.

Credit here plays a determining role, even though it only has a marginal impact on the spending budget. The idea is exemplary. Presented under the guise of gratification, of a facilitated access to affluence, of a hedonistic mentality, and of "freedom from the old taboos of thrift, etc.," credit is in fact the systematic socioeconomic indoctrination of forced economizing and an economic calculus for generations of consumers who, in a life of subsistence, would have otherwise escaped the manipulation of demands and would have been unexploitable as a force of consumption. Credit is a disciplinary process which extorts savings and regulates demand – just as wage labor was a rational process in the extortion of labor power and in the increase of productivity. The case cited by Galbraith, of the Puerto Ricans who, having been passive and carefree, were transformed into a modern labor force by being motivated to consume, is striking evidence of the tactical value of a regulated, forced, instructed, and stimulated consumption within the modern socioeconomic order. As Marc Alexandre demonstrates, this is achieved through credit (and the discipline and budget constraints it imposes), by the mental indoctrination of the masses to a planned calculus and to "basic" capitalist investment and behavior.[30] The rational and disciplinary ethics, which according to Weber was at the origin of modern capitalist productivism, in a way, has come to inhabit a whole domain which previously escaped it.

We don't realize how much the current indoctrination into systematic and organized consumption is *the equivalent and the extension, in the twentieth century, of the great indoctrination of rural populations into industrial labor, which occurred throughout the nineteenth century.* The same process of rationalization of productive forces, which took place in the nineteenth century in the sector of *production* is accomplished, in the twentieth century, in the sector of *consumption*. Having socialized the masses into a labor force, the industrial system had to go further in order to fulfill itself and to socialize the masses (that is, to control them) into a force of consumption. The small investors or the sporadic consumers of the pre-war era, who were free to consume or not, no longer had a place in the system.

The ideology of consumption would have us believe that we have entered a new era, and that a decisive "human revolution" separates the grievous and heroic Age of Production from the euphoric Age of Consumption, where justice has finally been restored to Man and to his desires. But there is no truth in this. Production and Consumption are *one and the same grand logical process in the expanded reproduction of the productive forces and of their control.* This imperative, which belongs to the system, enters in an inverted form into mentality, ethics, and everyday ideology, and that is its ultimate cunning: in the form of the liberation of needs, of individual fulfillment, of pleasure, and of affluence, etc. The themes of expenditure, pleasure, and non-calculation ("Buy now, pay later") have replaced the "puritan" themes of thrift, work, and patrimony. But this is only the appearance of a human revolution. In fact, this is the substitution of a new system of values for one that has become (relatively) ineffective: an internal substitution in a system essentially unchanged; a substitution within the guidelines of a more general process. What could have been a new finality, has become, stripped of any real content, an imposed mediation of the system's reproduction.

Consumer needs and satisfactions are productive forces which are now constrained and rationalized like all the others (labor power, etc.) From whichever perspective we chose (briefly) to examine it, consumption appeared quite opposite to the way we experience it as ideology, that is, as a dimension of constraint:

1   Governed by the *constraint of signification*, at the level of the
    structural analysis.
2   Governed by the *constraint of production* and the cycle of produc-
    tion in the analysis of strategies (socio-economico-political).

Thus, affluence and consumption are not the realization of Utopia,
but a new objective state, governed by the same fundamental processes, yet overdetermined by a new morality. This corresponds to a
new sphere of productive forces in the process of directed reintegra-
tion within the *same* expanded system. In this sense there is no
objective "progress" (nor *a fortiori* "revolution"): it is simply the
same thing and something else. What in fact results from the total
ambiguity of affluence and consumption, which can be observed at
the level of daily events, is that these are always lived as *myth* (the
assumption of happiness, beyond history and morality), while they
are simultaneously *endured as an objective process of adaptation* to a
new type of collective behavior.

On the issue of consumption as a civic restraint, Eisenhower stated
in 1958: "In a free society, government best encourages economic
growth when it encourages the *efforts* of individuals and private
groups. The government will never spend money as profitably as an
individual tax-payer would have were he freed from the burden of
taxation." He implies that consumption, not being directly imposed,
could effectively replace taxation as a social levy. "With nine billion
dollars of fiscal deductions," adds *Time* magazine, "the consumer
went to two million retail stores in search of prosperity... They
realized that they could increase economic growth by replacing their
fans with air conditioners. They *ensured the boom* of 1954 by purchasing five million miniaturized television sets, a million and a half
electric knives, etc." In short, they performed their civic duty. "Thrift
is un-American," said William H. Whyte.[31]

Regarding needs as productive forces, the equivalent in the heroic
epoch to "manual labor as natural resource," an advertisement for
movie advertising claims:

> The cinema allows you, thanks to its large screen, to present your
> product on site: colors, forms, conditioning. Each week 3,500,000
> spectators frequent the 2,500 cinemas in our advertising network; 67
> per cent of them are between the ages of fifteen and thirty-five. These
> are consumers *in the fullness of their needs*, who want and are able to
> purchase...

Exactly, they are individuals in full (labor) force.

The logistic function of the individual

> The individual serves the industrial system not by supplying it with
> savings and the resulting capital; he serves it by consuming its products.
> On no other matter, religious, political, or moral, is he so elaborately
> and skillfully and expensively instructed.[32]

The system needs people as workers (wage labor), and as econo-
mizers (taxes, loans, etc.), but increasingly they are needed *as
consumers*. Labor productivity is increasingly replaced by the
productivity obtained through technological and organizational
improvements and increasingly investments are being redirected to
the level of the corporation.[33] *But as consumer, the individual has
become necessary and practically irreplaceable.* In the process of the
extension of the techno-bureaucratic structures we can predict a
bright future and the eventual realization of the individualist system
of values, whose center of gravity will be displaced from the entre-
preneur and the individual investor, figurehead of competitive capitalism, to the individual consumer, subsequently encompassing all
individuals.

At the competitive stage, capitalism still sustained itself, for better
or for worse, with an individualist system of values bastardized with
altruism. The fiction of a social, altruistic morality (inherited
from traditional spiritualism) "softened" the antagonisms of social
relations. The "moral law" resulted from individual antagonisms, just
as "the law of the market" resulted from competitive processes; they
preserved the fiction of stability. For a long time we have believed in
individual salvation for the community of all Christians, and in
individual rights limited only by the rights of others. But this is
impossible today. In the same way that "free enterprise" has virtually
disappeared giving way to monopolistic, state and bureaucratic control, so the altruistic ideology is no longer sufficient to reestablish a
minimum of social integration. No other collective ideology has come
to replace these values. Only the collective constraint of the state has
thwarted the exacerbations of multiple individualisms. From this
arises the profound contradiction of civil and political society as
"consumer society": the system is forced to produce more and more
consumer individualism, which at the same time it is forced to
repress more and more severely. This can only be resolved by an
increase in altruistic ideology (which is itself bureaucratized, a "social
lubrication" through concern, social reform, the gift, the handout,
welfare propaganda and humane relations). But this incorporation

of altruism in the system of consumption will not be sufficient to stabilize it.

Consumption is therefore a powerful element in social control (by atomizing individual consumers); yet at the same time it requires the intensification of *bureaucratic control* over the processes of consumption, which is subsequently heralded, with increased intensity, as the *reign of freedom*. We will never escape it.

Traffic and the automobile provide the classic example of this contradiction, where there is the unlimited promotion of individual consumption; the desperate call to collective responsibility and social morality; and increasingly severe restraints. The paradox is the following: one can not simultaneously remind the individual that "the level of consumption is the just measure of social merit" and expect of him or her a different type of social responsibility, since in the act of personal consumption the individual already fully assumes a social responsibility. Once again, consumption is *social labor*. The consumer is conscripted and mobilized as a laborer at this level *as well* (today perhaps just as much as at the level of "production"). All the same, one should not ask the "laborer of consumption" to sacrifice his income (his individual satisfactions) for the collective good. Somewhere in their social subconsciousness, these millions of consumers have a sort of practical intuition of their new status as alienated laborer. The call for public solidarity is immediately perceived as a mystification. Their tenacious resistance here is simply a reflex of *political* defense. The consumer's "fixated egoism" is also the gross subconscious re-cognition of being the new exploited subject of modern times, despite all the non-sense about affluence and well-being. The fact that resistance and "egoism" drives the system to insoluble contradictions, to which it responds by reinforcing constraints, only confirms that consumption is a gigantic *political* field, whose analysis, as well as that of production, is still to be achieved.

The entire discourse on consumption aims to transform the consumer into the Universal Being, the general, ideal, and final incarnation of the human species. It attempts also to make of consumption the premise for "human liberation", to be attained in lieu of, and despite the failures of, social and political liberation. The consumer is in no way a universal being, but rather a social and political being, and a productive force. As such, the consumer revives fundamental *historical* problems: those concerning the ownership of the means of consumption (and no longer the means of production), those regarding economic responsibility (responsibility towards the *content* of production), etc. There is here the potential for a deep crisis and for new contradictions.

Ego consumans

Nowhere, up to the present day, have these contradictions been consciously manifested, except perhaps in a few strikes among American housewives and in the sporadic destruction of commodities (May 1968, the *No Bra Day*[34] when American women publicly burned their bras). "What does the consumer represent in the modern world? Nothing. What could he be? Everything, or almost everything. Because he stands alone next to millions of solitary individuals, he is at the mercy of all other interests."[35] One must add that the individualist ideology is an important element here (even though, as we saw, its contradictions are latent): since it affects the collective domain of social labor, exploitation by *dispossession* (of labor power), it produces (at a certain point) an effective solidarity. And this leads to a (relative) class consciousness. Whereas the directed *acquisition* of objects and commodities is individualizing, atomizing, and dehistoricizing. As a producer, and as a consequence of the division of labor, each laborer presupposes all others: exploitation is for everyone. As a consumer, humans become again solitary, cellular, and at best *gregarious* (for example in a family viewing TV, the crowd at a stadium or in a movie house, etc.) The structures of consumption are simultaneously fluid and enclosed. Can we imagine a coalition of drivers against car registration? Or a collective opposition to television? Even if every one of the million viewers is opposed to television advertising, advertisements will nevertheless be shown. That is because consumption is primarily organized as a discourse to oneself, and has a tendency to play itself out, with its gratifications and deceptions, in this minimal exchange. The object of consumption isolates. The private sphere lacks concrete negativity because it is collapsed on objects which themselves lack negativity. It is structured from outside by the system of production, whose strategy is no longer ideological at this level, but still political; whose strategy of desire invests the materiality of our existence with its monotony and distractions. Or, as we saw, the object of consumption creates distinctions as a stratification of statuses: if it no longer isolates, it differentiates; it *collectively assigns* the consumers a place in relation to a code, without so much as giving rise to any *collective solidarity* (but quite the opposite).

In general then consumers, as such, are unconscious and unorganized, just as workers may have been at the beginning of the nineteenth century. As such consumers have been glorified, flattered, and eulogized as "public opinion," that mystical, providential, and *sovereign* reality. Just as The People is glorified by democracy provided they remain as such (that is provided they do not interfere on the political or social scene), the sovereignty of consumers is also recognized ("powerful consumers," according to Katona),[36] provided they do not try to act in this way on the social scene. The People – these are the laborers, provided they are unorganized; the Public, or public opinion – these are the consumers, provided they are content to consume.

NOTES

1 Karl Marx, *Contribution to a Critique of Political Economy* (NY: International Publishers, 1970) p. 87. [Trans.]
2 Baudrillard appears to be quoting from an advertising brochure here, and elsewhere in the text. But at times they sound contrived, and can easily be read as fictional. [Trans.]
3 Parly 2: a planned community (etymologically and geographically) between Paris and Orly (the airport in the southern suburb of Paris). Baudrillard offers his own description in the next section. [Trans.]
4 "Idleness-on-the-Wasteful" would be one anglo-saxon version of "Flaine-la-Prodigue," Baudrillard's parody of suburban communities around Paris. "Flaine": perhaps the conjunction of "flemme" (laziness) and "flâneur" (idle/loafer); "Prodigue" (extravagant/wasteful). [Trans.]
5 See chapter 1, note 24. [Trans.]
6 Printemps, B. H. V., Dior, Prisunic, Lanvin, Frank et Fils are department stores. [Trans.]
7 Originally in English. [Trans.]
8 Knight: unable to identify the source of this quotation. [Trans.]
9 A French sociologist, author of *Pour une sociologie des aspirations* (Paris: Denoël, 1969). [Trans.]
10 Originally in English. [Trans.]
11 Ibid.
12 Ibid.
13 The translator is unable to identify the source of this quotation.
14 The translator is unable to identify the source of this quotation from Talcott Parsons.
15 Originally in English. [Trans.]
16 A study in *Sélection du Reader's Digest* (A. Piatier: *Structure et perspectives de la consommation européenne*), found that consumption in Europe is the activity of a minority, in contrast to the large middle class in the USA, a consuming elite (the As) which serves as a model for a majority that does not yet have access to this display of luxury (sports car, stereo system, summer home), without which there are no Europeans worthy of the name.

17 For these references see chapter 1, nn. 9 and 11. [Trans.]
18 John Kenneth Galbraith, *The New Industrial State* (New York: Signet, 1967) p. 215. [Trans.]
19 Ibid., p. 222.
20 The translator and editor are unable to locate this wonderful reference from Galbraith.
21 This is the "anticoagulant" effect of advertising (Elgozy).
22 Galbraith, *The New Industrial State*, p. 281. [Trans.]
23 Ibid., p. 279. [Trans.]
24 Ibid., p. 280. [Trans.]
25 "Happy end" was originally in English. [Trans.]
26 "The ideological genesis of needs," in *For a Critique of the Political Economy of the Sign*, trans. Charles Levin (St Louis: Telos Press, 1981).
27 Originally in English. [Trans.]
28 "Fun-system" was originally in English. [Trans.]
29 Originally in English. [Trans.]
30 Marc Alexandre, "Sur la société de consommation," *La Nef*, 37.
31 Originally in English. The translator is unable to identify the source of this quotation.
32 *The New Industrial State*, p. 49. [Trans.]
33 Cf. Paul Fabra's article in *Le Monde*, June 26, 1969, "Les superbenefices et la monopolization de l'épargne par les grandes entreprises."
34 Originally in English. [Trans.]
35 *Le Cooperateur*, 1965.
36 Originally in English from George Katona, *The Mass Consumption Society* (New York: McGraw-Hill, 1964). The translator is unable to identify the page of this citation.

3

For a Critique of the Political Economy of the Sign

For a general theory

"The ideological genesis of needs"[1] postulated four different logics of value:

1 The functional logic of use value.
2 The economic logic of exchange value.
3 The differential logic of sign value.
4 The logic of symbolic exchange.

They have for their respective principles: utility, equivalence, difference, ambivalence.

The study of "The art auction"[2] explored a particular case of the strategy of values in the passage from economic exchange value to sign exchange value. Continuing from that point, it is tempting to lay out a hypothetical general conversion table of all values that could serve as an orientation table for a general anthropology.

Use Value (UV)
1 UV—EcEV
2 UV—SgEV
3 UV—SbE

Economic Exchange Value (EcEV)
1 EcEV—UV
2 EcEV—SgEV
3 EcEV—SbE

Sign Exchange Value (SgEV)

    1 SgEV—UV
    2 SgEV—EcEV
    3 SgEV—SbE

Symbolic Exchange (SbE)

    1 SbE—UV
    2 SbE—EcEV
    3 SbE—SgEV

Here there is no attempt at a theoretical articulation of these various logics. There is simply an attempt to mark out the respective fields and the transit from one to the other.

1   *UV—EcEV*: The field of the process of production of exchange value, of the commodity form (*forme-marchandise*) etc., described by political economy. Productive consumption.

2   *UV—SgEV*: The field of the production of signs originating in the destruction of utility ("conspicuous consumption;" sumptuary value). "Unproductive" consumption (of time as well, in conspicuous idleness and leisure), in fact productive of differences: it is functional difference playing as a statutory difference (semi-automatic vs entirely automatic washing machine). Here, the advertising process of conferring value transmutes use goods (*biens d'usage*) into sign values. Here technique and knowledge are divorced from their objective practice and recovered by the "cultural" system of differentiation. It is thus the extended field of *consumption*, in the sense we have given it of production, systems and interplay of signs. Of course, this field also includes the production of signs originating from economic exchange (see 5 below).

3   *UV—SbE*: The field of consumption (*consumption* as opposed to the usual French, *consommation*), that is, of the destruction of use value (or of economic exchange value, cf. 6); no longer, however, in order to produce sign values, but in the mode of a *transgression* of the economic, reinstating symbolic exchange. The presentation, the gift, the festival (*fête*).

4   *EcEV—UV*: This is the process of "consumption" in the traditional economic sense of the term, that is, the reconversion of exchange value into use value (by private individuals in the act of purchase or by production in the productive consumption). Fields 4 and 1 are the two moments of the cycle of classical (and Marxist) political economy, which does not take into account the political economy of the sign. It is also the field of the consecration of exchange value by use value, of the transfiguration of the commodity form into the object form (cf. below, Beyond use value).

5   *EcEV—SgEV*: The process of *consumption* according to its redefinition in the political economy of the sign. It includes the act of spending as production of sign value and, conjointly with 2, it comprises the field of sumptuary value. But here, more accurately, we have the ascension of the commodity form into the sign form, the transfiguration of the economic into sign systems and the transmutation of economic power into domination and social caste privilege.

6   *EcEV—SbE*: While 2 and 5 describe the *transfiguration* of use value and exchange value into sign value (or again: of the object form and commodity form into sign form), 3 and 6 mark the *transgression* of these two forms (that is, of the economic) in symbolic exchange. According to our reformulation, which implicates the sign form in the field of general political economy, 9 completes 3 and 6 as transgression of the sign form towards symbolic exchange. There is no articulation between these three forms (which describe general political economy) and symbolic exchange. There is, on the contrary, a radical separation and transgression, an eventual deconstruction of these forms, which are *codes of value*. Precisely speaking, there is no symbolic "value," there is only symbolic "exchange," which defines itself precisely as something distinct from, and beyond value and code. All forms of value (object, commodity or sign) must be negated in order to inaugurate symbolic exchange. This is the radical rupture of the field of value.

7   *SgEV—UV*: Signs, like commodities, are at once use value and exchange value. The social hierarchies, the invidious differences, the privileges of caste and culture which they support, are accounted as profit, as personal satisfaction, and lived as "need" (need of social value-generation to which corresponds the "utility" of differential signs and their "consumption").

8   *SgEV—EcEV*: This involves the reconversion of cultural privilege, of the monopoly of signs, etc., into economic privilege. Coupled with 5, this reconversion describes the total cycle of a political economy in which economic exploitation based on the monopoly of capital and "cultural" domination based on the monopoly of the code engender one another ceaselessly.

9   *SgEV—SbE*: The deconstruction and transgression of the sign form towards symbolic exchange (cf. 3 and 6).

10, 11 & 12   *SbE—UV, EcEV, SgEV*: All three describe a single process, the inverse of the transgression described in 3, 6, and 9: the process of breaking and reducing symbolic exchange, and the inauguration of the economic. Taken together, they amount to a kind of "cost analysis" of symbolic exchange under the abstract and rational jurisdiction of the various codes of value (use value, exchange value, sign value). For example: the objects involved in reciprocal exchange, whose uninterrupted circulation establishes social relationships, i.e. social *meaning*, annihilate themselves in this continual exchange without assuming any value of their own (that is, any appropriable value). Once symbolic exchange is broken, this same material is abstracted into utility value, commercial value, statutory value. The symbolic is transformed into the instrumental, either commodity or sign. Any one of the various codes may be specifically involved, but they are all joined in the single form of political economy which is opposed, as a whole, to symbolic exchange.

This "combined" interpretation of the matrix (*grille*) of values is only a first approach. It appears that certain correlations group together naturally, that certain are reversible, that certain values are convertible into one another, that certain are exclusive of each other. Some function term by term, others in a more complex cycle. Their general principles – utility, equivalence, difference, and ambivalence – are difficult to articulate clearly. And above all, it should be borne in mind that this remains a combinatory exploration, with its merely formal symmetries. There is no organizing theory behind it.

A second phase consists in extracting some dominant articulation from this moving ensemble of production and reproduction, of conversion, transgression and reduction of values. The first that presents itself can be formulated thus:

$$\frac{\text{SgEV}}{\text{SbE}} = \frac{\text{EcEV}}{\text{UV}}$$

or: sign value is to symbolic exchange what exchange value (economic) is to use value.

That is to say that between symbolic exchange and sign value there is the same reduction, the same process of abstraction and rationalization (cf. "Fetishism and ideology" concerning the body, the unconscious, etc.) as between the multiple "concrete" use values and the abstraction of exchange value in the commodity. Consequently, the form of the equation, if it is accepted, implies that an identical process is at work on both sides of the equation. This process is none other than that of political economy, traditionally directed upon the second relation:

$$\frac{\text{EcEV}}{\text{UV}}$$

This implies analyzing the first relation in terms of a *political economy of the sign*, which is articulated in the political economy of material production and *countersigns* it in the process of ideological labor. This sign economy exists, more or less, in the form of theoretical linguistics and, more generally, semiology. But these latter carefully avoid placing their analyses under the rubric of *political economy* (which implies a *critique* of the political economy of the sign, following the same theoretical procedure as that of Marx). This, however, is what they amount to without knowing it: they are simply the equivalent, in the domain of signs and meaning, of classical bourgeois political economy *prior* to its critique by Marx.

If the political economy of the sign (semiology) is susceptible to a critique in the same way as classical political economy is, it is because their form, not their content, is the same.

This second phase has moved from a matrix (*grille*) and from a more or less mechanical combination of values to a relation of forms and to a homology of the ensemble: it is a considerable advance, but not decisive. This relation effectively articulates the various logics of value; but if the homology is to be fully coherent, there must be a horizontal relation to reinforce the vertical one. Not only must sign value be to symbolic exchange what exchange value is to use value (the relation posited above), but also sign value must be to exchange value what symbolic exchange is to use value. That is:

$$\frac{SgEV}{EcEV} = \frac{SbE}{UV}$$

Now, if sign value and exchange value (sign form and commodity form) really are implicated, by reason of their logical form, in the framework of a general political economy, we can claim no affinity of the same order linking symbolic exchange and use value; quite the contrary, because the former implies the *transgression* of the latter, the latter the *reduction* of the former (cf. in 1, 3 and 10–12). The formula then is not coherent – in particular because the integration of symbolic exchange as a factor homogeneous to the others in the relation does not take into account what has been posited: that the symbolic is not a value (i.e. not positive, autonomiable, measurable or codifiable). It is the ambivalence (positive and negative) of personal exchange – and as such it is radically opposed to all values.

These incoherencies finally result in bursting the formula and in a general restructuring.

1   In place of the sign as global value, it is necessary to make its constituent elements, the signifier and the signified, appear.

2   Then, the definitive correlation between sign form and commodity form is established thus:

$$\frac{\text{EcEV}}{\text{UV}} = \frac{\text{Sr}}{\text{Sd}}$$

or: exchange value is to use value what the signifier is to the signified. The horizontal implication – exchange value is to the signifier what use value is to the signified (i.e. the logical affinity of exchange value and the signifier on the one hand, and of use value and the signified on the other) – will emerge from the analysis of the respective vertical implications. On this basis, we will say that this homologous relation (this time coherent) describes the field of general political economy.

3   The homologous relation being saturated, symbolic exchange finds itself expelled from the field of value (or the field of general political economy). This corresponds to the radical definition as the alternative to and transgression of value.

4   The bar marking the process of reduction, or of rational abstraction, which (it is believed) separates use value from exchange value, and signified from signifier, is displaced. The fundamental reduction no longer takes place between UV and EV, or between signifier and signified; it takes place between the system as a whole and symbolic exchange.

The bar which separates use value from exchange value, and that which separates the signified from the signifier is a line of formal logical implication. It does not radically separate these respective terms; rather, it establishes a structural relation between them (and similarly between exchange value and signifier, between use value and signified). In fact, *all these relations form a system in the framework of political economy.* And the logical organization of this entire system denies, represses and reduces symbolic exchange. The bar that separates all these terms from symbolic exchange is not a bar of structural implication, it is a line of radical exclusion (which presupposes the radical alternative of transgression). Thus we arrive at the following general distribution of terms:

$$\frac{\text{EcEV}}{\text{UV}} = \frac{\text{Sr}}{\text{Sd}} / \text{SbE (symbolic exchange)}$$

that is to say, a single great opposition between the whole field of value (where the process of material production (commodity form) and the process of sign production (sign form) are articulated through the same systematic logic) and the field of non-value, of symbolic exchange.

General political economy / Symbolic exchange

A critique of general political economy (or a critical theory of value) and a theory of symbolic exchange are one and the same thing. It is the basis of a revolutionary anthropology. Certain elements of this anthropology have been elaborated by Marxist analysis, but it has since proved unable to develop them to the critical point of departure.

The present theory posits three essential tasks, beginning from and going beyond Marxist analysis.

1   The extension of the critique of political economy to a *radical critique of use value*, in order to reduce the idealist anthropology which it still subtends, even in Marx (whether at the level of "needs" of individuals or at the level of the "use value of labor"). A critique of use-value fetishism is necessary – an analysis of the object form in its relations to the commodity form.

2   The extension of the critique of political economy to the sign and to systems of signs is required in order to show how the logic, free play and circulation of signifiers is organized like the logic of the exchange value system; and how the logic of signifieds is subordinated to it tactically, as that of use value is subordinated to that of exchange value. Finally, we need a critique of signifier fetishism – an analysis of the sign form in its relation to the commodity form. In the global relation

$$\frac{EcEV}{UV} = \frac{Sr}{Sd}$$

these two initial points aim towards a critical theory of the three terms which Marxist analysis has not yet mastered. In fact, strictly speaking, Marx offers only a critical theory of exchange value. The *critical* theory of use value, signifier, and signified remains to be developed.

3   A theory of symbolic exchange.

Beyond use value

The status of use value in Marxian theory is ambiguous. We know that the commodity is both exchange value and use value. But the latter is always concrete and particular, contingent on its own destiny, whether this is in the process of individual consumption or in the labor process. (In this case, lard is valued as lard, cotton as cotton: they cannot be substituted for each other, nor thus "exchanged.") Exchange value, on the other hand, is abstract and general. To be sure, there could be no exchange value without use value – the two are coupled; but neither is strongly implied by the other:

> In order to define the notion of commodity, it is not important to know its particular content and its exact destination. It suffices that before it is a commodity – in other words, the vehicle (support) of exchange value – the article satisfy a given social need by possessing the corresponding useful property. That is all.[3]

Thus, use value is not implicated in the logic peculiar to exchange value, which is a logic of equivalence. Besides, there can be use value without exchange value (equally for labor power as for products, in the sphere outside the market). Even if it is continually reclaimed by the process of production and exchange, use value is never truly inscribed in the field of the market economy: it has its own finality, albeit restricted. And within it is contained, from this standpoint, the promise of a resurgence beyond the market economy, money and exchange value, in the glorious autonomy of the simple relation of people to their work and their products.

So it appears that commodity fetishism (that is, where social relations are disguised in the qualities and attributes of the commodity itself) is not a function of the commodity defined *simultaneously* as exchange value and use value, but of exchange value alone. Use value, in this restrictive analysis of fetishism, appears neither as a social relation nor hence as the locus of fetishization. Utility as such escapes the historical determination of class. It represents an objective, final relation of intrinsic purpose (*destination propre*), which does not mask itself and whose transparency, as form, defies history (even if its content changes continually with respect to social and cultural determinations). It is here that Marxian idealism goes to work; it is here that we have to be more logical than Marx himself – and more radical, in the true sense of the word. For use value – indeed, utility itself – is a fetishized social relation, just like the abstract equivalence of commodities. Use value is an abstraction. It is an abstraction of the *system of needs* cloaked in the false evidence of a concrete destination and purpose, an intrinsic finality of goods and products. It is just like the abstraction of social labor, which is the basis for the logic of equivalence (exchange value), hiding beneath the "innate" value of commodities.

In effect, our hypothesis is that needs (i.e. the system of needs) are the *equivalent of abstract social labor*: on them is erected the system of use value, just as abstract social labor is the basis for the system of exchange value. This hypothesis also implies that, for there to be a system at all, use value and exchange value must be regulated by an identical abstract logic of equivalence, an identical code. The code of utility is also a code of abstract equivalence of objects and subjects (for each category in itself and for the two taken together in their relation); hence, it is a combinatory code involving potential calculation (we will return to this point). Furthermore, it is in itself, as system, that use value can be "fetishized," and certainly not as a practical operation. It is always the systematic abstraction that is fetishized. The same goes for exchange value. And it is the *two* fetishizations, reunited – that of use value and that of exchange value – that constitute commodity fetishism.

Marx defines the form of exchange value and of the commodity by the fact that they can be equated on the basis of abstract social labor. Inversely, he posits the "incomparability" of use values. Now, it must be seen that:

1   For there to be economic exchange and exchange value, it is also necessary that the principle of utility has already become the reality principle of the object or product. To be abstractly and generally exchangeable, products must also be thought and rationalized in terms of utility. Where they are not (as in primitive symbolic exchange), they can have no exchange value. The reduction to the status of utility is the basis of (economic) exchangeability.

2   If the exchange principle and the utility principle have such an affinity (and do not merely coexist in the commodity), it is because utility is already entirely infused with the logic of equivalence, contrary to what Marx says about the "incomparability" of use values. If use value is not quantitative in the strictly arithmetical sense, it still involves equivalence. Considered as useful values, all goods are already comparable among themselves, because they are assigned to the same rational-functional common denominator, the same abstract determination. Only objects or categories of goods cathected in the singular and personal act of symbolic exchange (the gift, the present) are strictly incomparable. The personal relation (noneconomic exchange) renders them absolutely unique. On the other hand, as a useful value, the object attains an abstract universality, an "objectivity" (through the reduction of every symbolic function).

3 What is involved here, then, is an object form whose general equivalent is utility. And this is no mere "analogy" with the formulas of exchange value. The same logical form is involved. Every object is translatable into the general abstract code of equivalence, which is its rationale, its objective law, its meaning – and this is achieved independently of who makes use of it and what purpose it serves. It is functionality which supports it and carries it along as code; and this code, founded on the mere adequation of an object to its (useful) end, subordinates all real or potential objects to itself, without taking any one into account at all. Here, the economic is born: the economic calculus. The commodity form is only its developed form, and returns to it continually.

4 Now, contrary to the anthropological illusion that claims to exhaust the idea of utility in the simple relation of a human need to a useful property of the object, use value is very much a social relation. Just as, in terms of exchange value, the producer does not appear as a creator, but as abstract social labor power, so in the system of use value, the consumer never appears as desire and enjoyment, but as abstract social need power (one could say *Bedürfniskraft, Bedürfnisvermögen*, by analogy with *Arbeitskraft, Arbeitsvermögen*).

The abstract social producer is man conceived in terms of exchange value. The abstract social individual (the person with "needs") is man thought of in terms of use value. There is a homology between the "emancipation" in the bourgeois era of the private individual given final form by his or her needs and the functional emancipation of objects as use values. This results from an objective rationalization, the surpassing of old ritual and symbolic constraints. In a radically different type of exchange, objects did not have the status of "objectivity" that we give them at all. But henceforward secularized, functionalized and rationalized in purpose, objects become the promise of an ideal (and idealist) political economy, with its watchword "to each according to his needs."

At the same time, individuals, now disengaged from all collective obligations of a magical or religious order, "liberated" from archaic, symbolic or personal ties, at last private and autonomous, define themselves through an "objective" activity of transforming nature – labor – *and* through the destruction of utility for their benefit: needs, satisfactions, use value.

Utility, needs, use value: none of these ever come to grips with the finality of subjects who face their ambivalent object relations, or with symbolic exchange between subjects. Rather, it describes the relation of individuals to themselves conceived in economic terms – better still, the relation of the subject to the economic system. Far from the individual expressing his or her needs in the economic system, it is the economic system that induces the individual function and the parallel functionality of objects and needs.[4] The individual is an ideological structure, a historical form correlative with the commodity form (exchange value), and the object form (use value). The individual is nothing but the subject thought in economic terms, rethought, simplified, and abstracted by the economy. The entire history of consciousness and ethics (all the categories of occidental psycho-metaphysics) is only the history of the political economy of the subject.

Use value is the expression of a whole metaphysic: that of utility. It registers itself as a kind of *moral law* at the heart of the object – and it is inscribed there as the finality of the "need" of the subject. It is the transcription at the heart of things of the same moral law (Kantian and Christian) inscribed on the heart of the subject, positivizing it in its essence and instituting it in a *final* relation (with God, or to some transcendent reality). In both cases, the circulation of value is regulated by a providential code that watches over the correlation of the object with the needs of the subject, under the rubric of functionality – as it assures, incidentally, the coincidence of the subject with divine law, under the sign of morality.

This is the same teleology that seals the essence of the subject (his or her self-identity through the recognition of this transcendent finality). It establishes the object in its truth, as an essence called use value, transparent to itself and to the subject, under the rational banner of utility. And this moral law effects the same fundamental reduction of all the symbolic virtualities of the subject and the object. A simple finality is substituted for a multiplicity of meanings. And it is still the principle of equivalence that functions here as the reducer of symbolic ambivalence:

1   It establishes the object in a functional equivalence to itself in the single framework of this determined valence: utility. This absolute signification, this rationalization by identity (its equivalence to itself) permits the object to enter the field of political economy as a positive value.

2   The same absolute simplification of the subject as the subject of moral consciousness and needs permits him or her to enter the system of values and practices of political economy as an abstract individual (defined by identity, equivalence to himself or herself).

Thus the functionality of objects, their moral code of utility, is as entirely governed by the logic of equivalence as is their exchange value status. Hence, functionality falls just as squarely under the jurisdiction of political economy. And if we call this abstract equivalence of utilities the object form, we can say that *the object form is only the completed form of the commodity form*. In other words, the same logic (and the same fetishism) plays on the two sides of the commodity specified by Marx: use value and exchange value.

By not submitting use value to this logic of equivalence in radical fashion, by maintaining use value as the category of "incomparability," Marxist analysis has contributed to the mythology (a veritable rationalist mystique) that allows the relation of the individual to objects conceived as use values to pass for a concrete and objective – in sum, "natural" – relation between man's needs and the function proper to the object. This is all seen as the opposite of the abstract, reified "alienated" relation the subject would have toward products as exchange values. The truth of the subject would lie here, in usage, as a concrete sphere of the private relation, as opposed to the social and abstract sphere of the market.[5] (Marx does provide a radical analysis of the abstraction of the private individual as a social relation in another connection, however.) Against all this seething metaphysic of needs and use values, it must be said that abstraction, reduction, rationalization and systematization are as profound and as generalized at the level of "needs" as at the level of commodities. Perhaps this was not yet very clear at an anterior stage of political economy, when one could imagine that if individuals were alienated by the system of exchange value, at least they would return to themselves, become themselves again in their needs and in the moment of use value. But it has become possible today, at the present stage of consummative mobilization, to see that needs, far from being articulated around the desire or the demand of the subject, find their coherence elsewhere: in a generalized system that is to desire what the system of exchange value is to concrete labor, the source of value. All the drives, symbolic relations, object relations and even perversions – in short, all the subject's *labor* of cathexis – are abstracted and given their general equivalent in utility and the system of needs, as all values and real social labor find their general equivalent in money. Everything surging from the subject, his or her body and desire, is dissociated and catalyzed in terms of needs, more or less specified in advance by objects. All instincts are rationalized, finalized and objectified in needs – hence symbolically cancelled. *All ambivalence is reduced by equivalence.* And to say that the system of needs is a system of general equivalence is no metaphor: it means that we are completely immersed in political economy. This is why we have spoken of *fetish-ism of use value*. If needs were the singular, concrete expression of the subject, it would be absurd to speak of fetishism. But when needs erect themselves more and more into an abstract system, regulated by a principle of equivalence and general combinatory, then certainly the same fetishism is in play. For this system is not only homologous to that of exchange value and the commodity; *it expresses the latter in all its depth and perfection.*

Indeed, just as exchange value is not a substantial aspect of the product, but a form that expresses a social relation, so use value can no longer be viewed as an innate function of the object, but as a social determination (at once of the subject, the object, and their relation). In other words, just as the logic of the commodity indifferently extends itself to people and things and makes people (all obedient to the same law) appear only as exchange value – thus the restricted finality of utility imposes itself on people as surely as on the world of objects. It is illogical and naive to hope that, through objects conceived in terms of exchange value, that is, in his needs, humans can fulfill themselves *otherwise than as use value*. However, such is the modern humanist vulgate: through the functionality, the domestic finality of the exterior world, man is supposed to fulfill himself *qua man*. The truth is something else entirely. In an environment of commodities and exchange value, man is no more himself than he is exchange value and commodity. Encompassed by objects that function and serve, man is not so much himself as the most beautiful of these functional and servile objects. It is not only *homo economicus* who is turned entirely into use value during the process of capitalist production. This utilitarian imperative even structures the relation of the individual to himself or herself. In the *process of satisfaction*, individuals valorize and make fruitful their own potentialities for pleasure; they "realize" and manage, to the best of their ability, their own "faculty" of pleasure, treated literally like a productive force. Isn't this what all of humanist ethics is based on: the "proper use" of oneself?

In substance, Marx says: "Production not only produces goods; it produces people to consume them, and the corresponding needs." This proposition is most often twisted in such a way as to yield simplistic ideas like "the manipulation of needs" and denunciations of "artificial needs."[6] It is necessary to grasp that what produces the commodity system in its general form is the *concept* of need itself, as constitutive of the very structure of the individual; that is, the histor-ical concept of social beings who, in the rupture of symbolic exchange, autonomize themselves and rationalize their desire, their relation to others and to objects, in terms of needs, utility, satisfaction and use value.

Thus, it is not merely such and such a value that reduces symbolic exchange, or emerges from its rupture; it is first the structural opposition of two values: exchange value and use value, whose logical form is the same, and whose dual organization punctuates the economic. We are faced here at a global anthropological level with the same schema of "semiological reduction" analyzed in "Fetishism and ideology."[7] In that study, I tried to demonstrate the way in which this binary oppositive structuration constituted the very matrix of ideological functioning; I started from the fact that this structuration is never purely structural: it always plays to the advantage of one of the two terms. *Structural logic* always redoubles in a strategy (thus masculine–feminine, to the profit of masculinity, conscious–unconscious, to the advantage of consciousness, etc.)

Precisely the same thing is going on here. In the correlation

$$\frac{EV}{UV} = \frac{Sr}{Sd}$$

use value and signified do not have the same weight as exchange value and signifier respectively. Let us say that they have a tactical value; whereas exchange value and signifier have strategic value. The system is organized along the lines of a functional but hierarchized bipolarity. Absolute preeminence redounds to exchange value and the signifier. Use value and needs are only an effect of exchange value. Signified (and referent) are only an effect of the signifier (we will return to this point later).[8] Neither is an autonomous reality, one that either exchange value or the signifier would express or translate in their code. At bottom, they are only simulation models, produced by the play of exchange value and of signifiers. They provide signifiers with the guarantee of the real, the lived, the concrete; they are the guarantee of an objective reality for which, however, in the same moment, these systems qua systems substitute their own total logic. (Even the term "substitute" is misleading, in this context. It implies the existence somewhere of a fundamental reality that the system appropriates or distorts. In fact, there is no reality or principle of reality other than that directly produced by the system as its ideal reference.) Use value and the signified do not constitute an *elsewhere* with respect to the systems of the other two; they are only their alibis.

We have seen, in a first approximation, that the field of political economy generalizes and saturates itself through the system of use value (that is, the extension of the process of abstraction and productive rationality to the entire domain of consumption through the system of needs as system of values and productive forces). In this sense, use value appears as the completion and fulfillment of exchange value (of political economy in general). The fetishism of use value redoubles and deepens the fetishism of exchange value.

That is a starting point. But it is necessary to see that the system of use value is *not only* the double, transposition or extension of that of exchange value. It functions simultaneously as the latter's ideological guarantee (and once again, if this is so, it is because it is logically structured in the same way). It is understood, of course, that it is a naturalizing ideology we are concerned with here. Use value is given fundamentally as the instance (i.e. tribunal) before which all people are equal. On this view, need, leaving aside any variation in the means of satisfying it, would be the most equally distributed thing in the world.[9] People are not equal with respect to goods taken as exchange value, but they would be equal as regards goods taken as use value. One may dispose of them or not, according to one's class, income, or disposition; but the *potentiality* for availing oneself of them nevertheless exists for all. Everyone is equally rich in *possibilities* for happiness and satisfaction. This is the secularization of the potential equality of all people before God: the democracy of "needs." Thus use value, reflected back to the anthropological sphere, reconciles in the universal those who are divided socially by exchange value.

Exchange value erases the real labor process at the level of the commodity, such that the commodity appears as an autonomous value. Use value fares even better: it provides the commodity, inhuman as it is in its abstraction, with a "human" finality. In exchange value, social labor disappears. The system of use value, on the other hand, involves the resorption without trace of the entire ideological and historical labor process that leads subjects in the first place to think of themselves as individuals, defined by their needs and satisfaction, and so ideally to integrate themselves into the structure of the commodity.

Thus, without ceasing to be a system in historical and logical solidarity with the system of exchange value, the system of use value succeeds in naturalizing exchange value and offers it that universal and atemporal guarantee without which the exchange value system simply couldn't reproduce itself (or doubtless even be produced in its general form).

Use value is thus the crown and scepter of political economy:

1 In its lived reality: it is the immanence of political economy in everyday life, down to the very act in which man believes he has

rediscovered himself. People do not rediscover their objects except in what they serve; and they do not rediscover themselves except through the expression and satisfaction of their needs – in what they serve.

2   In its strategic value: ideologically, it seals off the system of production and exchange, thanks to the institution of an idealist anthropology that screens use value and needs from their historical logic in order to inscribe them in a formal eternity: that of utility for objects, that of the useful appropriation of objects by man in need.

This is why use-value fetishism is indeed more profound, more "mysterious" than the fetishism of exchange value. The mystery of exchange value and the commodity can be unmasked, relatively – it has been since Marx – and raised to consciousness as a social relation. But value in the case of use value is enveloped in total mystery, for it is grounded anthropologically in the (self-) "evidence" of a naturalness, in an unsurpassable original reference. This is where we discover the real "theology" of value – in the order of finalities: in the "ideal" relation of equivalence, harmony, economy and equilibrium that the concept of utility implies. It operates at all levels: between man and nature, man and objects, man and his body, the self and others. Value becomes absolutely self-evident, *la chose la plus simple.* Here the mystery and cunning (of history and of reason) are at their most profound and tenacious.

If the system of use value is produced by the system of exchange value as its own ideology – if use value has no autonomy, if it is only the *satellite* and *alibi* of exchange value, though systematically combining with it in the framework of political economy – then it is no longer possible to posit use value as an alternative to exchange value. Nor, therefore, is it possible to posit the "restitution" of use value, at the end of political economy, under the sign of the "liberation of needs" and the "administration of things" as a revolutionary perspective.

Every revolutionary perspective today stands or falls on its ability to reinterrogate radically the repressive, reductive, rationalizing metaphysic of utility. All critical theory depends on the analysis of the object form.[10] This has been absent from Marxist analysis. With all the political and ideological consequences that this implies, the result has been that all illusions converged on use value, idealized by opposition to exchange value, when it was in fact only the latter's naturalized form.

Marx and Crusoe

Marx says in volume 1 of *Capital* (part 1, section 4):

> So far as (a commodity) is a value in use, there is nothing mysterious
> about it, whether we consider it from the point of view that by its
> properties it is capable of satisfying human wants, or from the point
> that those properties are the product of human labor. It is as clear as
> noonday that man, by his industry, changes the forms of the materials
> furnished by Nature, in such a way as to make them useful to him...
> The mystical character of commodities does not originate, therefore,
> in their use value...
> The categories of bourgeois economy consist of... forms of thought
> expressing with social validity the conditions and relations of a definite
> historically determined mode of production, viz., the production of
> commodities. The whole mystery of commodities, all the magic and
> necromancy that surrounds the products of labor as long as they take
> the form of commodities, vanishes therefore, so soon as we come to
> other forms of production.
> Since Robinson Crusoe's experiences are a favorite theme with
> political economists, let us take a look at him on his island... All the
> relations between Robinson and the objects that form this wealth of his
> own creation are here so simple and clear as to be intelligible without
> exertion, even to Mr Baudrillard.[11] And yet those relations contain all
> that is essential to the determination of value.

Having quite justifiably played his joke at the expense of the
bourgeois economists and their interminable references to Robinson,
Marx would have done well to examine his own use of the Crusoe
myth. For by opposing the obscure mysticism of commodity value to
the simplicity and transparency of Crusoe's relation to his wealth, he
fell into a trap. If one hypothesizes (as Marxists do) that all the
ideology of bourgeois political economy is summed up in the myth
of Robinson Crusoe, then it must be admitted that everything in the
novel itself agrees with the mystical theology and metaphysics of
bourgeois thought, including (and above all) this "transparency" in
man's relation to the instruments and products of his labor.

This ideal confrontation of man with his labor capacity (*Arbeitsvermögen*) and with his needs is not only abstract because it is
separated out from the sphere of political economy and commercial
social relations; it is abstract *in itself*: not abstracted from political
economy, but abstract because it epitomizes the abstraction of political economy itself; that is, the ascension of exchange value via use

value, the apotheosis of the economic in the providential finality of utility.

Robinson Crusoe is the outcome of a total mutation that has been in progress since the dawn of bourgeois society (though only really theorized since the eighteenth century). Man was transformed simultaneously into a productive force and a "man with needs." The manufacturers and the ideologues of Nature divided him between themselves. In his labor, he became a use value for a system of production. Simultaneously, goods and products became use values for him, taking on a meaning as functions of his needs, which were henceforth legalized as "nature." He entered the regime of use value, which was also that of "Nature." But this was by no means according to an original finality rediscovered: all these concepts (needs, nature, utility) were born together, in the historical phase that saw the systematization of both political economy and the ideology that sanctions it.

The myth of Robinson Crusoe is the bourgeois avatar of the myth of terrestrial paradise. Every great social order of production (bourgeois or feudal) maintains an ideal myth, at once a myth of culmination and a myth of origin. Theology supported itself on the myth of the fulfillment of man in the divine law; political economy is sustained on the great myth of human fulfillment according to the natural law of needs. Both deal in the same finality: an ideal relation of man to the world through his needs and the rule of Nature; and an ideal relationship with God through faith and the divine rule of Providence. Of course, this ideal vocation is lived from the outset as lost or compromised. But the finality tarries, and use value, entombed beneath exchange value, like the natural harmony of earthly paradise broken by sin and suffering, remains inscribed as an invulnerable essence to be disinterred at the last stage of History, in a promised future redemption. The logic and ideology are the same: under the sign of a bountiful nature, where the primitive hunting and gathering mode of production, anterior to the feudal mode, is highlighted, and from which serfdom and labor are made to disappear, the myth of earthly paradise describes the ideality of feudal relations (suzerainty and fealty of vassals). Likewise, the Crusoe myth describes, in "transparent" isolation (where the anterior mode of agriculture and craftsmanship reappears, and the laws of the market and exchange disappear), the ideality of bourgeois relations: individual autonomy, to each according to their labor and their needs; moral consciousness bound to nature – and, if possible, some Man Friday, some aboriginal servant. (But if Crusoe's relations to his labor and his wealth are so "clear," as Marx insists, what on earth has Friday got to do with this set-up?)

In fact, nothing is clear about this fable. Its evidence of simplicity and transparency is, as that of the commodity for Marx, "abounding in metaphysical subtleties and theological niceties." There is nothing clear and natural in the fact of "transforming nature according to one's needs" or in "rendering oneself useful" as well as things. And there was no need for this moral law of use value to have escaped the critique of political economy: the whole system and its "mystery" were already there with Robinson on his island, and in the fabricated immediacy of his relation to things.

Toward a critique of the political economy of the sign

The critique of the political economy of the sign proposes to develop the analysis of the sign form, just as the critique of political economy once set out to analyze the commodity form.

Since the commodity comprises simultaneously exchange value and use value, its total analysis must encompass the two sides of the system. Similarly, the sign is at once signifier and signified; and so the analysis of the sign form must be established on two levels. Concurrently, of course, the logical and strategic analysis of the relation between the two terms is pressed upon us, thus:

1 Between the system of exchange value (EV) and that of use value (UV), or between the commodity form and the object form: this was the attempt in the preceding section.
2 Between the systems of the signifier and the signified (or between their respective codes, which define the articulation or sign value and the sign form).

In both cases, this (internal) relation is established as a hierarchical function between a dominant form and an alibi (or satellite) form, which is the logical crowning and ideological completion of the first.

The magical thinking of ideology

The effect of this homological structuration of values in what can conveniently be called the fields of economy and signification is to displace the whole process of ideology and to theorize it in radically different terms. Ideology can no longer be understood as an infra-structural – superstructural relation between a material production (system and relations of production) and a production of signs (culture, etc.), which expresses and masks the contradictions at the "base." Henceforth, all of this comprises, with the same degree of objectivity, a general political economy (its critique), which is traversed throughout by the same form and administered by the same logic.

It should be recalled that the traditional vision of ideology still proves incapable of grasping the "ideological" function of culture and of signs – except at the level of the signified. This follows inevitably from its separation of culture (and signs) in the artificial distinction between the economic and the ideological, not to mention the desperate contortions ("superstructure," "dialectic," "structure in dominance") that this entails. Thus, ideology (of such-and-such a group, or of the dominant class) always appears as the overblown discourse of some great theme, content, or value (patriotism, morality, humanism, happiness, consumption, the family) whose *allegorical* power somehow insinuates itself into consciousness (this has never been explained) in order to integrate them. These become, in turn, the *contents of thought* that come into play in real situations. In sum, ideology appears as a sort of cultural surf frothing on the beachhead of the economy.

It is then clear that ideology is actually *that very form* that traverses both the production of signs and material production; or rather, it is the logical bifurcation of this form into two terms:

$$\text{EV} \Big/ \text{UV}$$
$$\cdot \ \ \text{Sr} \Big/ \text{Sd}$$

This is the functional, strategic split through which the form reproduces itself. It signifies that ideology lies *already whole in the relation of EV to UV, that is, in the logic of the commodity*, as is so in the relation of Sr to Sd, that is in the internal logic of the sign.

Marx demonstrated that the objectivity of material production did not reside in its materiality, but in its *form*. In fact, this is the point of departure for all critical theory. The same analytical reduction must be applied to ideology: its objectivity does not reside in its "ideality," that is, in a realist metaphysic of thought contents, but in its form.

The "critique" (not excluding here the Marxist critique of ideology) feeds off a magical conception of its object. It does not unravel ideology as form, but as content, as given, transcendent value – a sort of mana that attaches itself to several global representations that magically impregnate those floating and mystified subjectivities called "consciousnesses." Like the concept of need, which is presented as the link between the utility of an object and the demand of a subject, ideology appears as the relation between the projection of a consciousness and the ideality of – vaguely – an idea, or a value. Transposed from the analysis of material goods to collective representations and values, the same little magic footbridge is suspended between artificial, even metaphysical, concepts.[12]

In fact, ideology is the process of reducing and abstracting symbolic material into a form. But this reductive abstraction is given immediately as value (autonomous), as content (transcendent), and as a representation of consciousness (signified). It is the same process that lends the commodity an appearance of autonomous value and transcendent reality – a process that involves the misunderstanding of the form of the commodity and of the abstraction of social labor that it operates. In bourgeois (or, alas, Marxist) thought, culture is defined as a *transcendence of contents* correlated with consciousnesses by means of a "representation" that circulates among them like positive values, just as the fetishized commodity appears as a real and immediate value, correlated with individual subjects through "need" and use value, and circulating according to the rules of exchange value.

It is the cunning of form to veil itself continually in the evidence of content. It is the cunning of the code to veil itself and to produce itself in the obviousness of value. It is in the "materiality" of content that form consumes its abstraction and reproduces itself as form. That is its peculiar magic. It simultaneously produces the content and the consciousness to receive it (just as production produces the product and its corresponding need). Thus, it installs culture in a dual transcendence of values (of contents) and consciousness, and in a metaphysic of exchange between the two terms. And if the bourgeois vulgate enshrines it in this transcendence precisely in order to exalt it as *culture*, the Marxist vulgate embalms it in the very same transcendence in order to denounce it as *ideology*. But the two scriptures rejoin in the same magical thinking.[13]

Just about all contemporary thought in this area confounds itself with false problems and in endless controversies ensuing from artificial disjunctions:

1   The subject–object dichotomy, bridged by the magical concept of need. Things might run quite smoothly here if the general system of production-consumption were not disrupted by the insoluble problem of supply and demand. Can one still speak of autonomy of choice, or is it a question of manipulation? Perhaps the two perspectives can be synthesized? This is mere pseudo-dialectic. It is all an eternal litany. And over a false problem anyway.

2   The infrastructure–superstructure dichotomy, which, as we have seen, covers over again the implacable disjunction between the materiality of contents and the ideality of consciousness, reuniting the two thereby separated poles with the magical conception of ideology. Even here, matters would run more smoothly if the problem of the "determinant instance" were not held eternally in suspense (since it is usually "in the last instance," it doesn't actually appear on the stage), with all the acrobatics of "interaction," "dialectic," "relative autonomy," and "overdetermination" that follow in its wake (and whose interminable careers have redounded to the glory of generations of intellectuals).

3   The exploitation–alienation distinction, which reiterates this false problem at the level of political analysis. The endless debate over whether exploitation is the ground of alienation or vice versa; or whether the second succeeds the first as "the most advanced stage of capitalism" – all this is absurd. Not for the first time, the confusion arises from an artificial separation – this time of the sign and the commodity, which are not analyzed in their form, but posed instead as contents (the one of signification, the other of production). Whence emerges the distinction between an "exploitation" of labor power and an "alienation by signs." As if the commodity and the system of material production "signified" nothing! As if signs and culture were not immediately abstract social production at the level of the code and models, in a generalized exchange system of values.

Ideology is thus properly situated on neither side of this split. Rather, it is the one and only form that traverses all the fields of social production. Ideology seizes all production, material or symbolic, in the same process of abstraction, reduction, general equivalence, and exploitation.

1   It is because *the logic of the commodity and of political economy is at the very heart of the sign*, in the abstract equation of signifier and signified, in the differential combinatory of signs, that signs can function as exchange value (the discourse of communication) and as use value (rational decoding and distinctive social use).

2   It is because *the structure of the sign is at the very heart of the commodity form* that the commodity can take on, immediately, the effect of signification: not epiphenomenally, in excess of itself, as "message" or connotation, but because its very form establishes it as a total *medium*, as a *system of communication* administering all social exchange. Like the sign form, the commodity is a code managing the exchange of values. It makes little difference whether the contents of

material production or the immaterial contents of signification are involved; it is the code that is determinant: the rules of the interplay of signifiers and exchange value. Generalized in the system of political economy, it is the code which, in both cases, reduces all symbolic *ambivalence* in order to ground the "rational" circulation of values and their play of exchange in the regulated equivalence of values.

It is here that the concept of alienation proves useless, by dint of its association with the metaphysic of the subject of consciousness. The code of political economy, which is the fundamental code of our society, does not operate by alienating consciousness from contents. A parallel confusion arises in the view of "primitive" myths as false stories or histories that consciousnesses recount to themselves. Here the pregnant effects of mythic contents are held to bind society together (through the "cohesion" of belief systems). But actually, these myths make up a code of signs that exchange among themselves, integrating the group through the very process of their circulation. Likewise, the fundamental code of our societies, the code of political economy (both commodity form and sign form) does not operate through the alienation of consciousness and contents. It rationalizes and regulates exchange, makes things communicate, but only under the law of the code and through the control of meaning.

The division of labor, the functional division of the terms of discourse, does not mystify people; it socializes them and informs their exchange according to a general, abstract model. The very concept of the individual is the product of this general system of exchange. And the idea of "totality" under which the subject (either that of consciousness or that of History) thinks itself in its ideal reference is nothing but the effect and the symptom of the system – the shadow that it wears. The concept of alienation involves a kind of wizardry in which consciousness thinks of itself as its own ideal content (its rediscovered totality): it is an ideological concept. And ideology is, in its version as a superstructure of contents of consciousness, in these terms, an alienated concept.

Today consumption – if this term has a meaning other than that given it by vulgar economics – defines precisely *the stage where the commodity is immediately produced as a sign, as sign value, and where signs (culture) are produced as commodities*. But this whole area of study is still occupied, "critically" or otherwise, by specialists of production (economy, infrastructure); or ideology specialists (signs, culture); or even by a kind of monolithic dialectician of the totality. This partitioning of the object domain obscures even the simplest realities. If any progress is to be made at this point, "research" –

especially Marxist research – must come to terms with the fact that nothing produced or exchanged today (objects, services, bodies, sex, culture, knowledge, etc.) can be decoded exclusively as a sign, nor solely measured as a commodity; that everything appears in the context of a general political economy in which the determining instance is neither the commodity nor culture (not even the updated commodity, revised and reinterpreted in its signifying function, with its message, its connotations, but always as if there still existed an objective substrate to it, the potential objectivity of the *product* as such; nor culture in its "critical" version, where signs, values, ideas are seen as everywhere commercialized or recuperated by the dominant system, but again, as if there subsisted through all this something whose transcendence could have been rationalized and simply compromised – a kind of sublime use value of culture distorted in exchange value). The object of this political economy, that is its simplest component, its nuclear element – that which precisely the commodity was for Marx – is no longer today properly either commodity or sign, but indissolubly both, and *both only in the sense that they are abolished as specific determinations, but not as form.* Rather, this object is perhaps quite simply the *object*, the object form, on which use value, exchange value and sign value converge in a complex mode that describes the most general form of political economy.

The metaphysics of the sign

The meaning value of the sign asserts itself with the same apparent obviousness as the natural evidence of the value of the commodity to the predecessors of Marx. These, as they say, are "the simplest of matters"; and yet they are the most mysterious. Like political economy before it, semiology accomplishes little more than a description of their circulation and structural functioning.[14]

We have seen, in the preceding section, that the abstraction of the exchange value system is sustained by the effect of concrete reality and of objective purpose exhaled by use value and needs. This is the strategic logic of the commodity; its second term acts as the satellite and alibi for the first. The present hypothesis is that the same analysis holds true for the logic and strategy of the sign, thus exploding the "scientific postulates" of semio-linguistics – the arbitrary character of the sign in particular, as originally defined by Saussure and modified by Benveniste.

The arbitrariness of the sign does not reside in its non-motivation – in the commonplace that the signifier "table" has no "natural" vocation to signify the concept of the reality of the table (any more than *Tisch* in German, etc.); it is rooted in the very fact of positing an equivalence between such and such an Sr and such and such an Sd. In this sense, arbitrariness is total even in the case of the symbol,[15] where the principle of equivalence between signifier and signified is fully retained in their analogy. Arbitrariness arises from the fundamental institution of an exact correlation between a given "discrete" Sr and an equally discrete Sd. In other words, arbitrariness lies in the "discretion" which alone grounds the possibility of the equational relation of the sign, so that *this* equals this, and nothing else. This discretion is thus the very principle of the sign's rationality; it functions as the agent of abstraction and universal reduction of all potentialities and qualities of meaning (*sens*) that do not depend on or derive from the respective framing, equivalence, and specular relation of a signifier and a signified. This is the directive and reductive rationalization transacted by the sign – not in relation to an exterior, immanent "concrete reality" that signs would supposedly recapture abstractly in order to express, but in relation to all that which overflows the schema of equivalence and signification; and which the sign reduces, represses and annihilates in the very operation that constitutes it (the sudden crystallization of an Sr and an Sd). The rationality of the sign is rooted in its exclusion and annihilation of all symbolic ambivalence on behalf of a fixed and equational structure. The sign is a discriminant: it structures itself through exclusion. Once crystallized on this exclusive structure, the sign aligns its fixed field, resigns the differential, and assigns Sr and Sd each its sphere of systemic control. Thus, the sign proffers itself as full value: positive, rational, exchangeable value. All virtualities of meaning are shorn in the cut of structure.

This one-to-one assignation of Sr to Sd can be complicated quite easily into an equivocal or multivocal relation without violating the logic of the sign. A signifier may refer to many signifieds, or vice versa: the principle of equivalence, ergo of exclusion and reduction, which roots the arbitrariness of the sign, remains untouched. While still opposing itself as radically as ever to *ambivalence, equivalence* has simply transmuted into *polyvalence.* Ambiguity itself is only the vacillation of a principle which, for all intents and purposes, rests intact. Nor does the "dissolve" effect (of signification) jeopardize the principle of the rationality of the sign; that is, its reality principle. While retaining their discreteness, Sr and Sd are capable of multiple connections. But (through all these combinatory possibilities) the code of signification never ceases to monitor and systematically control meaning.

Only ambivalence (as a *rupture* of value, of another side or beyond of sign value, and as the *emergence* of the *symbolic*) sustains a challenge to the legibility, the false transparency of the sign; only ambivalence questions the evidence of the use value of the sign (rational decoding) and of its exchange value (the discourse of communication). *It brings the political economy of the sign to a standstill;* it dissolves the respective definitions of Sr and Sd – concepts emblazoned with the seal of signification; and since they assume their meaning through the process of signification in the classical sense, Sr and Sd would be doomed by the shattering of the semiologic. In the logic of ambivalence and of the symbolic, we are dealing with a process of the resolution of the sign, a resolution of the equation on which the sign is articulated, and which, in communicative discourse, *is never resolved*: integrated, opaque, never elucidated, the sign gives rise, in communicative discourse, to the same type of social mystery as that other medium, the commodity, which also depends on an abstract equation of all values.[16]

The critique of political economy, worked out by Marx at the level of exchange value, but whose total scope implies also that of use value, is quite precisely this *resolution* of the commodity and of its implicit equation – a resolution of the commodity as the form and code of general equivalence. It is this same critical resolution that must be extended to the field of signification, in a critique of the political economy of the sign.

The mirage of the referent

Where the sign presents itself as a unity of discrete and functional meaning, the Sr refers to an Sd, and the ensemble to a referent. The sign as abstract structure refers to a fragment of objective reality. It is, moreover, between these two terms that Benveniste, modifying Saussure, relocates the arbitrariness of the sign – which is between the sign and that which it designates, and not between the Sr and the Sd, which are both of a psychic nature and necessarily associated in the mind of the subject by a veritable consubstantiality.

> What is arbitrary is that a certain sign, and not another, is applied to a certain element of reality, and not to any other. In this sense, and only in this sense, it is permissible to speak of contingency, and even in so doing we would seek less to solve the problem than simply to pinpoint it in order to set it aside provisionally... The domain of arbitrariness is thus left outside the comprehension (logical intention) of the linguistic sign.[17]

But banishing arbitrariness to the exterior of the sign does no more than displace the problem; and to believe in the possibility of deferring it is here only another way of providing a solution which, far from being merely provisional and methodological, risks reviving its eternal metaphysical formulation.

For Saussure the internal contingency of the sign was an obstacle that always threatened the reciprocal coherence of the Sr and the Sd. Through the expulsion of the arbitrary, Benveniste attempts to rescue the inner organization and logical necessity of the sign (not to mention that of semio-linguistics). But this adjustment is only possible on the basis of a separation between the sign and reality (the referent). As we have seen, Benveniste seems quite content to refer the solution to the problem that this creates back to philosophy; but in fact he responds to the question himself, and very metaphysically, like all linguists and semiologists – with the concepts of "motivation" and of "arbitrariness."

In the end, the difficulty with Benveniste's analysis (and the analyses of others) comes down to the fact that things are just not cut out according to his idealist scheme. The scission (*coupure*) does not occur between a sign and a "real" referent. It occurs between the Sr as form and, on the other side, the Sd and the Rft, which are registered together as content – the one of thought, the other of reality (or rather, of perception) – under the aegis of the Sr. The referent in question here is no more external to the sign than is the Sd: indeed, it is governed by the sign. It is carved out and projected as its function; its only reality is of that which is *ornamentally inscribed on the sign itself*. In a profound sense, the referent is the reflection of the sign, and this profound collusion, which depends on form, is "instinctively" translated at the level of contents by the speaking subject. Benveniste declares: "For the speaking subject, there is complete adequation between language and reality. The sign recovers and commands reality; better still, it *is* that reality..."[18] The poor speaker evidently knows nothing of the arbitrary character of the sign (but then, he probably isn't a semiologist)! Yet there is a certain truth to his naive metaphysic, for Benveniste's "arbitrary" link between the sign and reality has no more existence than the one postulated by Saussure between Sr and Sd.

So Benveniste's argument ultimately turns back on itself. For if one admits, with him, and against Saussure, that the Sd is consubstantial with the Sr, then so must be the referent (reality), since the Sd and Rft are both cut from the same cloth (as assigned to them by the Sr). The process of carving out and separation, of abstract formalization, is continuous from one end to the other of the chain – from Sr to Rft inclusive. In fact, it makes little difference whether one claims either:

1 That *motivation* is general throughout the chain: but then it is no longer the substantial motivation of the psychologistic type (that of content) that emanates somehow from the Rft toward the Sr; it is a kind of formal motivation "from on high" – it is the law of the code and the signifier that informs and determines (to the point of) "reality." The code becomes a veritable reality principle.

2 Or that it is *arbitrariness*, the conventionality of the sign, that reigns over the entire chain. Then the concrete ceases to exist, and the very perception of it hinges on the abstraction and the "discretion" of the Sr. The *specter* of the Sr extends onto the world (in two senses: it "analyzes" it spectrally, and it haunts it).

The crucial thing is to see that the separation of the sign and the world is a fiction, and leads to a science fiction. The logic of equivalence, abstraction, discreteness and projection of the sign engulfs the Rft as surely as it does the Sd. This "world" that the sign "evokes" (the better to distance itself from it) is nothing but the effect of the sign, the shadow that it carries about, its "pantographic" extension. Even better: this world is quite simply the Sd-Rft. As we have seen, the Sd-Rft is a single and compact thing, an identity of content that acts as the moving shadow of the Sr. It is the reality effect in which the play of signifiers comes to fruition and deludes the world.

Now the homology between the logic of signification and the logic of political economy begins to emerge. For the latter exploits its reference to needs and the actualization of use value as an anthropological horizon while precluding their real intervention in its actual functioning and operative structure. Or so it appears. Similarly, the referent is maintained as exterior to the comprehension of the sign: the sign alludes to it, but its internal organization excludes it. In fact, it is now clear that the system of needs and of use value is thoroughly implicated in the form of political economy as its completion. And likewise for the referent, this "substance of reality," in that it is entirely bound up in the logic of the sign. Thus, in each field, the dominant form (system of exchange value and combinatory of the Sr respectively) provides itself with a referential rationale (*raison*), a content, an alibi and, significantly, in each this articulation is made *under the same metaphysical "sign," i.e. need or motivation.*

All of this venerable old psychology nourishes the semiological organism:

1 The referent, the "real" object, is the phenomenal object, the perceptual contents and lived experience of the subject – situated

halfway between phenomenology and Bergsonian substance opposed to form.

2 In a manner of speaking, this perceptual content emerges flush; it is shifted to the level of the sign by the signified, the content of thought. Between the two, one is supposed to glide in a kind of frictionless space from the perceptual to the conceptual, in accordance with the old recipes of philosophical idealism and the abstract associationism that was already stale in the nineteenth century.

And how is the articulation established between the sign and referent (or between the Sr and the Sd), subtly differentiated as they are (so subtly, in fact, as to preserve them in each other's image!)? We have already broached the term: it is by *motivation*. Whether it is in order to deny motivation, according to the Saussurian theory of the sign (to relativize it, to proportion it in the definition of the symbol), or simply to affirm it, like Benveniste in his critique of the Saussurian theory (justified, to be sure, but only from the internal perspective of semio-linguistics) – the only relation thinkable, the only concept under which the articulation of the phenomenal (psychological) and the sign can be thought is that of motivation. It is a hollow and somewhat supernatural concept. But it can hardly be otherwise, once one has granted this metaphysical representation of the referent, this abstract separation between the sign and the world. *Some* form of wizardry is required to rejoin them: and – what a coincidence! – it is with this very term that political economy attempts to reunite the subject and the object it posits as separate: need. *Need, motivation*: one never escapes this circle. Each term conceals the same metaphysical wile. In the latter version, the term has a rather more logical resonance; in the other, a more psychological one. But let us not be mistaken here. The logical and the psychological are here indissolubly mixed: semiological motivation has all of psychology behind it. As for economic need, it is much more than a question of the "demand" of the subject: the entire logical articulation of economic science demands it as a functional postulate.

These concepts are not accidentally nebulous. Concepts are quite meaningless when they are busy bridging nonexistent gaps. There is no distinction between the sign and the phenomenal referent, except from the metaphysical perspective that simultaneously idealizes and abstracts the sign and the *Lebenswelt*, the one as form, the other as content, in their formal opposition. Having provided itself with false distinctions, it cannot be expected to resolve them except with false concepts. But such distinctions are strategic and operational –

that is the point. To resolve them (and to rupture the conceptual unreality, which would be the only means of resolving the false problem of the arbitrariness and motivation of the sign) would amount to shattering the possibility of all semiology.

The emptiness of the concepts in question evidently hides a strategy that can be analyzed simultaneously in the field of signification and of the economy. Motivation (need) only describes, behind the formal opposition between two terms, a kind of circuit, a sort of specular and tautological process between two modalities of the same form, via the *detour* of a self-proclaimed content; and the reproduction of a systematic abstraction (whether it is that of the exchange value or of the code of the signifier) via the detour of the real. We have seen that needs (UV system) do not constitute a qualitative, incommensurable, concrete reality exterior to political economy, but rather a system that is itself induced by the EV system and which functions according to the same logic. If the two systems are in some way matched up in an identical form, then it is evident that the concept of need (like motivation) analyzes nothing at all. It only describes, through an illusory articulation, the general circulation of the same model and its internal operation. A typical rendition of this (necessarily) tautological definition of need might read: people appropriate a given object for themselves as use value "because they need it."

Benveniste's motivation partakes of the same circularity, the same psychological tautology.

1 The sign derives its necessity from a psychological consensus that inescapably binds a given Sr to a given Sd (some fraction of the "real" of thought).
2 But: the objectivity of this "denoted" fraction of the real is evidently the perceptive consensus of (speaking) subjects.
3 And this is supported no less evidently by the psychological consensus that links any given Sr to a given Sd.

The circle that legitimates the sign by the real and which founds the real by the sign is strictly vicious; but this circularity is the very secret of all metaphysical (ideological) operationality.

Needs are not the actuating (*mouvante*) and original expression of a subject, but the functional reduction of the subject by the system of use value in solidarity with that of exchange value. Similarly, the referent does not constitute an autonomous concrete reality at all; it is only the extrapolation of the excision (*decoupage*) established by the logic of the sign onto the world of things (onto the phenomenological universe of perception). It is the world such as it is seen and interpreted through the sign – that is, *virtually excised and excisable at pleasure*. The "real" table does not exist. If it can be registered in its identity (if it exists), this is because it has already been *designated*, abstracted and rationalized by the separation (*decoupage*) which establishes it in this equivalence to itself. Once again, given this line of reasoning, there is no fundamental difference between the referent and the signified, and the spontaneous confusion which so often arises here can only be symptomatic: the referent has no other value than that of the signified, of which it wants to be the substantial reference *in vivo*, and which it only succeeds in extending *in abstracto*.[19] Thus the strategy repeats itself: the double aspect of the commodity (UV/EV) in fact conceals a formal homogeneity in which use value, regulated by the system of exchange value, confers on the latter its "naturalist" guarantee. And the double face of the sign (Sr/Sd, generalizable into Sr/Sd–Rft) obscures a formal homogeneity in which Sd and Rft (administered by the same logical form, which is none other than that of the Sr), serve together as the reference-alibi – precisely the guarantee of "substance" for the Sr.

Saussure's sheet of paper theory of language (the double face of the sign one "cuts up") is thus perfectly idealist.[20] By giving the Sr and the Sd "in equivalence" as constitutive agencies (instances) of the sign, it veils the strategic apparatus of the sign, which rests precisely on the disparity of the two terms and on the fundamental circularity of the dominant term:

1   To summarize what we have so far, there is a metaphysic of the Sd–Rft, homologous with that of needs and use value. The Sd–Rft is taken for an original reality, a substance of value and recurring finality through the supporting play of signifiers (cf. the analysis of *Tel Quel*, in particular Derrida). Similarly, use value is given as origin and purpose (*finalité*) and needs as the basic motor of the economic – the cycle of exchange value appearing here as a necessary detour, but incompatible with true finalities.

2   In reality, this moral and metaphysical privilege of contents (UV and Sd–Rft) only masks the decisive privilege of form (EV and Sr). These two terms are respectively the last "Reason," the structural principle of the entire system, of which the former terms are only the detour. It is the rational abstraction of the system of exchange value and of the play of signifiers which commands the whole. But this fundamental strategy (of which it is impossible[21] here to demonstrate the operational repercussions at every level of contemporary society – from cybernetic programming to bureaucratic systems, and to the system of "consumption") is carefully hidden by the spreading

out of the signification process over the two (or three) agencies (Sr, Sd, Rft), and the play of their distinction and of their equivalence.

Denotation and connotation

The entire conceptual battery of semio-linguistics must be subjected to the same radical analysis that Marx applied to the concepts of classical political economy. And so we shift to the level of the message, where, as we shall see, the by now familiar metaphysics reappears in the concepts of denotation and connotation.

Denotation maintains itself entirely on the basis of the myth of "objectivity" (whether the denotation is that of the linguistic sign, the photographic analagon, iconic, etc.). Objectivity in this case is the direct adequation of an Sr to a precise reality. Even the difficulty which arises in the case of the image (i.e. its nondiscreteness, the fact that its Sr and Sd form a continuum, etc.) poses no fundamental challenge to the rule of the equivalence of the sign: that assignation of two terms which makes possible the further assignation of a fictive real to the contoured image (*decoupé*) of the sign – and thus to the rationalization and general control of meaning.

The Sd of connotation[22] is quite certainly amenable to the same analysis, since it also reemerges as a "denotation effect" of the *new* process of "staggered" signification. Barthes' analysis of the advertisement for Panzani pasta, with its connotation of "Italianity" is an example.[23] "Italianity" is only apparently of the Sd, conceptual content, etc. In fact, it constitutes a code unto itself – a myth, if you wish. But myths are not comprised of content. They are a process of exchange and circulation of a code whose *form* is determinant. And so it is for the role of connotation here. And if it is the locus of ideology, this is not a question of its having grafted annex and parasitical significations onto an "objective" denotative process; nor that it has smuggled in parallel contents, foreign to the infrastructure of the sign that would otherwise constitute the process of denotation:[24] what is involved here is precisely a free play of concatenation and exchange of Srs – a process of indefinite reproduction of the code (cf. "Fetishism and Ideology": ideology is bound to form, not content: it is the passion of the code).

Having said this, we can return to the process of denotation in order to show that it differs in no way from connotation: the denoted Sd, this objective "reality," is itself nothing more than a coded form (code of perception, "psychological" code, code of "realistic" values, etc.). In other words, ideology is as rife with the denotative as with the connotative process and, in sum, denotation is never really anything more than the most attractive and subtle of connotations.

As Barthes says in *S/Z*:

> Denotation is not the first among meanings, but pretends to be so; under this illusion, it is ultimately no more than the *last* of the connotations (the one that seems both to establish and to close the reading), the superior myth by which the text pretends to return to the nature of language, to language as nature: doesn't a sentence, whatever meaning it releases, subsequent to its utterance, it would seem, appear to be telling us something simple, literal, primitive: something *true*, in relation to which all the rest is literature?[25]

So it all parallels use value as the "denotative" function of objects. Indeed, doesn't the object have that air, in its "being serviceable," of having said something objective? This manifest discourse is the subtlest of its mythologies. A false ingenuity, and a perversion of objectivity is involved. Utility, like the literality of which Barthes speaks, is not a nature; it is a code of natural evidence which has the advantage over many other possible codes (the moral, the aesthetic, etc.) of appearing *rational*, while the others seem like mere rationalizations of more or less "ideological" purposes. Denotation or use value; objectivity or utility: it is always the complicity of the real with the code under the sign of evidence which generates these categories. And just as use value, the "literal" and ideal finality of the object, resurges continually from the system of exchange value, the effect of concreteness, reality and denotation results from the complex play of interference of networks and codes – as white light results from the interference of the colors of the spectrum. So the white light of denotation is only the play of the spectrum – the chromatic ghost – of connotations.

Thus the denotation–connotation distinction appears unreal and itself ideological. It could, however, be restored in a paradoxical sense, exactly opposed to the current accepted use. For denotation distinguishes itself from other significations (connoted) by its singular function of effacing the traces of the ideological process by restoring its universality and "objective" innocence. Far from being the objective term to which connotation is opposed as an ideological term, denotation is thus (since it naturalizes the very process of ideology) *the most ideological term* – ideological to the second degree. It is the "superior myth" of which Barthes speaks. This is exactly the same ideological function we have discerned of use value in its relation to exchange value. Hence, the two fields reciprocally illuminate each other in the totality of the ideological process.[26]

Beyond the sign: the symbolic

A critique of the political economy of the sign implies certain perspectives of transcendence: a "beyond" of the signification process through which sign exchange value organizes itself; and thus also a "beyond" of semiology which, in its quite "objective innocence," simply details the functioning of sign exchange value.

In general, the critical perspectives of transcendence of the sign (of its abstract rationality, its "arbitrariness") are generated in the spirit of one of the two terms that comprise it: that is, either in the name of the Sd (or the Rft: same thing), which it is then necessary to liberate from the stranglehold of the code (of the Sr) – or in the name of the Sr, which must be liberated from that of the Sd.

The first perspective, the party of the Sd, is to be analyzed in the framework of Derrida's (and *Tel Quel*'s critique of the primacy of the signified in the occidental process of meaning, which moralizes the sign in its content (of thought or of reality) at the expense of form, and confers an ethical and metaphysical status on meaning itself. This "natural philosophy" of signification implies an "idealism of the referent." It is a critique of the abstraction and arbitrariness of the sign in the name of "concrete" reality. Its phantasm is that of a total resurrection of the "real" in an immediate and transparent intuition, which establishes the economy of the sign (of the Sr) and of the code in order to release the Signifieds (subjects, history, nature, contradictions) in their actuating, dialectical, authentic truth. Today, this vision is developed largely in the critique of the abstraction of systems and codes in the name of authentic values (which are largely derived from the bourgeois system of individualist values). It amounts to a long sermon denouncing the alienation of the system, which becomes, with the expansion of this very system, a kind of universal discourse.

The temptation to criticize the Sr in the name of the Sd (Rft), to make of the "real" the ideal alternative to the formal play of signs, is congruent with what we have analyzed as the idealism of use value.[27] The salvation of UV from the system of EV, without realizing that UV is a satellite system in solidarity with that of EV: this is precisely the idealism and transcendental humanism of contents which we discover again in the attempt to rescue the Sd (Rft) from the terrorism of the Sr. The velleity of emancipating and liberating the "real" leaves intact the entire ideology of signification – just as the ideology of political economy is preserved in toto in the ideal autonomization of use value.

Because it confirms the separation which establishes the logic of the sign, every attempt to surpass the political economy of the sign which takes its support from one of its constituent elements is condemned to reproduce its arbitrary character (ergo, ideology) in the alternated mode of Sd or Sr. Any basis for a crucial interrogation of the sign must be situated from the perspective of what it expels and annihilates in its very institution, in the respective emergence and structural assignation of the Sr and the Sd. The process of signification is, at bottom, nothing but a gigantic *simulation model of meaning.* Clearly, neither the real, the referent, nor some substance of value banished to the exterior shadow of the sign can abolish this process. It is the symbolic that continues to haunt the sign, for in its total exclusion it never ceases to dismantle the formal correlation of Sr and Sd. But the symbolic, whose virtuality of meaning is so subversive of the sign, cannot, for this very reason, be named except by allusion, by infraction (*effraction*). For signification, which names everything in terms of itself, can only speak the language of values and of the *positivity* of the sign.

Indeed, in the final analysis, the whole problem revolves around the question of the positivity of the sign, its "assumption of value" (*prise de valeur*). Of what is outside the sign, of what is other than the sign, *we can say nothing,* really, except that it is ambivalent; that is, it is impossible to distinguish respective separated terms and to positivize them as such. And we can say that in this ambivalence is rooted a type of exchange that is radically different from the exchange of values (exchange values or sign values). But this (symbolic) exchange is foreclosed and abolished by the sign in its simultaneous institution of: (1) a separation, a distinctive structure; and (2) a positive relation, a sort of structural copulation between the two terms, which clearly only eternalizes their separation. This copulation is objectified in the bar of structural inclusion between Sr and Sd (Sr/Sd).[28] It is then even further objectified and positivized in the "R" of Hjemslev's formula: E R C.[29] It is this positive relation that makes a value of the sign. Whether it is understood to be arbitrary or motivated makes little difference. These terms divert the problem by inscribing it in an already established logic of the sign. Its true arbitrariness, or true motivation, is its positivization, which creates its rationality. And this is nothing other than the radical *reduction* of all ambivalence, through its dual abstraction. The motivation of the sign is thus purely and simply its strategy: structural crystallization and the liquidation of ambivalence by the "solidification" of value. And this motivation evidently functions by means of the arbitrariness of its form: foreclosure and reduction. The concepts of arbitrariness and motivation are thus hardly contradictory from a strategic (political) perspective.

Still, the arbitrariness of the sign is at bottom untenable. The sign value cannot admit to its own deductive abstraction any more than exchange value can. Whatever it denies and represses, it will attempt to exorcise and integrate into its own operation: such is the status of the "real," of the referent, which are only the simulacrum of the symbolic, its form reduced and intercepted by the sign. Through this mirage of the referent, which is nothing but the phantasm of what the sign itself represses during its operation,[30] the sign attempts to mislead: it permits itself to appear as totality, to efface the traces of its abstract transcendence, and parades itself as the reality principle of meaning.[31]

As the functional and terrorist organization of the control of meaning under the sign of the positivity of value, signification is in some ways kin to the notion of reification. It is the locus of an elemental objectification that reverberates through the amplified systems of signs up to the level of the social and political terrorism of the bracketing (*encadrement*) of meaning. All the repressive and reductive strategies of power systems are already present in the internal logic of the sign, as well as those of exchange value and political economy. Only total revolution, theoretical and practical, can restore the symbolic in the demise of the sign and of value. Even signs must burn.

NOTES

1 In *For a Critique of the Political Economy of the Sign*, trans. Charles Levin (St Louis: Telos Press, 1981).

2 Ibid.

3 Marx, *Capital*, vol. I. I have been unable to find this passage in the exact form Baudrillard cites it. But see Marx's *Grundrisse* (New York: Vintage, 1975), for example at the bottom of p. 404.

4 By the same token, there is no fundamental difference between "productive" consumption (direct destruction of utility during the process of production) and consumption by persons in general. The individual and his or her "needs" are produced by the economic system like unit cells of its reproduction. We repeat that "needs" are a *social labor*, a productive discipline. Neither the actual subjects nor their desires are addressed in this scheme. It follows that there is only productive consumption at this level.

5 Consumption itself is only apparently a concrete operation (in opposition to the abstraction of exchange). For what is consumed isn't the product itself, but its utility. Here the economists are right: consumption is not the destruction of products, but the destruction of utility. In the economic cycle, at any rate, it is an abstraction that is produced or consumed as *value* (exchangeable in one case, useful in another).

Nowhere is the "concrete" object or the "concrete" product concerned in the matter (what do these terms mean, anyway?): but, rather, an abstract cycle, a value system engaged in its own production and expanded reproduction. Nor does consumption make sense as a *destruction* (of "concrete" use value). Consumption is a labor of expanded reproduction of use value as an abstraction, a system, a universal code of utility – just as production is no longer in its present finality the production of "concrete" goods, but the expanded reproduction of the exchange value system. Only consummation (*consommation*) escapes recycling in the expanded reproduction of the value system – not because it is the destruction of substance, but because it is a transgression of the law and finality of objects, the abolition of their abstract finality. Where it appears to consume (destroy) products, consumption only consummates their utility. Consumption destroys objects as substance the better to perpetuate this substance as a universal, abstract form – hence, the better to reproduce the value code. *Consummation* (play, gift, destruction as pure loss, symbolic reciprocity) attacks the code itself, breaks it, deconstructs it. The symbolic act is the destruction of the value code (exchange and use), not the destruction of objects in themselves. Only this act can be termed "concrete," since it alone breaks with and transgresses the abstraction of value.

6   It should be pointed out that Marx's formulations in this domain (and the anthropology that they imply) are so vague as to permit culturalist interpretations of the type: "Needs are functions of the historical and social context." Or in its more radical version: "Needs are produced by the system in order to assure its own expanded reproduction"; that is, the sort of interpretation that takes into account only the multiple *content* of needs, without submitting the concept of need itself and the system of needs as form to a radical critique. [As in Marx's *Grundrisse*, p. 527, where both the "culturalist" and "more radical" position are mixed. Trans.]

7   In *For a Critique.*

8   In *Toward a critique of the political economy of the sign.*

9   Here Baudrillard alludes to the rationalist lineage of anthropological substantialism. See the first paragraph of Descartes' *Discourse on Method*, which Baudrillard parodies here. [Trans.]

10 Critical theory must also take the sign form into account. We shall observe that an identical logic regulates the organization of the sign in the present-day system; it turns the signified (referent) into the *satellite* term, the *alibi* of the signifier, the play of signifiers, and provides the latter with a reality guarantee.

11 Any resemblance to a living person is purely coincidental.

12 It should be noted here that alienation itself is one of these magical concepts devoted to sealing up an artificial disjunction; here, the disjunction between the consciousness of the subject and his or her own ideal content (rediscovered totality).

13 Thus the "critical" denunciation of artificial needs and the manipulation of needs converges in the same mystification the unconditional exaltation of consumption.

14 Two types of analysis have grappled with this parallel fetishism of the commodity and the sign: the critique of political economy, or theory of material production, inaugurated by Marx; and critical semiology, or the theory of textual production, led by the *Tel Quel* group.

15 The term "symbol" is here intended in the classic semio-linguistic sense of an analogical variant of the sign. For contrast, we will always use the term symbol (the symbolic, symbolic exchange) in opposition to and as a radical alternative to the concept of the sign and of signification.

16 The resolution of the sign entails the abolition of the Sr and the Sd as such, but not the abolition, toward some mystical nothingness, of the material and operation of meaning. The symbolic operation of meaning is also exercised upon phonic, visual, gestural (and social) material, but according to an entirely different logic, to the question of which we shall return later.

17 Emile Benveniste, *Problems in General Linguistics* (University of Miami, 1971).

18 Ibid.

19 This facsimile of the concrete concept (concept "*en dur*") only transliterates the fetish of realism, and of substance, the last stage of idealism fantasizing matter. (For more on "*en dur*," cf. J.-M. Lefebvre, *NRF 1* (February 1970): "The referent is not truly reality...it is the image we make of reality. It is a signified determined by an intention carried toward things (!) and not considered in its simple relation to the Sr, as is usual in linguistics. From the Sd concept, I pass to the referent as a concrete approach to the world.") It is, however, on these intermingled vestiges of idealism and materialism, deriving from all the confines of Western metaphysics, that semiology is based. The position of Lefebvre is moreover characteristic of the cunning with which "reality" succeeds in resurrecting itself surreptitiously behind all semiological thought, however critical, in order to establish more firmly the strategy of the sign. It thus gives witness to the impossibility of escaping the metaphysical problems posed by the sign without radically challenging semiological articulation itself. In effect, Lefebvre says: "The referent is not reality (i.e. an object whose existence I can test, or control): we relate to it as real, but this intentionality is precisely an act of mind that belies its reality, which makes a fiction, an artificial construction out of it." Thus, in a kind of flight in advance, the referent is drained of its reality, becomes again a simulacrum, behind which, however, the tangible object immediately reemerges. Thus, the articulation of the sign can gear down in infinite regress, while continually reinventing the real as its beyond and its consecration. At bottom, the sign is haunted by the nostalgia of transcending its own convention, its arbitrariness; in a way,

it is obsessed with the idea of *total motivation*. Thus it alludes to the real as its beyond and its abolition. But it can't "jump outside its own shadow": for it is the sign itself that produces and reproduces this real, which is only its *horizon* – not its transcendence. Reality is the phantasm by means of which the sign is indefinitely preserved from the symbolic deconstruction that haunts it.

20 Ferdinand de Saussure, *Course in General Linguistics* (New York, 1959) p. 113.

21 Of course, it is not impossible at all. But such an analysis would depend for its full impact on our grasp of the whole process of development of the political economy of the sign. To this we shall return later.

22 In the "staggered scheme of connotation, the entire sign is transformed into the signifier of another signified:

$$\frac{\dfrac{Sr/Sd}{Sr}}{Sd}$$

[See part IV of "Elements of semiology," in Roland Barthes, *Writing Degree Zero* and *Elements of Semiology* (Boston, 1968), p. 89, and also his discussion of "Myth as a semiological system," in *Mythologies* (Frogmore: St Albans, 1973), esp. p. 115. [Trans.]

23 Roland Barthes, "Rhetorique de l'image," in *Communications* 4 (1964); "Rhetoric of the image," *Image-Music-Text*, trans. Stephen Heath, (Fontana/Collins, 1977).

24 It is no accident here if the mythical scheme of infrastructure and super-structure resurfaces at least implicitly in the field of signification: *denotative infrastructure* and *ideological* superstructure.

25 Roland Barthes, *S/Z* (New York, 1974), p. 9.

26 The analysis could be extended to the level of metalanguage (a system of signification staggered in reverse)

$$\frac{\dfrac{Sr/Sd}{Sd}}{Sr}$$

where the entire sign is transformed into the Sd of a new Sr. In the end, the signified of metalinguistic denotation is only an effect of the Sr, only a simulation model whose coherence derives from the regulated exchange of signifiers. It would be interesting to push, to the verge of paradox:

1 The hypothesis (though it is scarcely even that) that the historical event is volatilized in its successive coding by the media; that it is invented and manipulated by the simple operation of the code. The historical event then appears as a combinatory effect of discourse.

2 The hypothesis, in the same mode, at the metalinguistic level, that the object of a (given) science is only the effect of its discourse. In the carving out and separation of the field of knowledge the rationality of a science is established through its exclusion of the remainder (the same process, as we have seen, is involved in the institution of the sign itself); or, to take this even further, that this (scientific) discourse posits its object as a simulation model, purely and simply. It is known, after all, that a science is established in the last instance as the language consensus of a scientific community.

27 See Beyond use value, in this chapter.

28 All the arbitrariness and positivity of the sign is amassed on this line separating the two levels of the sign. This structural-inclusive copula establishes the process of signification as *positive* and occults its prior function – the process of reducing and abolishing meaning (or nonmeaning: ambivalence); the process of misunderstanding and denegation with which, moreover, the sign never finishes. This line is in fact the barrier whose raising would signify the deconstruction of the sign, its resolution, and the dissolution of its constituent elements, Sr and Sd, as such. Lacan's formulation of the linguistic sign reveals the true meaning of this line: s/s. It becomes the line (barrier) of repression itself – no longer that which articulates, but that which censors – and thus the locus of transgression. This line highlights what the sign denies, that upon which the sign establishes itself negatively, and of which it is only, in its positive institution, the symptom.

However, Lacan's formula introduces this radically new line in terms of the *traditional* schema of the sign, maintaining the usual place of the Signified. This Signified is not the Sd–Rft of linguistics; it is the repressed. It still retains a sort of content, and its representation is always that of a substance, though no longer assigned term for term, but only coinciding at certain points with the metaphoric chain of Srs ("anchoring points" – *points de capiton*). [On "points de capiton" and other matters concerning Lacan see Anthony Wilden, *The Language of the Self* (New York: Delta, 1968): "Perhaps language is in fact totally tautologous in the sense that it can only in the end talk about itself, but in any event, Lacan has suggested that there must be some privileged 'anchoring points', points like the buttons on a mattress or the intersections of quilting, where there is a 'pinning down' (*capitonnage*) of meaning, not to an object, but rather by 'reference back' to a symbolic function" (p. 273). For Lacan's version of the Saussurian formula, see Jacques Lacan, "The insistence of the letter in the unconscious," in Jacques Ehrmann, ed., *Structuralism* (New York, 1970). [Trans.]

According to the very different logic of linguistics, it is a question of the partition of two agencies (instances), where the *reference* is only representative of one. It appears on the contrary that to conceive the sign as censor, as a barrier of exclusion, is not to wish to retain for the repressed its position as signifiable, its position of latent value. Rather, it is to conceive it as that which, denied by the sign, in turn denies the sign's form, and can never have any place within it. It is a nonplace and nonvalue in opposition to the sign. Barred (*barrée*) and deleted (*rayée*) by the sign, it is a symbolic ambivalence that only reemerges fully in the total resolution of the sign, in the explosion of the sign and of value. The symbolic is not inscribed anywhere. It is not what comes to be registered beneath the repression barrier (line), the Lacanian Sd. It is rather what tears all Srs and Sds to pieces, since it is what dismantles their pairing off (*appareillage*) and their simultaneous carving out (*découpe*). See note 16 above.

29 See Roland Barthes, "Elements of Semiology". "It will be remembered that any system of signification comprises a plane of expression (E) and a plane of content (C) and that the signification coincides with the relation (R) of the two planes: E R C [Trans.]

30 One could say that the referent becomes "symbolic" again, by a curious inversion – not in the radical sense of the term, but in the sense of a "symbolic" gesture, that is, its meager reality. Here the referent is *only* "symbolic," the principle of reality having passed over into the code.

31 Even exchange value could not exist in its pure state, in its total abstraction. It can only function under the cover of use value, where a simulacrum of totality is restored at the horizon of political economy, and where it resuscitates, in the functionality of needs, the phantom of precisely what it abolishes: the symbolic (*le symbolique*) of desire.

4

The Mirror of Production

In order to achieve a radical critique of political economy, it is not enough to unmask what is hidden behind the concept of consumption: the anthropology of needs and of use value. We must also unmask everything hidden behind the concepts of production, mode of production, productive forces, relations of production, etc. All the fundamental concepts of Marxist analysis must be questioned, starting from its own requirement of a radical critique and transcendence of political economy. What is axiomatic about productive forces or about the dialectical genesis of modes of production from which springs all revolutionary theory? What is axiomatic about the generic richness of man who is labor power, about the motor of history, or about history itself, which is only "the production by men of their material life?" "The first historical act is thus the production of the means to satisfy these needs, the production of material life itself. And indeed this is an historical act, a fundamental condition of all history, which today, as thousands of years ago, must daily and hourly be fulfilled merely in order to sustain human life."[1]

The liberation of productive forces is confused with the liberation of man: is this a revolutionary formula or that of political economy itself? Almost no one has doubted such ultimate evidence, especially not Marx, for whom men "begin to distinguish themselves from animals as soon as they begin to *produce* their means of subsistence..."[2] (Why must man's vocation always be to distinguish himself from animals? Humanism is an *idée fixe* which also comes from political economy – but we will leave that for now.) But is man's existence an end for which he must find the means? These innocent little phrases are already theoretical conclusions: the separation of the end from the means is the wildest and most naive postulate about the human race. Man has needs. Does he have needs? Is he pledged to satisfy them? Is he labor power (by which he separates himself as means from himself as his own end)? These prodigious metaphors of the system that dominates us are a fable of political economy retold to generations of revolutionaries infected even in their political radicalism by the conceptual viruses of this same political economy.

Critique of use value and labor power

In the distinction between exchange value and use value, Marxism shows its strength but also its weakness. The presupposition of use value – the hypothesis of a concrete value beyond the abstraction of exchange value, a human purpose of the commodity in the moment of its direct relation of utility for a subject – is only the effect of the system of exchange value, a concept produced and developed by it.[3] Far from designating a realm beyond political economy, use value is only the horizon of exchange value. A radical questioning of the concept of consumption begins at the level of needs and products. *But this critique attains its full scope in its extension to that other commodity, labor power.* It is the concept of production, then, which is submitted to a radical critique.

We must not forget that according to Marx himself the revolutionary originality of his theory comes from releasing the concept of labor power from its status as an unusual commodity whose insertion in the cycle of production *under the name of use value* carries the X element, a differential extra-value that generates surplus value and the whole process of capital. (Bourgeois economics would think instead of simple "labor" as one factor of production among others in the economic process.)

The history of Marx's concept of the use value of labor power is complex. With the concept of labor, Adam Smith attacked the physiocrats and the exchangists. In turn, Marx deconstructed labor into a double concept of labor power commodity: abstract social labor (exchange value) and concrete labor (use value). He insisted on the need to maintain these two aspects in all their force. Their articulation alone could help decipher objectively the process of capitalist labor. To A. Wagner, who reproached him for neglecting use value, Marx replied:

> the *vir obscurus* overlooks the fact that even in the analysis of the commodity I do not stop at the double manner in which it is represented, but immediately go on to say that in this double being of the

commodity is represented *the two-fold character of the labor* whose product it is: *useful labor,* i.e., the concrete modes of the labors which create use values, and *abstract labor, labor as expenditure of labor power,* irrespective of whatever "useful" way it is expended...that in the development of the *value form of the commodity,* in the last instance of its money form and hence of *money,* the *value* of a commodity is represented in the *use value* of the other, i.e., in the natural form of the other commodity; that surplus value itself is derived from a *"specific" use value of labor power* exclusively pertaining to the latter, etc., etc., that thus for me use value plays a far more important part than it has in economics hitherto, however, that it is only ever taken into account where this springs from the analysis of a given economic constellation, not from arguing backwards and forwards about the concepts or words "use value" and "value." (Emphasis added)[4]

In this passage it is clear that the use value of labor, losing its "naturalness," takes on a correspondingly greater "specific" value in the *structural* functioning of exchange value. In maintaining a kind of dialectical equilibrium between concrete, qualitative labor and abstract, quantitative labor, Marx gives logical priority to exchange value (the given economic formation). But in so doing, he retains something of the *apparent movement of political economy*: the concrete positivity of use value – a kind of concrete antecedent within the structure of political economy. He does not radicalize the schema to the point of reversing this appearance and revealing use value *as produced by the play of exchange value*. We have shown this regarding the products of consumption; it is the same for labor power. The definition of products as useful and as responding to needs is the most accomplished, most internalized expression of abstract economic exchange: it is its subjective closure. The definition of labor power as the source of "concrete" social wealth is the complete expression of the abstract manipulation of labor power: the truth of capital culminates in this "evidence" of man as producer of value. Such is the twist by which exchange value retrospectively originates and logically terminates in use value. In other words, the signified "use value" here is still a code effect, the final precipitate of the law of value. Hence it is not enough to analyze the operation of the quantitative abstraction of exchange value *starting from* use value, but it is also necessary to bring out the condition of the possibility of this operation: the production of the concept of the use value of labor power itself, of a specific rationality of productive man. Without this generic definition there is no political economy. In the last instance, this is the basis of political economy. This generic definition must be shattered in unmasking the "dialectic" of quantity and quality, behind which hides the definitive structural institution of the field of value.

The concrete aspect of labor: the "dialectic" of quality and quantity

"The quantitative aspect of labour could not emerge until it was universalized during the 18th century in Europe... Until then, the different forms of activity were not fully comparable... labor appeared then as diverse qualities."[5] During the historical epoch of the artisanal mode of production, qualitative labor was differentiated in relation to its process, to its product, and to the destination of the product. In the subsequent capitalist mode of production labor is analyzed under a double form: "While labor which creates exchange values is *abstract, universal* and *homogeneous,* labor which produces use values is concrete and special and is made up of an endless variety of kinds of labor according to the way in which and the material to which it is applied."[6] Here we rediscover the moment of use value: concrete, differentiated, and incommensurable. In contrast to the quantitative measure of labor power, labor use value remains nothing more or less than a qualitative potentiality. It is specified by its own end, by the material it works on, or simply because it is the expenditure of energy by a given subject at a given time. The use value of labor power is the moment of its actualization, of man's relation to his useful expenditure of effort. Basically, it is an act of (productive) *consumption*; and in the general process, this moment retains all its uniqueness. At this level labor power is incommensurable.

There is, moreover, a profound enigma throughout the articulation of Marx's theory: how is surplus value born? How can labor power, by definition qualitative, generate a measurable actualization? One would have to assume that the "dialectical" opposition of quantity and quality expresses only an apparent movement.

In fact, the *effect* of quality and of incommensurability once again partakes of the *apparent* movement of political economy. What produces the universalization of labor in the eighteenth century and consequently reproduces it is not the reduction of concrete, qualitative labor by abstract, quantitative labor but, from the outset, the structural articulation of the two terms. Work is really universalized at the base of this "fork," not only as market value but as human value. Ideology always thus proceeds by a binary, structural scission, which works here to universalize the dimension of labor. By dividing (or redividing into the qualitative structural effect, a *code* effect), quantitative labor spreads throughout the field of possibility. Henceforth there can be only labor: qualitative or quantitative. The quantitative still signifies only the commensurability of all forms of labor in abstract value; the qualitative, under the pretext of incommensurability, goes much further. It signifies *the comparability of all human practice in terms of production and labor.* Or better: the abstract and formal universality of the commodity labor power is what supports the "concrete" universality of qualitative labor.

But this "concrete" is an abuse of the word. It seems opposed to the abstract at the base of the fork, but in fact the fork itself is what establishes the abstraction. The autonomization of labor is sealed in the play of the two: from the abstract to the concrete; from the qualitative to the quantitative; from the exchange value to the use value of labor. In this structuralized play of signifiers, the fetishism of labor and productivity crystallizes.[7]

And what is this concrete aspect of labor? Marx says:

> The indifference as to the particular kind of labor implies the existence of a highly developed aggregate of different species of concrete labor, none of which is any longer the predominant one. So do the most general abstractions commonly arise only where there is the highest concrete development, where one feature appears to be jointly possessed by many, and to be common to all.[8]

But if one type of labor no longer dominates all others, it is because labor itself dominates all other realms. Labor is substituted for all other forms of wealth and exchange. Indifference to determined labor corresponds to a much more total determination of social wealth by labor. And what is the conception of this social wealth placed entirely under the sign of labor, if not use value? The "richest concrete development" is the qualitative and quantitative multiplication of use values.

> The greater the extent to which historic needs – needs created by production itself, social needs – needs which are themselves the offspring of social production and intercourse, are posited as *necessary,* the higher the level to which real wealth has become developed. Regarded *materially,* wealth consists only in the manifold variety of needs.[9]

Is this not the program of advanced capitalist society? Failing to conceive of a mode of social wealth other than that founded on labor and production, Marxism no longer furnishes in the long run a real alternative to capitalism. Assuming the generic schema of production and needs involves an incredible simplification of social exchange by the law of value. Viewed correctly, this fantastic proposition is both arbitrary and strange with respect to man's status in society. The analysis of all primitive or archaic organizations contradicts it, as does the feudal symbolic order and even that of our societies, since all perspectives opened up by the contradictions of the mode of production drive us hopelessly into political economy.

The dialectic of production only intensifies the abstractness and separation of political economy. This leads us to the radical questioning of Marxist theoretical discourse. When in the last instance Marx defines the dialectical relation of abstract—concrete as the relation between "scientific representation and real movement" (what Althusser will analyze precisely as the *production* of a theoretical object), this theoretical production, itself taken in the abstraction of the representation, apparently only redoubles its object (in this case, the logic and movement of political economy). Between the theory and the object – and this is valid not only for Marxism – there is, in effect, a dialectical relation, in the bad sense: they are locked into a speculative dead end.[10] It becomes impossible to think outside the form production or the form representation.

Man's double "generic" face

In fact the use value of labor power does not exist any more than the use value of products or the autonomy of signified and referent. The same fiction reigns in the three orders of production, consumption, and signification. Exchange value is what makes the use value of products appear as its anthropological horizon. The exchange value of labor power is what makes its use value, the concrete origin and end of the act of labor, appear as its "generic" alibi. This is the logic of signifiers which produces the "evidence" of the "reality" of the signified and the referent. In every way, exchange value makes concrete production, concrete consumption, and concrete signification appear only in distorted, abstract forms. But it foments the concrete as its ideological ectoplasm, its phantasm of origin and transcendence (*dépassement*). In this sense need, use value, and the referent "do not exist."[11] They are only concepts produced and projected into a generic dimension by the development of the very system of exchange value.

By the same token, the double potentiality of man as needs and labor power, this double "generic" face of universal man, is only man as produced by the system of political economy. And productivity is not primarily a generic dimension, a human and social kernel of all wealth to be extracted from the husk of capitalist relations of production (the eternal empiricist illusion). Instead, all this must be overturned to see that the abstract and generalized development of productivity (the developed form of political economy) is what makes the *concept of production* itself appear as man's movement and generic end (or better, as the concept of man as producer).

In other words, the system of political economy does not produce only the individual as labor power that is sold and exchanged: it produces the very conception of labor power as the fundamental human potential. More deeply than in the fiction of individuals freely selling their labor power in the market, the system is rooted in the identification of individuals with their labor power and with their acts of "transforming nature according to human ends." In a word, man is not only quantitatively exploited as a productive force by the *system* of capitalist political economy, but is also metaphysically overdetermined as a producer by the *code* of political economy.[12] In the last instance, the system rationalizes its power here. *And in this Marxism assists the cunning of capital. It convinces men that they are alienated by the sale of their labor power, thus censoring the much more radical hypothesis that they might be alienated as labor power, as the "inalienable" power of creating value by their labor.*

If on the one hand Marx is interested in the later fate of the labor power objectified in the production process as abstract social labor (labor as its exchange value), Marxist theory, on the other hand, never challenges human capacity of production (energetic, physical, and intellectual), this productive potential of every man in every society "of transforming his environment into ends useful for the individual or the society," this *Arbeitsvermögen*. Criticism and history are strangely arrested before this anthropological postulate: a curious fate for a Marxist concept.

The same fate has befallen the concept of need in its present operation (the consumption of use value). It presents the same characteristics as the concrete aspects of labor: uniqueness, differentiation, and incommensurability – in short, "quality." If the one can be defined as "a specific type of action that produces its own product," the other is also defined as "a specific kind of tendency (or other psychologistic motivation, since all of this is only bad psychology) seeking its own satisfaction." Need also "decomposes both matter and form... into infinitely varied types of consumption." In concrete labor man gives a useful, objective end to nature; in need he gives a useful, subjective end to products. Needs and labor are man's double

potentiality or double generic quality. This is the same anthropological realm in which the concept of production is sketched as the "fundamental movement of human existence," as defining a rationality and a
sociality appropriate for man. Moreover, the two are logically united
in a kind of ultimate perspective: "In a higher stage of community
society...work will not be simply a means of living but will become
the prime, vital need itself."[13]

Radical in its *logical* analysis of capital, Marxist theory nonetheless
maintains an *anthropological* consensus with the options of Western
rationalism in its definitive form acquired in eighteenth-century bourgeois thought. Science, technique, progress, history – in these ideas we
have an entire civilization that comprehends itself as producing its
own development and takes its dialectical force toward completing
humanity in terms of totality and happiness. Nor did Marx invent the
concepts of genesis, development, and finality. He changed nothing
basic: nothing regarding the *idea* of man *producing* himself in his
infinite determination, and continually surpassing himself toward his
own end.

Marx translated this concept into the logic of material production
and the historical dialectic of modes of production. But differentiating
modes of production renders unchallengeable the evidence of production as the determinant instance. It generalizes the economic mode of
rationality over the entire expanse of human history, as the generic
mode of human becoming. It circumscribes the entire history of man
in a gigantic simulation model. It tries somehow to turn against the
order of capital by using as an analytic instrument the most subtle
ideological phantasm that capital has itself elaborated. Is this a "dialectical" reversal? Isn't the system pursuing *its* dialectic of universal
reproduction here? If one hypothesizes *that there has never been and
will never be anything but the single mode of production ruled by
capitalist political economy* – a concept that makes sense only in
relation to the economic formation that produced it (indeed, to the
theory that analyzes this economic formation) – then even the "dialectical" generalization of this concept is merely the *ideological* universalization of this system's postulates.

Ethic of labor; aesthetic of play

This logic of material production, this dialectic of modes of production, always returns beyond history to a generic definition of man as a
dialectical being; a notion intelligible only through the process of the
objectification of nature. This position is heavy with consequences to

the extent that, even through the vicissitudes of his history, man (whose history is also his "product") will be ruled by this clear and definitive reason, this dialectical scheme that acts as an implicit philosophy. Marx develops it in the *1844 Manuscripts*. Marcuse revives it in his critique of the economic concept of labor: "labor is an ontological concept of human existence as such." He cites Lorenz von Stein:

> Labor is...in every way the actualization of one's infinite determinations through the self-positing of the individual personality [in which the personality itself] makes the content of the external world its own and in this way forces the world to become a part of its own internal world.[14]

Marx: "Labor is *man's coming-to-be for himself* within *externalization* or as *externalized* man...[that is], the *self-creation* and self-objectification [of man]."[15] And even in *Capital*:

> So far therefore as labor is a creator of use-value, is useful labor, it is a necessary condition, independent of all forms of society, for the existence of the human race; it is an external nature-imposed necessity, without which there can be no material exchanges between man and nature, and therefore no life.[16]

And again:

> Labor is, in the first place, a process in which both man and nature participate, and in which man of his own accord starts, regulates, and controls the material reactions between himself and nature. He opposes himself to nature as one of her own forces, setting in motion arms and legs, head and hands, the natural forces of his body, in order to appropriate nature's productions in a form adapted to his own wants.[17]

The dialectical culmination of all of this is the concept of nature as "the inorganic body of man": the naturalization of man and the humanization of nature.[18]

On this dialectical base, Marxist philosophy unfolds in two directions: an ethic of labor and an aesthetic of nonlabor. The former traverses all bourgeois and socialist ideology. It exalts labor as value, as end in itself, as categorical imperative. Labor loses its negativity and is raised to an absolute value. But is the "materialist" thesis of man's generic productivity very far from this "idealist" sanctification of labor? In any case, it is dangerously vulnerable to this charge. In the same article, Marcuse says:

– insofar as they take the concept of "needs" and its satisfaction in the world of goods as the starting point, all economic theories fail to recognize the full factual content of labor... The essential factual content of labor is not grounded in the scarcity of goods, nor in a discontinuity between the world of disposable and utilizable goods and human needs, but, on the contrary, in an essential excess of human existence beyond every possible situation in which it finds itself and the world.[19]

On this basis he separates off play as a secondary activity: "In the structural sense, within the totality of human existence, labor is necessarily and eternally 'earlier' than play: it is the starting point, foundation, and principle of play insofar as play is precisely a breaking off *from* labor and a recuperation *for* labor."[20] Thus, labor alone founds the world as objective and man as historical. In short, labor alone founds a real dialectic of transcendence (*dépassement*) and fulfillment. Even metaphysically, it justifies the painful character of labor. "In the last analysis, the burdensome character of labor expresses nothing other than a negativity rooted in the very essence of human existence: man can achieve his own self only by passing through otherness: by passing through 'externalization' and 'alienation'."[21] I cite this long passage only to show how the Marxist dialectic can lead to the purest Christian ethic. (Or its opposite. Today there is a widespread contamination of the two positions on the basis of this transcendence of alienation and this intrawordly asceticism of effort and overcoming where Weber located the radical germ of the capitalist spirit.) I have cited it also because this aberrant sanctification of work has been the secret vice of Marxist political and economic strategy from the beginning. It was violently attacked by Benjamin:

Nothing was more corrupting for the German workers' movement than the feeling of swimming with the current. It mistook technical development for the current, the direction it believed it was swimming in. From there, there was only one step to take in order to imagine that industrial labor represented a political performance. With German workers the old Protestant ethic of work celebrated, in a secular form, its resurrection. The Gotha Program bore traces of this confusion. It defined work as "the source of all wealth and culture." To which Marx, even worse, objected that man possesses only his labor power, etc. However, the confusion spread more and more: and Joseph Dietzgen announced, "Work is the Messiah of the modern world. In the amelioration of labor resides the wealth that can now bring what no redeemer has succeeded in."[22]

Is this "vulgar" Marxism, as Benjamin believes? It is no less "vulgar" than the "strange delusion" Lafargue denounced in *The Right to be Lazy*: "A strange delusion possesses the working classes of the nations where capitalist civilization holds its sway."[23] Apparently, "pure and uncompromising" Marxism itself preaches the liberation of productive forces under the auspices of the *negativity* of labor. But, confronted by the "vulgar" idealism of the gospel of work, isn't this an "aristocratic" idealism? The former is positivist and the latter calls itself "dialectical." But they share the hypothesis of man's productive vocation. If we admit that it raises anew the purest metaphysics,[24] then the only difference between "vulgar" Marxism and the "other" Marxism would be that between a religion of the masses and a philosophical theory – not a great deal of difference.

Confronted by the *absolute* idealism of labor, dialectical materialism is perhaps only a *dialectical* idealism of productive forces. We will return to this to see if the dialectic of means and end at the heart of the principle of the transformation of nature does not already virtually imply the autonomization of means (the autonomization of science, technology, and labor; the autonomization of production as generic activity; the autonomization of the dialectic itself as the general scheme of development).[25]

The regressive character of this work ethic is evidently related to what it represses: Marx's chief discovery regarding the double nature of labor (his discovery of abstract and measurable social labor). In the fine points of Marxist thought, confronting the work ethic is an aesthetic of nonwork or play itself based on the dialectic of quantity and quality. Beyond the capitalist mode of production and the quantitative measure of labor, this is the perspective of a definitive qualitative mutation in communist society: the end of alienated labor and the free objectification of man's own powers.

> In fact, the realm of freedom actually begins only where labor which is determined by necessity and mundane considerations ceases; thus in the very nature of things it lies beyond the sphere of actual material production.
>   ... Freedom in this field can only consist in socialized man, the associated producers, rationally regulating their interchange with Nature, bringing it under their common control, instead of being ruled by it as by the blind forces of Nature; and achieving this with the least expenditure of energy and under conditions most favorable to, and worthy of, their human nature. But it nonetheless still remains

a realm of necessity. Beyond it begins that development of human energy which is an end in itself, the true realm of freedom which, however, can blossom forth only with this realm of necessity as its basis.[26]

Even Marcuse, who returns to the less puritanical (less Hegelian) conceptions, which, however, are totally philosophical (Schiller's aesthetic philosophy), says that

Play and display, as principles of civilization, imply not the transformation of labor but its complete subordination to the freely evolving potentialities of man and nature. The ideas of play and display now reveal their full distance from the values of productiveness and performance. Play is *unproductive* and *useless* precisely because it cancels the repressive and exploitative traits of labor and leisure...[27]

This realm beyond political economy called play, nonwork, or nonalienated labor, is defined as the reign of a finality without end. In this sense it is and remains an *aesthetic*, in the extremely Kantian sense, with all the bourgeois ideological connotations which that implies. Although Marx's thought settled accounts with bourgeois morality, it remains defenseless before its aesthetic, whose ambiguity is more subtle but whose complicity with the general system of political economy is just as profound. Once again, at the heart of its strategy, in its analytic distinction between quantity and quality, Marxist thought inherits the aesthetic and humanistic virus of bourgeois thought, since the concept of quality is burdened with all the finalities – whether those concrete finalities of use value, or those endless ideal and transcendent finalities. Here stands the defect of all notions of play, freedom, transparence, or disalienation: it is the defect of the *revolutionary imagination* since, in the ideal types of play and the free play of human faculties, we are still in a process of repressive desublimation. In effect, the sphere of play is defined as the fulfillment of human rationality, the dialectical culmination of man's activity of incessant objectification of nature and control of his exchanges with it. It presupposes the full development of productive forces; it "follows in the footsteps" of the reality principle and the transformation of nature. Marx clearly states that it can flourish only when founded on the reign of necessity. Wishing itself beyond labor but *in its continuation*, the sphere of play is always merely the aesthetic sublimation of labor's constraints. With this concept we remain rooted in the problematic of necessity and freedom, a typically bourgeois problematic whose double ideological expression has always been the institution of a reality principle (repression and sublimation, the principle of labor) and its formal overcoming in an ideal transcendence.

Work and nonwork: here is a "revolutionary" theme. It is undoubtedly the most subtle form of the type of binary, structural opposition discussed above. The end of the end of exploitation by work is this reverse fascination with nonwork, this reverse mirage of free time (forced time—free time, full time—empty time: another paradigm that fixes the hegemony of a temporal order which is always merely that of production). Nonwork is still only the repressive desublimation of labor power, the antithesis which acts as the alternative. Such is the sphere of nonwork: even if it is not immediately conflated with leisure and its present bureaucratic organization, where the desire for death and mortification and its management by social institutions are as powerful as in the sphere of work; even if it is viewed in a radical way which *represents it* as other than the mode of "total disposability" or "freedom" for the individual to "produce" himself as value, to "express himself," to "liberate himself" as a (conscious or unconscious) authentic *content*; in short, as the ideality of time and of the individual as an empty form to be filled finally by his or her freedom. The finality of value is always there. It is no longer inscribed in *determined* contents as in the sphere of productive activity; henceforth it is a *pure form*, though no less determining. Exactly as the pure institutional form of painting, art, and theater shines forth in antipainting, anti-art, and anti-theater, which are emptied of their contents, the pure form of labor shines forth in nonlabor. Although the concept of nonlabor can thus be fantasized as the abolition of political economy, it is bound to fall back into the sphere of political economy as the sign, and only the sign, of its abolition. It already escapes revolutionaries to enter into the programmatic field of the "new society."

Marx and the hieroglyph of value

Julia Kristeva writes in *Semiotica*:

> From the viewpoint of social distribution and consumption (of communication), labour is always a value of use or exchange...Labor is measurable according to the value which it is, and not in any other way. Value is measured by the quantity of time socially necessary for production. But Marx clearly outlined another possibility: *work could be apprehended outside value*, on the side of the commodity produced and circulating in the chain of communication. Here labor

no longer represents any value, meaning, or signification. It is a question only of a *body* and a *discharge*.[28]

Marx writes,

> The use values, coat, linen, etc., i.e., the bodies of commodities, are combinations of two elements – matter and labor... We see, then, that labor is not the only source of material wealth, of use-values produced by labor, as William Petty puts it, labor is its father and the earth its mother... Productive activity, if we leave out of sight its special form, viz., the useful character of the labor, is nothing but the expenditure of human labor-power.[29]

Is there a conception of labor in Marx different from that of the production of useful ends (the canonical definition of labor as value in the framework of political economy and the anthropological definition of labor as human finality)? Kristeva attributes to Marx a radically different vision centered on the body, discharge, play, anti-value, nonutility, nonfinality, etc. She would have him read Bataille before he wrote – but also forget him when it is convenient. If there was one thing Marx did not think about, it was discharge, waste, sacrifice, prodigality, play, and symbolism. Marx thought about *production* (not a bad thing), and he thought of it in terms of value.

There is no way of getting around this. Marxist labor is defined in the absolute order of a natural necessity and its dialectical overcoming as rational activity producing value. The social wealth produced is *material*; it has nothing to do with *symbolic* wealth which, mocking natural necessity, comes conversely from destruction, the deconstruction of value, transgression, or discharge. These two notions of wealth are irreconcilable, perhaps even mutually exclusive; it is useless to attempt acrobatic transfers. According to Bataille, "sacrificial economy or symbolic exchange is exclusive of political economy (and of its critique, which is only its completion). But this is just to render to political economy what belongs to it: the concept of labor is consubstantial with it and therefore cannot be switched to any other analytical field. Above all, it cannot become the object of a science that pretends to surpass political economy. "The labor of the sign," "productive intertextual space," etc., are thus ambiguous metaphors. There is a choice to be made between value and nonvalue. Labor is definitely within the sphere of value. This is why Marx's concept of labor (like that of production, productive force, etc.) must be submitted to a radical critique as an *ideological* concept. Thus, with all its ambiguities, this is not the time to generalize it as a *revolutionary* concept.

The quotations from Marx to which Kristeva refers do not at all carry the meaning she gives them. The genesis of wealth by the genital combination of labor-father and earth-mother certainly reinstates a "normal" productive reproductive scheme – one makes love to have children but not for pleasure. The metaphor is that of genital, reproductive sexuality, not of a discharge of the body in enjoyment! But this is only a trifle. The "discharge" of human power Marx speaks of is not a discharge with a pure waste, a symbolic discharge in Bataille's sense (pulsating, libidinal): it is still an economic, productive, finalized discharge precisely because, in its mating with the other, it begets a productive force called the earth (or matter). It is a useful discharge, an investment, not a gratuitous and festive energizing of the body's powers, a game with death, or the acting out of a desire. Moreover, this "discharge of the body" does not, as in play (sexual or otherwise), have its response in other bodies, its echo in a nature that plays and discharges in exchange. It does not establish a symbolic exchange. What man gives of his body in labor is never *given* or *lost* or *rendered* by nature in a reciprocal way. Labor only aims to "make" nature "yield." This discharge is thus immediately an investment of value, a *putting into value* opposed to all symbolic *putting into play* as in the gift or the discharge.

Kristeva poses the problem of redefining labor beyond value. In fact, as Goux has shown, for Marx the demarcation line of value cuts between use value and exchange value.

> If we proceed further, and compare the process of producing value with the labor-process, pure and simple, we find that the latter consists of the useful labor, the work, that produces use-values. Here we contemplate the labor as producing a particular article; we view it under its qualitative aspect alone, with regard to its end and aim. But viewed as a value creating process, the same labor-process presents itself under its quantitative aspect alone. Here it is a question merely of the time occupied by the laborer in doing the work; – of the period during which the labor-power is usefully expended.[30]

Hence the abstraction of value begins only in the second stage of exchange value. Thus use value is separated from the sphere of the production of value; or the realm beyond value is confounded with the sphere of use value (this is Goux's interpretation, in which he extends this proposition to the use value of the sign). As we have seen, this is a very serious idealization of the process of concrete, qualitative labor and, ultimately, a compromise with political economy to the extent that the entire theoretical investment and strategy crystallizes on this line of demarcation within the sphere of value, leaving the "external" line of closure of this sphere of political economy in the shadows. By positing use value as the realm beyond exchange value, all transcendence is locked into this single alternative within the field of value. Qualitative production is already the realm of rational, positive finality; the transformation of nature is the occasion of its objectification as a productive force under the sign of utility (the same is true simultaneously of human labor). Even before the stage of exchange value and the equivalence through time of abstract social labor, labor and production constituted an abstraction, a reduction, and an extraordinary rationalization in relation to the richness of symbolic exchange. This "concrete" labor carries all the values of repression, sublimation, objective finality, "conformity to an end," and rational domestication of sexuality and nature. In relation to symbolic exchange, this *productive Eros* represents the real rupture which Marx displaces and situates between abstract quantitative labor and concrete qualitative labor. The process of "valorization" begins with the process of the useful transformation of nature, the insaturation of labor as generic finality, and the stage of use value. The real rupture is not between "abstract" labor and "concrete" labor, but between symbolic exchange and work (production, economics). The abstract social form of labor and exchange is only the completed form, overdetermined by capitalist political economy, of a scheme of rational valorization and production inaugurated long before, which breaks with every symbolic organization of exchange.[31]

Kristeva would gladly be rid of value, but neither labor nor Marx. One must choose. Labor is defined (anthropologically and historically) as what disinvests the body and social exchange of all ambivalent and symbolic qualities, reducing them to a rational, positive, unilateral investment. The productive Eros represses all the alternative qualities of meaning and exchange in symbolic discharge toward a process of production, accumulation, and appropriation. In order to question the process which submits us to the destiny of political economy and the terrorism of value, and to rethink discharge and symbolic exchange, the concepts of production and labor developed by Marx (not to mention political economy) must be resolved and analyzed as ideological concepts interconnected with the general system of value. And in order to find a realm beyond economic value (which is in fact the only revolutionary perspective), then the *mirror of production*, in which all Western metaphysics is reflected, must be broken.

Epistemology I

In the shadow of Marxist concepts

Historical materialism, dialectics, modes of production, labor power – through these concepts Marxist theory has sought to shatter the abstract universality of the concepts of bourgeois thought (Nature and Progress, Man and Reason, formal Logic, Work, Exchange, etc.). Yet Marxism in turn universalizes them with a "critical" imperialism as ferocious as the others'.

The proposition that a concept is not merely an interpretive hypothesis but a translation of universal movement depends upon pure metaphysics. Marxist concepts do not escape this lapse. Thus, to be logical, the concept of history must itself be regarded as historical, turn back upon itself, and only illuminate the context that produced it by abolishing itself. Instead, in Marxism history is transhistoricized: it redoubles on itself and thus is universalized. To be rigorous the dialectic must dialectically surpass and annul itself. By radicalizing the concepts of production and mode of production at a given moment, Marx made a break in the social mystery of exchange value. The concept thus takes all its strategic power from its irruption, by which it dispossesses political economy of its imaginary universality. But, from the time of Marx, it lost this advantage when taken as a principle of explication. It thus cancelled its "difference" by universalizing itself, regressing to the dominant form of the code (universality) and to the strategy of political economy. It is not tautological that the concept of history is historical, that the concept of dialectic is dialectical, and that the concept of production is itself produced (that is, it is to be judged by a kind of self-analysis). Rather, this simply indicates the explosive, mortal, present form of critical concepts. As soon as they are constituted as universal they cease to be analytical and the religion of meaning begins. They become canonical and enter the general system's mode of theoretical representation. Not accidentally, at this moment they also take on their scientific cast (as in the scientific canonization of concepts from Engels to Althusser). They set themselves up as expressing an "objective reality." They become signs: signifiers of a "real" signified. And although at the best of times these concepts have been practised as concepts without taking themselves for reality, they have nonetheless subsequently fallen into the *imaginary of the sign*, or the *sphere of truth*. They are no longer in the sphere of interpretation but enter that of *repressive simulation*.

From this point on they only evoke themselves in an indefinite metonymic process which goes as follows: man is historical; history is dialectical; the dialectic is the process of (material) production; production is the very movement of human existence; history is the history of modes of production, etc. This scientific and universalist discourse (code) immediately becomes imperialistic. All possible societies are called on to respond. That is, consult Marxist thought to see if societies "without history" are something other than "pre"-historical, other than a chrysalis or larva. The dialectic of the world of production is not yet well developed, but nothing is lost by waiting – the Marxist egg is ready to hatch. Moreover, the psychoanalytic egg is in a similar condition. What we have said about the Marxist concepts holds for the unconscious, repression, Oedipus complex, etc., as well. Yet here, it is even better: the Bororos[32] are closer to primitive processes than we are.

This constitutes a most astonishing theoretical aberration – and a most reactionary one. There is *neither a mode of production nor production* in primitive societies. There is *no dialectic* and *no unconscious* in primitive societies. These concepts analyze only our own societies, which are ruled by political economy. Hence they have only a kind of boomerang value. If psychoanalysis speaks of the unconscious in primitive societies, we should ask about what represses psychoanalysis or about the repression that has produced psychoanalysis itself. When Marxism speaks of the mode of production in primitive societies, we ask to what extent this concept fails to account even for our own historical societies (the reason it is exported). And where all our ideologues seek to finalize and rationalize primitive societies according to their own concepts – to encode the primitives – we ask what obsession makes them see this finality, this rationality, and this code blowing up in their faces. Instead of exporting Marxism and psychoanalysis (not to mention bourgeois ideology, although at this level there is no difference), we bring all the force and questioning of primitive societies to bear on Marxism and psychoanalysis. Perhaps then we will break this fascination, this self-fetishization of Western thought. Perhaps we will be finished with a Marxism that has become more of a specialist in the impasses of capitalism than in the roads to revolution; finished with a psychoanalysis that has become more of a specialist in the impasses of libidinal economy than in the paths of desire.

The critique of political economy is basically completed

Comprehending itself as a form of the rationality of production superior to that of bourgeois political economy, the weapon Marx created turns against him and turns his theory into the dialectical apotheosis of political economy. At a much higher level, his critique falters under his own objection to Feuerbach of making a radical critique of the *contents* of religion but in a completely religious *form*. Marx made a radical critique of political economy, but still in the form of political economy. These are the rushes of the dialectic, undoubtedly the limit of all "critique." The concept of critique emerged in the West at the same time as political economy and, as the quintessence of Enlightenment rationality, is perhaps only the subtle, long-term expression of the system's expanded reproduction. The dialectic does not avoid the fate of every critique. Perhaps the inversion of the idealist dialectic into a materialist dialectic was only a metamorphosis; perhaps the very logic of political economy, capital, and the commodity is dialectical; and perhaps, under the guise of producing its fatal internal contradiction, Marx basically only rendered a descriptive theory. The logic of representation – of the duplication of its object – haunts all rational discursiveness. Every critical theory is haunted by this surreptitious religion, this desire bound up with the construction of its object, this negativity subtly haunted by the very form that it negates.

This is why Marx said that after Feuerbach the critique of religion was basically completed (cf. *Critique of Hegel's Philosophy of Right*) and that, to overcome the ambiguous limit beyond which it can no longer go (the reinversion of the religious form beneath the critique), it is necessary to move resolutely to a different level: precisely to the critique of political economy, which alone is radical and which can definitively resolve the problem of religion by bringing out the true contradictions. *Today we are exactly at the same point with respect to Marx. For us, the critique of political economy is basically completed.* The materialist dialectic has exhausted its content in reproducing its form. At this level, the situation is no longer that of a critique: it is inextricable. And following the same revolutionary movement as Marx did, we must move to a radically different level that, beyond its critique, permits the definitive resolution of political economy. This level is that of symbolic exchange and its theory. And just as Marx thought it necessary to clear the path to the critique of political economy with a critique of the philosophy of law, the preliminary to this radical change of terrain is the critique of the metaphysic of the signifier and the code, in all its current ideological extent. For lack of a better term, we call this the critique of the political economy of the sign.

NOTES

1 *The German Ideology* (New York: International Publishers, 1947) p. 16.
2 Ibid., p. 7.
3 Cf. Baudrillard, *Pour une critique de l'économie politique du signe* (Paris: Gallimard, 1972), and chapter 4 above.
4 "Notes on Wagner," in *Theoretical Practice 5* (Spring, 1972) 51–2.
5 Pierre Naville, *Le nouveau léviathan* (Paris: Riviare, 1954) p. 371.
6 Marx, *Contribution to the Critique of Political Economy* (New York: International Publishers, 1904) p. 33.
7 There is a further great disjuncture through which the critique of political economy is articulated: the split between the technical and the social division of labor, which is subject to the same analysis. Transfiguring the technical division as both sides of the social division, it thus preserves the fiction of an ideal distribution of labor, of a concrete "nonalienated" productivity; and it universalizes the technical mode or technical reason. Thus the dialectic of productive forces—relations of production: everywhere the "dialectical" contradiction ends up as a Moebius band. But meanwhile this contradiction has circumscribed and universalized the field of production.
8 *Contribution to the Critique of Political Economy* pp. 298–9.
9 *Grundrisse*, trans. M. Nicolaus (London: Pelican, 1973), p. 527.
10 We will return to this reciprocal neutralization of the theory and the object when we deal with the relations between Marxist theory and the workers' movement.
11 This does not mean *that they have never existed*. Hence we have another paradox that we must return to later.
12 Similarly for nature: there is not only the exploitation of nature as a productive force, but overdetermination of nature as referent, as "objective" reality, by the code of political economy.
13 *1844 Manuscripts*. [I have not been able to locate this quotation. Trans.]
14 "On the concept of labor," *Telos 16* (Summer 1973) 11–12.
15 Easton and Guddat eds, *Writings of the Young Man on Philosophy and Society* (New York: Anchor, 1969) pp. 321, 332.
16 *Capital*, vol. I (Moscow: Foreign Languages Publishing House) pp. 42–3.
17 Ibid., p. 177.
18 Engels, always a naturalist, goes so far as to exalt the role played by work in the transition from ape to man.
19 Marcuse, "Concept of labor," p. 22.
20 Ibid., p. 15.
21 Ibid., p. 25.
22 Walter Benjamin, *Poésie et révolution* (Paris: Denoël, 1971) p. 283.
23 Paul Lafargue, *The Right to be Lazy*, trans. C. Kerr (Chicago: Kerr, 1917) p. 9.

24 Such as conceiving man as the union of a soul and a body – which gave rise to an extraordinary "dialectical" efflorescence in the Christian Middle Ages.

25 But this autonomization is the key which turns Marxism toward social democracy, to its present revisionism, and to its total positivist decay (which includes bureaucratic Stalinism as well as social democratic liberalism).

26 *Capital*, vol. III, pp. 799–800.

27 Marcuse, *Eros and Civilization* (New York: Vintage, 1962) p. 178.

28 Julia Kristeva, "La sémiotique et la production," *Semiotica* 2. [I have not been able to complete this reference. Trans.]

29 *Capital*, vol. I, pp. 43–4.

30 Ibid., p. 195.

31 For example, look at this passage from Marx on the social hieroglyph: "Value, therefore, does not stalk about with a label describing what it is. It is value, rather, that converts every product into social hieroglyphic. Later on, we try to decipher the hieroglyphic, to get behind the secret of our own social products; for to stamp an object of utility as a value, is just as much a social product as language" (*Capital*, vol. I, p. 74). This entire analysis of the mystery of value remains fundamental. But rather than being valid only for the product of labor in distribution and exchange, it is valid even for the product of labor (and for labor itself) taken as a "useful object." Utility (including labor's) is already a socially produced and determined hieroglyphic abstraction. The whole anthropology of "primitive" exchange compels us to break with the natural evidence of utility and to reconceive the social and historical genesis of use value as Marx did with exchange value. Only then will the hieroglyph be totally deciphered and the spell of value radically exorcized.

32 The Bororos are a South American society studied by Lévi-Strauss in *Tristes Tropiques*. [Trans.]

5

Symbolic Exchange and Death

Introduction

Symbolic exchange is no longer an organizing principle; it no longer functions at the level of modern social institutions. Of course, the symbolic still haunts them as the prospect of their own demise. But this is only an obsessive memory, a demand ceaselessly repressed by the law of value. And if a certain conception of the Revolution since Marx has tried cutting a path through this law of value, it has in the end remained a revolution according to the Law. As for psychoanalysis, although it acknowledges the ghostly presence of the symbolic, it averts its power by circumscribing it in the individual unconscious, reducing it, under the Law of the Father, to the threat of Castration and the subversiveness of the Signifier. Always the Law.

Nevertheless, beyond the topographical and economic schemas of psychoanalysis and politics, which always revolve around some kind of production (whether material or desiring) on the scene of value, we can still perceive the outline of a social relation based on the extermination of value. For us, the model for this derives from primitive formations, but its radical utopian version is beginning to explode slowly at all levels of our society, in the vertigo of a revolt which has nothing to do with the revolution or the laws of history, nor even with the "liberation" of a "desire" – though this latter truth will take longer to appear obvious, since the value problematic of desire has emerged only recently and will take time to dissipate.

In this perspective, other theoretical developments take on a central meaning: Saussure's anagrams and Marcel Mauss's gift-exchange will appear, in the long term, as more radical hypotheses than those of

Freud and Marx. In fact, it is precisely the imperialism of Marxist and Freudian interpretations that has censured these new points of view. The anagram and the gift are not just curiosities of linguistics and anthropology; they cannot be viewed as secondary issues with respect to the great machines of the unconscious and the revolution. On the contrary, we may discover in them an outline of a single form from which psychoanalysis and Marxism are derived only by virtue of a misunderstanding – a form that relates political economy and libidinal economy intimately, so that we can glimpse, in the present, a beyond of value, of the law, of repression, and of the unconscious. In fact, a supersession such as this is inevitable.

For this writer, there is only one comparable theoretical event: Freud's death instinct. At least, this is the case, so long as we radicalize Freud against himself. In all three instances, in fact, it is a question of counterreference: Mauss must be turned against Mauss, Saussure against Saussure, Freud against Freud. We must line up the principle of reversion (the countergift) against all the economistic, psychological, or structuralist interpretations to which Mauss's work has led. We must oppose the Saussure of the *Anagrams* against that of linguistics, and even against his own restrictive hypothesis about the anagrams. The Freud of the death instinct must be played off against the whole previous edifice of psychoanalysis, and even against Freud's own version of the death instinct.

At this paradoxical price – that of theoretical violence – we see the three hypotheses traced within their respective fields; but their discreteness is dissolved in the general form of the symbolic, a functioning principle that is sovereignly external and antagonistic to our economic "reality principle."

The reversibility of the gift in the countergift, of exchange in the sacrifice, of time in the cycle, of production in destruction, of life in death, and of each linguistic value term in the anagram: in all domains, reversibility – cyclical reversal, annulment – is the one encompassing form. It puts an end to the linearity of time, language, economic exchange and accumulation, and power. For us, it takes on the form of extermination and death. It is the form of the symbolic, neither mystical nor structural, but ineluctable.

The reality principle coincided with a determinate phase of the law of value. Today, the entire system is fluctuating in indeterminacy, all of reality absorbed by the hyperreality of the code and of simulation. It is now a principle of simulation, and not of reality, that regulates social life. The finalities have disappeared; we are now engendered by models. There is no longer such a thing as ideology; there are only simulacra. To grasp the hegemony and the spectacle of the present system, we have to retrace an entire genealogy of the law of value and of successive simulacra – the structural revolution of value. Political economy has to be resituated within this genealogy: it thus appears as a simulacrum of the second order, in which only the so-called "real" is ever put into play: the real of production, of signification, in consciousness, or in the unconscious.

Capital no longer corresponds to the order of political economy; it uses political economy as a simulation model. The whole apparatus of the commodity law of value is absorbed and recycled in the larger machinery of the structural law of value, and thus connects with the third order of simulation (see below). Hence, in a way, political economy is assured a kind of second life, in the framework of an apparatus where it loses all self-determination, but where it retains its efficacy as a referential of simulation. The same goes for the previous apparatus of the natural law of value, which had been taken up as an imaginary referential ("Nature") by the system of political economy and the law of the commodity. This was use value, which led a kind of phantom existence at the heart of exchange value. But in the subsequent twist of the spiral, exchange value was in turn seized as an alibi in the dominant order of the code. Each configuration of value is resumed by the following in a higher order of simulation. And each phase of value integrates into its own apparatus the anterior apparatus as a phantom reference, a puppet or simulation reference.

A revolution separates each order from the next one: these are the true revolutions. We are in the third order, no longer the order of the real, but of the hyperreal, and it is only in the third order that theory and practice, themselves floating and indeterminate, can catch up with the hyperreal and strike it dead.

The current revolutions index themselves on the immediately prior phase of the system. They arm themselves with a nostalgic resurrection of the real in all its forms; in other words, with simulacra of the second order: dialectics, use value, the transparency and finality of production, the "liberation" of the unconscious, or of repressed meaning (of the signifier, or of the signified called desire), and so on. All of these liberations offer, as ideal content, the phantoms which the system has devoured in successive revolutions and which it subtly resuscitates as revolutionary fantasies. All these liberations are just transitions toward a generalized manipulation. The revolution itself is meaningless at the present level of random processes of control.

To the industrial machine corresponds the rational, referential, functional, historical consciousness. But it is the unconscious – non-referential, transferential, indeterminate, floating – that corresponds to the aleatory machin(ations) of the code. Yet even the unconscious has been reinserted into the game: it long ago relinquished its own reality principle in order to become an operational simulacrum. At the exact point where its psychic principle of reality is confused with its psychoanalytic reality principle, the unconscious becomes, like political economy, another simulation model.

The entire strategy of the system lies in this hyperreality of floating values. It is the same for money and theory as for the unconscious. Value rules according to an ungraspable order: the generation of models, the indefinite chaining of simulation.

Cybernetic operationality, the genetic code, the random order of mutations, the principle of uncertainty, and so on: all of these replace a determinist and objectivist science, a dialectical vision of history and consciousness. Even critical theory and the revolution belong to the second-order simulations, as do all determinate processes. The installation of third-order simulacra upsets all of this, and it is useless to resurrect the dialectic, "objective" contradictions and the like, against them; that is a hopeless political regression. You cannot beat randomness with finality; you cannot beat programmed dispersion with *prises de conscience* or dialectical transcendence; you cannot defend against the code with political economy or "revolution." All these old weapons (including those of the first order, the ethics and metaphysics of man and nature, use value, and other liberatory referentials) have been progressively neutralized by the general system, which is of a higher order. Everything that gets inserted into the definalized space-time of the code, or tries to interfere with it, is disconnected from its own finalities, disintegrated and absorbed – this is the well-known effect of recuperation, or manipulation: cycling and recycling at each level. "All dissent must be of a higher logical type than that to which it is opposed."[1]

Is it thus necessary to play a game of at least equal complexity, in order to be in opposition to third-order simulations? Is there a subversive theory or practice more random than the system itself? An undetermined subversion, which would be to the order of the code what revolution was to political economy? Can we fight DNA? Certainly not with the blows of class struggle. Can we invent simulacra of an even higher logical (or illogical) order, beyond the current third order, beyond determination and indetermination? If so, would they still be simulations? Perhaps only death, the reversibility of death, is of a higher order than the code. Only symbolic disorder can breach the code.

Any system approaching perfect operationality is approaching its own death. When the system declares "A is A," or "two and two make four," it simultaneously arrives at the point of complete power and total ridicule – in other words, of probable immediate subversion. At this point, it takes only a straw to collapse the whole system. We know the power of tautology when it redoubles this systemic pretension in perfect sphericity: the belly of Ubu Roi.

Identity is untenable: it is death, since it fails to inscribe its own death. Such is the case with closed, or metastable, or functional, or cybernetic systems, which are all eventually waylaid by laughter, instantaneous subversion (and not by a long dialectical labor), because all the inertia of these systems works against them. Ambivalence lies in wait for the most accomplished systems, those that have succeeded in construing their own functional principles, like the binary God of Leibniz. The fascination that they exercise because they are constructed on such profound denials, as in the case of fetishism, can be reversed in an instant. Their fragility arises from this, and grows in proportion to their ideal coherence. These systems, even when they are based on a radical indeterminism (the loss of meaning), become once more the prey of meaning. They fall under the weight of their own monstrosity, like the dinosaurs, and decompose immediately.

Such is the fatality of every system devoted through its own logic to total perfection, and thus total defectiveness, to absolute infallibility and thus incorrigible extinction: all bound energies aim for their own demise. This is why the only strategy is *catastrophic*, and not in the least bit dialectical. Things have to be pushed to the limit, where everything is naturally inverted and collapses. At the peak of value, ambivalence intensifies; and at the height of their coherence, the redoubled signs of the code are haunted by the abyss of reversal. The play of simulation must therefore be taken further than the system permits. Death must be played against death – a radical tautology. The system's own logic turns into the best weapon against it. The only strategy of opposition to a hyperrealist system is paraphysical, a "science of imaginary solutions;" in other words, a science fiction about the system returning to destroy itself, at the extreme limit of simulation, a reversible simulation in a hyperlogic of destruction and death. Death is always simultaneously that which awaits us at the system's *term*, and the *extermination* that awaits the system itself. There is only one word to designate the finality of death that is internal to the system, the one that is everywhere inscribed in its operational logic, and the radical counter-finality, ex-scribed from the system as such, but which everywhere haunts it: the same term of death, and only it can manifest itself on either side. This ambiguity can already be seen in the Freudian death instinct. It is *not an ambiguity.* It simply translates the proximity of realized perfection and the immediate defection of the system.

A thoroughgoing reversibility: such is the symbolic obligation. That each *term* should be ex-*term*inated, that value should be abolished in this revolution of the term against itself – this is the only symbolic violence worthy of the structural violence of the code.

A dialectic of revolution counterposed the value law of the commodity and equivalence. To the indeterminism of the code and the structural law of value, only the fastidious (*minutieuse*) reversion of death can respond. Death should never be interpreted as an actual occurrence in a subject or a body, but rather as a *form*, possibly a form of social relation, where the determination of the subject and value disappears. The obligation of reversibility puts an end simultaneously to determinacy and indeterminacy. It puts an end to energies bound in regulated oppositions, and consequently joins the theories of fluxes and intensities, libidinal or schizo. But the release of energy is the actual form of the present system, the strategic floating of value. The system can be connected and disconnected: all energies released will eventually return to it, because it is the system that has produced the very concept of energy and intensity. Capital is an energetic and intense system. Thus it becomes impossible to distinguish (Lyotard) the libidinal economy from the system's economy (that of value). It becomes impossible to distinguish (Deleuze) the capitalist schizzes from the revolutionary schizzes. Because the system is the master: like God, it can bind and unbind energies; but what it cannot do (and also what it cannot escape), is to be reversible. The process of value is irreversible. Only reversibility then, and not release or drift, is fatal to the system. And this is exactly what is meant by the term symbolic "exchange."[2]

In truth, there is nothing left to ground ourselves on. All that is left is theoretical violence. Speculation to the death, whose only method is the radicalization of all hypotheses. Even the code and the symbolic are terms of simulation – it must be possible somehow to retire them, one by one, from discourse.

The structural revolution of value

Saussure offered two perspectives on the exchange of language terms when he compared them to money: a piece of money can be placed in relationship to all the other terms of the monetary system; and it can be exchanged against a real good of some value. It was for the former dimension that Saussure increasingly reserved the term "value": the relativity of all the terms among themselves, which is internal to the general system and composed of distinctive oppositions – as opposed to the other possible definition of value: the relation of each term to what it designates, of each signifier to its signified, as each monetary unit has something against which it can be exchanged. The first type of relationship corresponds to the structural dimension of language; the second to its functional aspect. The two dimensions are distinct, but articulated, which is to say, they work together and cohere – a view that characterizes the "classical" configuration of the linguistic sign, which can be placed with the commodity law of value, where the function of designation always appears as the goal or finality of the structural operation of language. At this "classical" stage of signification, there is a complete parallel with the mechanism of value in material production as Marx described it. Use value functions as the horizon and finality of the system of exchange value: use value qualifies the concrete operation of the commodity in (the act of) consumption (a moment of the process that is parallel to the sign's moment of designation); while exchange value refers to the interchangeability of all commodities under the law of equivalence (a moment parallel to the structural organization of the sign). Use value and exchange value are organized together dialectically throughout Marx's analyses and define a rational configuration of production regulated by political economy.

A revolution has put an end to this "classical" economy of value, a revolution which, beyond the commodity form, stretches value to its most radical form.

In this revolution, the two aspects of value, which sometimes used to be thought of as coherent and eternally linked, as if by natural law, are disarticulated; *referential value is nullified, giving the advantage to the structural play of value.* The structural dimension, in other words, gains autonomy, to the exclusion of the referential dimension, establishing itself on the death of the latter. Gone are the referentials of production, signification, affect, substance, history, and the whole equation of "real" contents that gave the sign weight by anchoring it with a kind of burden of utility – in short, its form as representative equivalent. All this is surpassed by the other stage of value, that of total relativity, generalized commutative, combinatory simulation. This means simulation in the sense that from now on signs will exchange among themselves exclusively, without interacting with the real (and this becomes the condition for their smooth operation). The emancipation of the sign: released from any "archaic" obligation it might have had to designate something, the sign is at last free for a structural or combinatory play that succeeds the previous role of determinate equivalence.

The same operation occurs at the level of labor power and the process of production: the elimination of all finalities of content allows production to function as a code, and permits the monetary sign, for example, to escape in indefinite speculation, beyond any reference to the real, or even to a gold standard. We are really witnessing a type of absolute liberty: disaffection, disobligation, disenchantment. It must indeed have been a sort of magic, a magical obligation that kept the sign chained to the real; but capital has liberated the sign from this "naivety" to deliver it over to pure circulation.

The floating suspension of money and signs, of needs and productive goals, and the flotation of labor itself: Marx and Saussure never foresaw this indeterminacy, this commutability of every kind of term, which accompanies such unlimited speculation and inflation. But they were writing in the golden age of the dialectic of signs and reality, the classical period of capital and value. Their dialectic has since disintegrated, and the real is dead from the blow of this fantastic autonomization of value. Determination is dead, indeterminism reigns. We have witnessed the ex-termination (in the literal sense of the word) of the reality of production, and of the real of the sign.

If it was just a question of the primacy of exchange value over use value (or of the structural dimension over the functional dimension of language), Marx and Saussure have already pointed it out. Marx is close to making use value the pure and simple medium or alibi of exchange value. And his whole analysis is based on the principle of equivalence that is at the heart of the system of exchange value. But if there is *equivalence* at the heart of the system, the global system is not *indeterminate* (there is always a dialectical determination and finality in the mode of production). The current system on the other hand is based on indeterminacy; it is driven by it; it is haunted by the death of all determinations.

To indicate the structural revolution in the law of value I have used the phrase the "political economy of the sign," but the phrase is makeshift, since:

1   Is it still a question of political economy? Yes, in the sense that it still concerns value and the law of value. But the mutation that has affected the political economy is so fundamental and definitive, its content so transformed, even nullified, that the expression is now merely allusive, or more specifically *political*, since it concerns the *destruction* of social relations regulated by value. Yet it has long since been a question of something other than economics.

2   Even the term sign is merely allusive. Since the structural law of value affects signification along with everything else, it takes the form, not of the sign in general, but of a certain organization which is that of the code – yet a code does not organize just any sign. Nor does the law of value of the commodity imply the existence of some kind of structural determination, at a given moment, by material production. Nor conversely does the structural law of value imply a kind of preeminence of the sign. Such an illusion arises, in the former case, with Marx in the shadow of the commodity, and, in the latter case, with Saussure in the shadow of the linguistic sign. We must shatter this illusion. The commodity law of value is a law of equivalences, a law which functions in every sphere: it equally refers to the configuration of signs where the equivalency of a signifier and a signified permits the regulated exchange of referential content (another parallel modality: the linearity of the signifier, the simultaneity of the linear and cumulative time of production).

This classical law of value thus simultaneously functions at every level (language, production, etc.), but each remains separate according to their referential sphere.

Conversely, the structural law of value means the indeterminacy of every sphere in relation to every other, as well as their specific content (and consequently the transition from the *determined* sphere of the sign to the *indeterminacy* of the code). To state that the sphere of production and the sphere of the sign exchange their respective content is inadequate: they literally disappear as such and lose their specificity, along with their determinacy, to the advantage of a form of value, a much more general form of organization, whereby determination and production are nullified.

The "political economy of the sign" was still conceptualized as the result of the extension of the commodity law of value and its verification at the level of the sign. Whereas the structural configuration of value purely and simply puts an end to the system of production and to political economy, as well as to the representational system and the system of signs. All of this, along with the code, migrates into the realm of simulation. Neither the "classical" economy of the sign, nor political economy, however, cease to exist in any literal sense: they lead a second life, they become a sort of phantom principle of dissuasion.

This is the end of labor, the end of production, and the end of political economy.

This is the end of the signifier—signified dialectic that permitted the accumulation of knowledge and meaning, the linear syntagm of cumulative discourse. Simultaneously, this is the end of the use value—exchange value dialectic, that which made social accumulation and production possible; the end of the linear dimension of discourse and commodities; the end of the classical era of the sign; and the end of the era of production.

It is not the revolution that puts an end to all of this, but capital itself. Capital abolishes social determination through the mode of production, and substitutes the structural form of value for the commodity form. And it is capital that determines the current strategy of the system.

This historical and social mutation can be observed at every level. The era of simulation is thus everywhere initiated by the interchangeability of previously contradictory or dialectically opposed terms. Everywhere the same "genesis of simulacra": the interchangeability of the beautiful and the ugly in fashion; of the right and the left in politics; of the true and false in every media message; of the useful and the useless at the level of objects; and of nature and culture at every level of meaning. All the great humanist criteria of value, all the values of a civilization of moral, aesthetic, and practical judgment, vanish in our system of images and signs. Everything becomes undecidable. This is the characteristic effect of the domination of the code, which is based everywhere on the principle of neutralization and indifference.[3] This is the generalized brothel of capital:[4] not the brothel of prostitution but the brothel of substitution and interchangeability.

This process, which has been at work for a long time in culture, art, politics, and even sexuality (in the domains labelled "superstructural") today affects the economy itself, the so-called "infrastructural" field. The same indeterminacy rules here. And of course, with the determination of the economic sphere there are no possibilities of conceiving the economic as a determining agency.

Because historical determination has been articulated around the economic for two centuries (or at least ever since Marx), it is here that we must first grasp the eruption of the code.

The end of production

We are at the end of production. Production coincides, in the West, with the formulation of the commodity law of value, that is with the reign of political economy. Before that nothing was *produced*, strictly speaking: everything was *deduced*, from grace (of God), or beneficence (of nature) of an agency that offered or refused its wealth. Value emanated from the reign of divine or natural qualities (for us in retrospect these converge). This was still how the Physiocrats perceived the cycle of land and labor: labor had no specific value. We can therefore question whether an actual *law* of value in fact exists, since it is *dispensed* without ever being expressed rationally. Its form is not separate, since it is bound to an inexhaustible referential substance. If there is a law here, it is, in contrast to the law of the market, a *natural* law of value.

As soon as value is *produced*, as soon as its reference becomes labor and its law becomes the general equivalence of all labor, a mutation topples this system of the natural distribution or dispensation of wealth. Value is henceforth assigned to the distinct and rational function of human labor (of social labor). It is measurable, and as a result so is surplus value.

The critique of political economy begins with social production and the mode of production as references. Only the concept of production allows us to extract, in the analysis of this peculiar commodity which is labor power, a *surplus* (a surplus value), which regulates the rational dynamics of capital, as well as the equally rational dynamics of the revolution.

Today everything has changed again. Production, the commodity form, labor power, equivalence and surplus value once sketched a quantitative, material and measurable configuration which is now irrelevant. Productive forces once pointed to a reference, in opposition to the relations of production, but nevertheless a reference, one of social wealth. Some aspect of production still supported a social form called capital and its internal criticism called Marxism. And the requirements of the revolution were based on the destruction of the *commodity* law of value.

Yet, we have gone from the commodity law to the structural law of value, and this coincides with the undermining of the social form called production. Are we therefore still in the capitalist mode? We could be in a hypercapitalist mode or in some quite different order. Is the form of capital linked to the law of value in general, or does it have a limited form of value? (Perhaps we are actually already in a socialist mode? Perhaps this metamorphosis of capital, under the sign of the structural law of value, is simply its socialist outcome? Ouch!) If the life and death of capital is contingent upon the *commodity* law of value, and if the revolution depends on the mode of production, then we are neither in capital, nor in the revolution. If the revolution means man's liberation from social and generic production, then there is no longer any revolution in sight, since there is no longer any production. If, on the contrary, capital is a *mode of domination*, then we are still well within it, since the structural law of value is the purest and the most illegible form of social domination, like the surplus value of a dominant class henceforth without reference, or like power relations without violence. It is completely absorbed, without a trace of blood, in the signs that surround us. It is everywhere functional in the code, where capital has finally attained its purest form of discourse, beyond the specific dialects of industry, of the market and of finance, beyond the dialects of class which held sway in the "productive" phase. A symbolic violence is everywhere inscribed in signs, including in the signs of the revolution.

The structural revolution of value nullifies the foundations of the "Revolution." The loss of referentials first mortally affects the referentials of the revolution, which can no longer find in any social substance of production, in any truth of labor power the certainty of political change. This is because labor is no longer a *force*. It has become a *sign* among signs, produced and consumed like the rest. It is interchangeable with nonlabor, leisure, according to an exact equivalence; it is commutable with every other sector of daily life. Labor is no longer "alienated" to a greater or lesser degree; no longer the locus of a specific historical "praxis" that is productive of specific social relations. It is, like most practices, no longer anything but a set of described [*signalétique*] operations. It enters the general life style; in other words it is encompassed by signs. Labor is no longer even that suffering, that historical prostitution which acted as the inverted promise of a final emancipation (or, as in Lyotard, the locus of worker *gratification*, the fulfillment of unrelenting desire in the abjectness of value and within the rules of capital). None of this is real any longer. The sign form has appropriated labor in order to empty it of all its historical and libidinal meaning, and to absorb it in the process of its own reproduction: the function of the *sign* is to redouble itself behind the empty allusion of what it designates. Labor was once able to designate the reality of social production, of a social objective that was cumulative wealth, even while exploited by capital and surplus value. Here precisely, labor maintained some use value for the expanded reproduction of capital, and for its ultimate destruction. In any case it was marked by a finality. Even if a worker is absorbed in the pure and simple reproduction of his own labor power, it is not the case that the labor process is experienced as meaningless repetition. Labor, through its very abjection, revolutionizes society in the form of a commodity whose potential always exceeds the pure and simple reproduction of value.

Today, no: labor is no longer productive; it has become reproductive of the *assignment to labor*, as the general habitus of a society
unsure whether it wants to produce or not. No more myths of production, no more content of production: GNPs merely recount a
numerical, statistical growth, void of meaning – an inflation of
accounting signs incapable of providing a fantasy for the collective
will. The pathos of growth is itself dead, like the pathos of production
which was its final panicked and paranoid erection – presently
detumescent according to the figures – which no one believes in any-
more. It remains even more indispensable to reproduce labor as social
status, as reflex, as morality, as consensus, as regulation, and as the
principle of reality. But now labor becomes the principle of reality *of
the code*: an enormous *ritual of signs of labor* extend across society –
no matter if it still produces or not, for it reproduces itself. Socialization by ritual, and by signs, is much more effective than socialization
by energies bound to production. All that is asked of you is not that
you produce, nor that you make an effort to surpass yourself (this
classical ethics would be rather suspect), but that you be socialized.
All that is asked is that you acquire value, according to the structural
definition which here takes on its full *social* significance only as a term
in relation to others; that you function as a sign within the general
scenario of production – just as labor and production now only
function as signs, as interchangeable terms with nonlabor, consumption, communication, etc. As a multiple, incessant, and spiralling
relation throughout the network of other signs, labor, thus emptied
of its energy and its substance (and quite generally disinvested),
reemerges as a model of social simulation, bringing all other
categories of political economy within the aleatory realm of the code.

The new situation elicits a disquieting strangeness of a sudden
plunge into a kind of second life, separated from you by all the
distance of a previous life, since there was a familiarity, an intimacy
in the traditional process of labor. At least the concreteness of exploitation, the violent sociality of labor, is familiar. Nothing like this today
– and this is not so much due to the *operative* abstraction of the labor
process which is so often blamed, as it is to the passage of each *sign* of
labor into an *operational* field where it becomes a floating variable,
bringing along with it all of the imaginary of a previous life.

Beyond the conception of the *mode* as an autonomous unit of
production (beyond the mode's internal convulsions, contradictions
and revolutions), the *code* of production must reemerge. This is the
form it presently takes, in the light of a "materialist" history that has
succeeded in legalizing production as the principle of the actual
development of societies. (For Marx, art, religion, law etc. do not

have a specific history; only production has a history, or better: production *is* history, it *grounds* history. This is the incredible fabrication of labor and production as a historical reason and as the generic model of fulfillment.)

At the conclusion of this religious formulation of the autonomy of production we begin to see that all of this could have recently been *produced* (this time in the sense of theatrical production and scenario), and for a purpose quite different from the internal finalities (such as the revolution) that production secretes.

To analyze production as a code is to transcend the material presence of machines, industry, labor time, products, wages, money, and those that are more formal, yet just as "objective," such as surplus value, the market, capital, in order to identify the rules of the game, and to destroy the logical connections in the determinations of capital, even in the critical connections of Marxist categories that analyze it. For these categories remain an appearance of capital to the second power, the categories of its apparent *criticality*, used to identify the elementary signifiers of production, and the social relations it produces, forever buried under the historical illusion of the producers (and the theoreticians).

Labor

Labor power is not a force, it is a definition, an axiom, and its "real" function in the labor process, its "use value," is merely the redoubling of this definition in the operation of the code. It is at the level of the sign, never at the level of energy, that violence is fundamental. The *mechanism* of capital (and not its law) operates on surplus value – the difference between wages and labor power. Even if the two were equivalent, meaning the end of surplus value, and even if wages (the sale of labor power) were eliminated, man would remain marked by this axiom, by this destiny of production, by this sacrament of labor which characterizes him like a sex. No, the laborer is no longer a man, neither man nor woman: it has a sex of its own; it is marked by this labor power that assigns it a purpose, just as woman is marked by her sex (her sexual definition), or as blacks are by skin color – these are also signs, and nothing but signs.

We must distinguish between what specifically derives from the *mode* of production and what derives from the *code* of production. Before it becomes an element in the commodity law of value, labor power is first a status, a structure of compliance to a code. Before it becomes exchange value and use value, it is already, like every commodity, a *sign* of nature's exploitability, upon which production is defined, and which is the underlying principle of our culture, and of no other. This message that underlies the commodity is much more fundamental than quantitative equivalences: the extraction of nature (and man) from indeterminacy to subject it (him) to the determination of value. This is what we experience as the constructive rage of bulldozers, the rage of highways and "infrastructures." The civilizing rage of the productive era is the rage of not letting a single parcel remain unproductive, of countersigning everything by production, without even the hope of abundant wealth: producing in order to mark; producing to reproduce a marked man. What is production today if not this terrorism of the code? This is becoming as clear to us as it was to the first industrial generations who reacted to machines as if they were mortal enemies, bearers of total destruction, before the lofty dream of the historical dialectic of production took over. Luddite activities springing up everywhere, savage attacks on the instruments of production (for the most part productive forces turning on themselves) and endemic sabotage and defection are all witness to the fragility of the productive order. The destruction of machines is a deviant act if machines are the *means* of production, or if there remains some ambiguity concerning their future use value. But if the *ends* of production collapse, then the respect due to the means also collapses. Machines then appear in the light of their true end: as immediate, direct indicators of the social relation of death upon which capital thrives. Thus nothing opposes their immediate destruction. In this sense, the Luddites were much more lucid than Marx concerning the impact of the industrial order. So today the *catastrophic* consequences of the industrial process, about which even Marx erred in his *dialectical* euphoria over productive forces, are in a sense the revenge of the Luddites.

When we say that labor is a sign we do not mean the connotations of prestige associated with specific kinds of work; nor the promotion that wage labor signifies for the Algerian immigrant in relation to his tribal community; nor what it means for the Moroccan boy from the Upper Atlas whose only dream is to work for Simca – these signs work in a similar way to the signification of women in our society today. In these particular cases labor refers to a specific value – either an increase or difference in status. In the present scenario, labor is no longer a function of this referential definition of the sign. Particular kinds of labor, even labor in general, no longer has its own specific meaning. There is now a system of labor where positions are interchanged. No more "right man in the right place":[5] an old adage of the era of the scientific idealism of production. Nor any longer are there individuals who are interchangeable yet indispensable in a determined labor process. It is the process of labor itself that has become interchangeable: a mobile, polyvalent, intermittent, system of socialization, indifferent to every objective, and to labor itself understood in the classical sense of the term. Its only function is to localize each individual in a social nexus where nothing ever converges, except perhaps in the immanence of this functional matrix, an indifferent paradigm that assigns individuals to the same radical, or a syntagm that associates them according to an indeterminate combinatorial mode.

Work (in the form of leisure as well) invades all of life as a fundamental repression, as control, and as a permanent job in specified times and places, according to an omnipresent code. People must be *positioned* at all times: in school, in the plant, at the beach or in front of the TV, or in job retraining – a permanent, general mobilization. But this form of labor is no longer productive in the original sense: it is now merely the mirror of society, its imaginary, its fantastic principle of reality. A death instinct perhaps.

This is the tendency of every current strategy that concerns labor: job enrichment,[6] flexible working time, mobility, retraining, continuing education, autonomy, joint worker—management control, and the decentralization of the labor process, including the Californian utopia of computerized homework. You are no longer brutally removed from daily life to be delivered up to machines. But rather you are integrated: your childhood, your habits, your human relations, your unconscious instincts, even your rejection of work. You will certainly find a place for yourself in all of this, a personalized job, and if not, there is social welfare provision that is calculated based on your individualized statistics.[7] In any case, you will never be left on your own. The important thing is that everyone be a terminal in the network, a tiny terminal, but a term nevertheless: certainly no inarticulate cry, but a linguistic term, and in terms of the whole structural network of language. The choice of occupation, the ideal of an occupation custom made for everyone means that the *die is cast*, that the system of socialization is complete. Labor power is no longer violently bought and sold; it is designed, it is marketed, it is merchandised.[8] Production thus joins the consumerist system of signs.

The first stage of the analysis was to conceptualize the realm of consumption as an extension of the realm of productive forces. Now we must do just the opposite. We must conceptualize the realm of production, labor, and productive forces as basking in the realm of "consumption" – here taken as a generalized axiomatic, a coded exchange of signs, and as a general lifestyle. Thus, knowledge, know-how, and attitudes (Verres: "Why not consider the attitudes of the personnel as one of the resources to be managed by the boss?"),[9] but also sexuality and the body, and imagination (Verres: "Imagination is the only thing still connected to pleasure, whereas the psychic apparatus is subordinated to the principle of reality [Freud]. We must stop this waste. Let imagination actualize itself as a productive force, let it invest itself. Power to imagination: the call to arms of technocracy");[10] and the unconscious, and the revolution, etc. Yes, all of this is in the process of "investment" and absorption within the sphere of value, but not so much in market value, as in computable value. It is not mobilized for production, but indexed, assigned, summoned to function as an operational variable. It has become, not so much a productive force, but the code's chess pieces, which follow the same rules of the game. The axiom of production still tends to reduce everything to *factors*. The axiom of the code reduces everything to *variables*. The former leads to equations and tests of strength. The latter leads to fluid and aleatory combinations that neutralize by *connection*, not by *annexation*, whatever resists or escapes them.

The three orders of simulation

Three orders of simulation, parallel to mutations in the law of value, have succeeded one another since the Renaissance:

1   The *counterfeit* is the dominant scheme of the "classical" epoch, from the Renaissance to the industrial revolution.
2   *Production* is the dominant scheme of the industrial era.
3   *Simulation* is the dominant scheme of the present phase of history, governed by the code.

Simulacra of the first order play on the natural law of value; those of the second order play on the commodity law of value; and those of the third order play on the structural law of value.

The stucco angel

The problem of the counterfeit (and of fashion) was born with the Renaissance, with the destructuration of the feudal order and the emergence of open competition at the level of distinctive signs. There is no fashion in societies of caste and rank; where social assignation is total, social mobility nil. In these societies, signs are shielded by a prohibition that assures their absolute clarity: each sign refers unequivocally to a (particular) situation and a level of status. Ceremony and counterfeit do not mix – unless we intend black magic and sacrilege; but it is precisely these categories that brand the crime of mingling signs as a breach of the order of things. If we start yearning nostalgically, especially these days, for a revitalized "symbolic order," we should have no illusions. Such an order once existed, but it was composed of ferocious hierarchies; the transparency of signs goes hand in hand with their cruelty.

Caste societies, feudal or archaic, were *cruel* societies, where signs were limited in number and restricted in scope. Each possessed its full interdictory value, and each was a reciprocal obligation between castes, or persons; hence they were not arbitrary. The arbitrary nature of the sign arises when, instead of linking two people in unbreachable reciprocity, the sign begins, in signifying, to refer to the disenchanted universe of the signified – the common denominator of the real world, to which nobody really has any further obligation.

With the end of the *bound* sign, the reign of the emancipated sign begins, in which all classes eventually acquire the power to participate. Competitive democracy succeeds the endogamy of the sign proper to orders of status. With the transition of the sign values of prestige from one class to another, we enter the world of the counterfeit in a stroke, passing from a limited order of signs, where taboos inhibit "free" production, to a proliferation of signs according to demand. But this multiplication of signs no longer bears any connection with the bound sign of restricted circulation. It is the counterfeit of it, not by virtue of having denatured some "original," but through the extension of a material whose clarity depended on the restrictions that stamped it. No longer discriminating (but only competitive), relieved of all barriers, universally available, the modern sign nevertheless simulates necessity by offering itself as a determinate link to the world. The modern sign dreams of the sign anterior to it and fervently desires, in its reference to the real, to rediscover some binding obligation. But it finds only a *reason*: a referential reason, the real – the "natural" on which it will feed. This lifeline of designation, however, is no more than a simulacrum of symbolic obligation. It produces only neutral values, those that exchange among each other in an objective world. Here, the sign undergoes the same destiny as work. The "free" laborer is only free to produce equivalences; the "free and emancipated" sign is only free to produce equivalent signifieds.

It is thus in a kind of simulacrum of a "nature" that the modern sign discovers its value. The problematic of the "natural," the metaphysics of appearance and reality, become the characteristic themes of the bourgeoisie since the Renaissance, the mirror of the bourgeois sign, the mirror of the classical sign. Even today, nostalgia for natural reference survives, in spite of numerous revolutions aimed at smashing this configuration, such as the revolution of production, in which signs ceased to refer to nature, but only to the law of exchange, under the commodity law of value. (We will return to these, for they are simulations of the second order.)

It was thus with the Renaissance that the false was born with the natural...

The industrial simulacrum

The industrial revolution gave rise to a whole new generation of signs and objects. These were signs with no caste tradition, which had never known the restrictions of status, and which would not have to be *counterfeited* because they were being *produced* on such a gigantic scale. The problem of the singularity and the origin of these signs no longer arises; technique is their origin. They have no meaning beyond the dimensions of the industrial simulacrum.

This is the phenomenon of the series; in other words, there is the very possibility of two or of *n* identical objects. The relation between them is not that of the original to its counterfeit, or its analogue, or its reflection; it is a relationship of equivalence, of indifference. In the series, objects are transformed indefinitely into simulacra of one another and, with objects, so are the people who produce them. Only the extinction of original reference permits the generalized law of equivalence, which is to say, the *very possibility of production*.

But the analysis of production is beginning to falter because it is no longer able to read production as an original process, a process that lies at the origin of all the others. In fact, it discovers the reverse: a process of resorption of every original being and its introduction to identical series of beings. Hitherto, production and labor have been viewed as potential and force, as historical process and as a generic activity. This is the modern energo-economic myth. But it is worth asking whether production does not intervene, *in the order of signs*, as a *particular phase*; whether it is not at bottom only one episode in the lineage of simulacra? It would be that which, thanks to technique, produces potentially identical beings (sign-objects) in indefinite series.

The fabulous energies released in the play of technique, industry, and economy should not obscure the fact that the ultimate point was to establish this condition of indefinite reproducibility. Although it certainly amounts to a major challenge to the "natural" order, it remains a "second order" simulacrum and a rather poor imaginary solution to the problem of mastering the world. Relative to the era of the counterfeit, the double, the mirror, of theater and the play of masks and appearances, the serial and technical age of reproduction commands, in the end, less scope (but the following era of simulation models, the third order, is of considerably greater dimensions).

It was Walter Benjamin who first separated the implications of this principle of reproduction. He showed that reproduction absorbs the process of production and alters its goals, the status of the product, and the producer. He established this on the terrain of art, cinema, and photography.... But we know now that today all production returns to this sphere. It is at the level of reproduction – fashion, media, advertising, information and communication networks – the level that Marx described as the *faux frais* of capital (you can almost measure the irony of history), it is in other words within the sphere of simulacra and the code, that the unity of the whole process of capital is tied together. Benjamin (and later McLuhan) grasped technique not as "productive force" (where Marxist analysis remains trapped) but as medium, as the form and principle of a whole new generation of meaning. The mere fact that any object can be reproduced, as such, in an exemplary double, is already a revolution.... That two products are *equivalent* by virtue of social necessary labor is less interesting in the long run than the serial repetition of the same object (which is the same for individuals considered as labor power). Technique as medium quashes not only the "message" of the product (its use value), but also labor power itself, which Marx wanted to make the revolutionary message of production. But Benjamin and McLuhan saw that the real message, *the real ultimatum*, lay in reproduction itself, and that production, as such, has no meaning: its social finality gets lost in seriality. Simulacra surpass history.

Moreover, the phase of serial production is ephemeral. Ever since dead labor began to predominate over living labor, in other words, since the end of primitive accumulation, serial production has been ceding precedence to generation by models. This is a matter of reversing origins and finalities, since all forms change from the moment they are no longer mechanically reproduced, but conceived instead in light of their reproducibility, as a diffraction from a generating nucleus called a model. With this, we find ourselves in the midst of third-order simulacra. Both the counterfeit of the original in the first order and the pure series of the second order disappear in favor of models from which all forms proceed according to the modulation of differences. Only an affiliation to the model generates meaning and makes sense (*fait sens*). Nothing functions according to an end, but proceeds from the model, the "signifier of reference," which acts like an anterior finality, supplying the only credible outcome (*la seule vraisemblance*). This is simulation in the modern sense of the term, where industrialization is only the primary form. In the end, serial reproducibility is less fundamental than modulation; quantitative equivalence less important than distinctive oppositions. The potential for commutation of terms takes precedence over the law of equivalence; the structural law of value replaces the commodity law of value. Not only does it make little sense to search for the secrets of the code in technique or the economy; the very possibility of industrial production has to be traced to the genesis of the code and of simulacra. As the order of the counterfeit was seized by serial production (viz., how art succumbed entirely to a kind of "machinality"), so the order of production is in the process of being undermined by operational simulation...

The metaphysics of the code

> The mathematical Leibniz saw in the mystic elegance of the binary system of *zero* and *one* the image of Creation. The unity of the Supreme Being operating in the void by binary function would, he felt, suffice to make all beings from the void.
>
> Marshall McLuhan

The great simulacra constructed by man evolve from a universe of natural laws to one of forces and tensions, and finally, today, to a universe of structures and binary oppositions. After the metaphysics of being and appearance, after that of energy and determination, we have the metaphysics of indeterminacy and the code. Cybernetic control, generation by models, differential modulation, feedback, questionnaires (*question/réponse?*): such is the new *operational* configuration (industrial simulacra were only *operative*). Digitality is its metaphysical principle (Leibniz's God) and DNA its prophet. In fact, it is in the genetic code that the "genesis of simulacra" finds its most developed form. At the limit of an always increasing elimination of references and finalities, an ever-increasing loss of resemblances and designations, we find the digital and programmatic sign, whose "value" is purely *tactical*, at the intersection of other signals ("bits" of information/tests) whose structure is that of a micromolecular code of command and control.

At this level, the question of signs and their rational destination; their *real* and their *imaginary*; their repression; their reversal; the illusions they sketch; what they hush up, or their parallel significations – all of these are swept from the table. We have already touched on first-order signs, complex and rich with illusions, and how they have been transformed, together with machines, into brute, flat, industrial, repetitive signs: echoless, efficient, operative. Yet much more radical is the evolution of the coded signal, which is in a sense unreadable, without possible interpretation, like a programmatic matrix buried for light-years at the foundation of the "biological" body: little black boxes where all the commands are formented with all the responses.

Surely this must mean the end of the theater of representation – the space of signs, their conflict and their silence. All this is replaced by the black box of the code, the molecular signal emitter with which we are irradiated. Our bodies are crisscrossed by question/answer formulas and tests, like programs inscribed in our cells. Bodily cells, electronic cells, party cells, microbiological cells: we are always on the lookout for the tiniest, indivisible element, whose organic synthesis arises from the givens of the code. But the code itself is only a genetic, generative cell where myriad intersections produce all the questions and all the possible solutions. The questions (the stimuli of data processing and information systems) have no finality beyond the programmed reply, which is genetically immutable, or inflected by infinitesimal and aleatory differences. This is the space of an unprecedented linearity and one-dimensionality: a cellular space for the indefinite generation of the same signals, like the ticks of a prisoner driven mad by loneliness and repetition. This is the genetic code, an unchanging, radiating disk of which we are no more than interpretive cells. The aura of the sign and of signification itself is resolved along with the possibility of determination; everything is resolved in inscription and decoding.

This is the current strategic model. It takes up where the old ideological model, political economy, left off, and reappears under the rigorous sign of science in Jacques Monod's *Chance and Necessity*. Dialectical evolution is over. Now it is the discontinuous indeterminism of the genetic code that regulates life – the *teleonomic* principle. Finality is no longer located at the conclusion; indeed, there is no end, and no determination. The finalities are established in advance, inscribed in the code. In a way, things have not really changed. The system of ends has only ceded to the play of molecules, as has the order of signifieds to the play of infinitesimal signifiers reduced to aleatory commutation. It is as if the transcendental ends have been revised into an instrument panel. However, what is always involved is a recourse to nature, to an inscription in a "biological" nature. In effect, this is a fantasized nature, as nature has always been. It is a metaphysical sanctuary no longer for the origin or for substances, but this time for the code. The code has to have an "objective" seat – what better throne than the molecule and genetics? Monod is the severe theologian of this molecular transcendence; Edgar Morin is his ecstatic acolyte (ADN = Adonaï)! In each, the phantasm of the code, which is equivalent to the reality of power, is combined with an idealism of the molecule.

In other words, we encounter once more the delirious dream of reunifying the world under a unitary principle. There was the homogeneous substance of the Jesuits during the Counter-Reformation; now there is the genetic code, whose precursor is Leibniz's binary Divinity. For the current program has nothing to do with genetics; it is a social and historical program. What biochemistry hypostatizes is the ideal of a social order regulated by a kind of genetic code or micromolecular calculus of PPBS (Planning Programming Budgeting System) that irradiates the social body with its operational circuits. Technocybernetics here unveils its "natural philosophy," as Monod calls it . . .

In its reproduction, the system puts an end to its own myth of origin and the referential values it has secreted during its process of development. By extinguishing its own foundational myth, the system also eliminates its internal contradictions (no more "reality" and no referent with which to challenge it). But it does away, in the same stroke, with its teleological myths, with the revolution itself. What the revolution always held out for was the triumph of the generic human reference, the original potential of man. If capital scratches generic man himself from the map (in favor of genetic man?), what then? The golden age of revolution was also the era of capital, when myths of origin and end were still in circulation. The irony is that the major historical threat to capital lay in the *mythic* imperative of rationality that characterized it from the beginning. But once it has short-circuited these myths in a factual operationalism, undermined rational discourse, and become its own myth, or more precisely, the indeterminate, random machine that it is today – something comparable to a genetic social code – then capital eliminates the opportunity for a determinate reversal. This is the essential violence of capital today. It remains to be seen whether this operationality is not also a myth – if, indeed, DNA itself is not a myth . . .

Regulation on the model of the genetic code is not confined to laboratory effects and the exalted visions of biological theoreticians. The most banal aspects of ordinary life are invested with these models. Digitality is among us: it preys on the messages and signs of modern societies. Its most concrete form is the test: question/ answer, stimulus/response. Content is steadily neutralized in a continual procedure of controlled interrogation, of verdicts and ultimatums to be decoded, none of which, this time, originate in the genetic code, but they partake nevertheless of the same tactical indetermination. The cycle of meaning is infinitesimally abridged into minute quantities of energy/information, bits, questions/answers, returning to their points of departure, describing only the perpetual reactualization of the same models. This is the equivalent of the code's neutralization of signifieds, the instantaneous verdicts of fashion, advertising, media messages. It dwells everywhere that supply engulfs demand, or the question devours the answer, or absorbs and regurgitates it in decodable form, or simply invents and then anticipates it. Everywhere, we find the same "scenario:" the "trial and error" scenario (of guinea pigs in laboratory tests); the scenario that gives you a "range of choices;" the multiple-choice testing offered everywhere ("test your personality"). The test appears as a fundamental social form of control, infinitely dividing practices and responses.

We live in the mode of the *referendum*, and this is precisely because there are no more referentials. All signs and messages (which include "functional" objects as well as fashion features, televised information, polls or electoral consultations) present themselves to us in the question/answer format. The social system of communication has evolved from a complex syntactic structure of language to the probing of a binary signaling system: a perpetual test. Yet, as we know, tests and referenda are perfect forms of simulation. The reply is induced by the question; it is, so to speak, designated in advance. Hence, the referendum is really just an ultimatum. The question, being unilateral, is therefore no longer properly interrogative, but rather the immediate imposition of a meaning whose cycle is instantly completed. Each message is a verdict, like the statistical ones announced in polls. The simulation of distance (that is, of contradiction) between the two poles of the communication process is, like the reality effect in the sign, just a tactical hallucination.... "Reality" has been analyzed into simple elements and recomposed into scenarios of regulated opposition....

It may seem that the historical movement of capital has carried it from the open competition of the oligopoly to outright monopoly;

that democracy has moved from the multiparty system to bipartisanism and finally to the single-party state. But this is not what is going on. The oligopoly, or contemporary diapoly, results from the monopoly's tactical division in two. In all domains, diapoly is the highest stage of monopoly. It is not political will that breaks the monopoly of the market (state intervention, antitrust laws, etc.); it is the fact that every unitary system, if it wants to survive, has to evolve a *binary* system of *regulation*. This changes nothing in the essence of monopoly; on the contrary, power is only absolute if it knows how to diffract itself in equivalent variations; that is, if it knows how to redouble itself through doubling. This goes for brands of detergent as much as for "peaceful coexistence." You need two superpowers to maintain a universe under control; a single empire collapses under its own weight. The equilibrium of terror is what permits a strategy of regulated oppositions to be established, since the strategy is really structural rather than atomic. This regulated opposition can be ramified into more complex scenarios, but the matrix remains binary. It looks as if, from now on, we shall be dealing not with duality or open competitive war, but with couples of simultaneous opposition.

From the tiniest disjunctive unities (the question/answer particle) to the macroscopic level of systems of alternation that preside over the economy, politics, and global coexistence, the matrix does not vary: it is always 0/1, the binary scansion that affirms itself as the metastable or homoeostatic form of contemporary systems. It is the processual node of the simulations that dominate us. They can be organized as an unstable play of variation, or in polyvalent or tautological modes, without endangering this central principle of bipolarity: digitality is, indeed, the divine form of simulation....

Why does the World Trade Center in New York City have *two* towers...?

The hyperrealism of simulation

What I have been describing so far defines a digital space, a magnetic field of the code, with polarizations, diffractions, gravitating models and always – *always* – the flux of tiniest disjunctive unities (the question/answer cell, which is a kind of cybernetic atom of signification). It is important now to gauge the difference between this field of control and the traditional space of repression – the police space – which still corresponded to a significative violence...

Totalitarian, bureaucratic concentration is an arrangement that dates from the era of the commodity law of value. That system of equivalences in effect imposed a form of general equivalence, and hence, the centralization of a global process. Its archaic rationality contrasts starkly with the meaning of simulation. Simulation does not secrete a single, general equivalent, but rather a diffraction of models playing a supervisory role. General equivalence is replaced by distinctive opposition. The code's disjunction supplants the centralist injunction. Solicitation is substituted for the ultimatum. Mandatory passivity evolves into models constructed directly from the "active responses" of the subject, his or her implication, "ludic" participation, etc., and finally toward a total, environmental model made up of incessant spontaneous responses, joyful feedback, and irradiated contact.

This is (according to Nicholas Schöffer) "the concretization of the general ambience" – the great Festival of Participation, composed of myriad stimuli, miniaturized tests, infinitely divisible nodes of query and reply, magnetized by a few overarching models illuminated by the code. The culture of tactile communication is in fact burgeoning in the techno-lumino-kinetic space provided by this total, spatio-dynamic theater. It brings with it a kind of contact Imaginary, a sensorial mimeticism, a tactile mysticism that grafts onto the universe of operational simulation, multistimulation, and multiresponse like an entire system of ecological concepts. Indeed, the rationality of adaptive testing awaits naturalization through assimilation with animal mimeticism: "Animal adaptation to the forms and colors of their milieu is a phenomenon valid also for man" (Schöffer). And even for Indians, with their "innate sense of ecology!"

Tropisms, mimeticism, empathy – the whole ecological Gospel of open system, with feedback, negative or positive, is on the verge of being swallowed up in this breach, as an ideology of regulation through information, which is surely just the modern-day avatar, dressed in a more flexible rationality, of Pavlovian reflex (psychology). Thus, we have evolved from electroshock therapy to bodily expression as mental health conditioning. The apparatuses of force and of "forcing" (*forçage*) have given way to those of ambience, which include the operationalization of the concepts of need, perception, desire, and so on. This is a generalized ecology, mystique of the (ecological) "niche," of context, and of simulations of milieu... The spectacle itself is engulfed in this total, fusional, tactile, aesthesic (no more aesthetics) environmentalism...

Reality itself founders in hyperrealism, the meticulous reduplication of the real, preferably through another, reproductive medium, such as photography. From medium to medium, the real is volatilized, becoming an allegory of death. But it is also, in a sense, reinforced through its own destruction. It becomes *reality for its own sake*, the fetishism of the lost object: no longer the object of representation, but the ecstasy of denial and of its own ritual extermination: the hyperreal.

Realism had already inaugurated this process. The rhetoric of the real signaled its gravely altered status (its golden age was characterized by an innocence of language in which it was not obliged to redouble what is said with a reality effect). Surrealism remained within the purview of the realism it contested – but also redoubled – through its rupture with the Imaginary. The hyperreal represents a much more advanced stage insofar as it manages to efface even this contradiction between the real and the imaginary. Unreality no longer resides in the dream or fantasy, or in the beyond, but in the *real's hallucinatory resemblance to itself*. To escape the crisis of representation, reality loops around itself in pure repetition, a tendency that was already apparent, before the days of pop art and pictorial neorealism, in the *nouveau roman*. There, the project was already to enclose the real in a vacuum, to extirpate all psychology and subjectivity in order to render a pristine objectivity. In fact, this objectivity was only that of the pure gaze – an objectivity at last liberated from the object, which is no more than the blind relay of the look that scans it. It attempts a kind of circular seduction in which one can easily mark the unconscious undertaking to become invisible.

This is certainly the impression created by the neonovel: the rage for eliding meaning in a blind and meticulous reality. Both syntax and semantics have disappeared. There is no longer an apparition, but an arraignment of the object, the eager examination of its scattered fragments: neither metaphor nor metonymy, but a successive immanence beneath the police agency of the look. This objective microscopics makes reality swim vertiginously, arousing the dizziness of death within the confines of representation for its own sake. The old illusions of relief, perspective, and spatial and psychological depth linked to the perception of the object give way to an optics functioning on the surface of things, as if the gaze had become the molecular code of the object...

A possible definition of the real is: *that for which it is possible to provide an equivalent representation*. This definition is contemporary with science, which postulates a universal system of equivalences (classical representation was not so much a matter of equivalence as of transcription, interpretation, commentary). At the conclusion of this process of reproduction, the real becomes not only that which can be reproduced, but that which is always already reproduced: the hyperreal. But this does not mean that reality and art are in some sense extinguished through total absorption in one another. Hyper-realism is something like their mutual fulfillment and overflowing into one another through an exchange at the level of simulation of their respective foundational privileges and prejudices. Hyperrealism is only beyond representation because it functions entirely within the realm of simulation. There, the whirligig of representation goes mad, but with an implosive insanity which, far from being ex-centric, casts longing eyes at the center, toward its own repetition *en abîme*. Like the distancing effect within a dream, which tells one that one is dreaming, but only in behalf of the censor, in order that we continue dreaming, hyperrealism is an integral part of a coded reality, which it perpetuates without modifying.

In fact, we must interpret hyperrealism inversely: today, *reality itself is hyperrealistic*. The secret of surrealism was that the most banal reality could become surreal, but only at privileged moments, which still derived from art and the imaginary. Now the whole of everyday political, social, historical, economic reality is incorporated into the simulative dimension of hyperrealism; we already live out the "aesthetic" hallucination of reality. The old saying, "reality is stranger than fiction," which belonged to the surrealist phase of the aesthet-icization of life, has been surpassed. There is no longer a fiction that life can confront, even in order to surpass it; reality has passed over into the play of reality, radically disenchanted, the "cool" cybernetic phase supplanting the "hot" and phantasmatic...

There once existed a specific class of objects that were allegorical, and even a bit diabolical, such as mirrors, images, works of art (and concepts?); of course, these too were simulacra, but they were trans-parent and manifest... they had their own style and characteristic savoir faire. In these objects, pleasure consisted more in discovering something "natural" in what was artificial and counterfeit. Today, the real and the imaginary are confounded in the same operational totality, and aesthetic fascination is simply everywhere. It involves a kind of subliminal perception, a kind of sixth sense for fakery, montage, scenarios, and the overexposure of reality in the lighting of models. This is no longer a productive space, but a kind of cipher-ing strip, a coding and decoding tape, a tape recording magnetized with signs. It is an aesthetic reality, to be sure, but no longer by virtue of art's premeditation and distance, but through a kind of elevation to the second power, via the anticipation and the immanence of the code. An air of nondeliberate parody clings to everything – a tactical simulation – like an undecidable game to which is attached a specifically aesthetic pleasure, the pleasure in reading (*lecture*) and in the rules of the game...

For a long time now art has prefigured this transformation of everyday life. Very quickly, the work of art redoubled itself as a manipulation of the signs of art: this oversignification, or as Lévi-Strauss would call it, this "academicism of the signifier," introduced art to the sign form. Thus art entered the phase of its own indefinite *reproduction*; everything that redoubles in itself, even ordinary, everyday reality, falls in the same stroke under the sign of art, and becomes aesthetic. The same goes for production, of which one can say that today it is commencing this aesthetic doubling at the point where, having expelled all content and finality, it becomes, in a way, abstract and nonfigurative. It begins to express the pure form of production; it takes itself, like art, as its own teleological value.

Art and industry can thus exchange signs: art, in order to become a reproductive machine (Andy Warhol), without ceasing to be art, since this machine is only a sign; and production, in order to lose all social purpose and thus to verify and exalt itself at last in the hyperbolic and aesthetic signs of prestige that are the great industrial combines, the 400-meter-high business blocks and the statistical mysteries of the GNP...In this vertigo of serial signs – shadowless, impossible to sublimate, immanent in their repetition – who can say where the reality of what they simulate resides? Apparently, these signs repress nothing...even the primary process is abolished. The cool universe of digitality absorbs the worlds of metaphor and of metonymy, and the principle of simulation thus triumphs over both the reality principle and the pleasure principle.

NOTES

1 Anthony Wilden, *System and Structure: Essays in Communication and Exchange* (London: Tavistock, 1977) p. xxvii.
2 See G. Deleuze and F. Guattari, *Anti-Oedipus* (Minneapolis: Minnesota Press, 1983) and J.-F. Lyotard, *Économie libidinale* (Paris: Minuit, 1974).
3 Theoretical production, like material production, is also losing its determinations and is beginning to spin on its own, disconnectedly, *en abîme*, towards an unknown reality. Today we are already at that point: in the realm of undecidability, in the era of *floating theories*, like floating currencies. Every current theory, from whatever horizon it originates (including psychoanalysis), with whatever violence it arms itself, pretending to recover an immanence or fluidity without referent (Deleuze, Lyotard, etc.) – all are floating, and their only purpose is to signal one

another. It is futile to fault them for lack of coherence by appealing to some sort of "reality." The system has removed from theoretical labor power all referential guarantees, as it did in the other realm. Theory no longer has any use value either. The mirror of theoretical production is also cracked. And this is in the order of things. What I mean to say is that the very undecidability of theory is an effect of the code. There is no illusion in fact: this flotation of theories is not some schizophrenic "drift" where fluxes might pass freely over the body without organs (of what? of capital?) It simply means that all theories are now interchangeable according to variable exchange rates, but they are that way without investing in anything, except perhaps in the mirror of their writing (*écriture*).

4   Baudrillard is playing with the dual semantic surface of *bordel*: "brothel" and "chaos." [Trans.]

5   "Right man in the right place" was originally in English. [Trans.]

6   "Job enrichment" was originally in English. [Trans.]

7   In France those unemployed for economic reasons received, for a period of time, social welfare provision proportionate to their previous salaries. [Trans.]

8   Baudrillard uses the Franglais terms: *design, markète, merchandise*. [Trans.]

9   Daniel Verres, et al., *Le Discours du capitalisme* (Paris: L'herne, 1971) p. 36.

10 Ibid., p. 74. Baudrillard paraphrases the last sentence of Verres's text but includes his paraphrase within the quotation mark. [Trans.]

6

On Seduction

The sacred horizon of appearances

Seduction is that which extracts meaning from discourse and detracts it from its truth. It would thus be the opposite of the psychoanalytic distinction between manifest and latent discourse. For latent discourse diverts manifest discourse not *from* its truth but *towards* it and makes it say what it did not wish to say. It uncovers determinations and deep-seated lack of determinations. It always suspects depth behind the rupture; always suspects meaning behind the bar. Manifest discourse has the status of a labored appearance, traversed by the emergence of meaning. Interpretation is that which, shattering appearances and the play of manifest discourse, will set meaning free by remaking connections with latent discourse.

In seduction, conversely, it is somehow the manifest discourse, the most "superficial" aspect of discourse, which acts upon the underlying prohibition (conscious or unconscious) in order to nullify it and to substitute for it the charms and traps of appearances. Appearances, which are not at all frivolous, are the site of play and chance taking the site of a passion for diversion – to reduce signs is here far more important than the emergence of any truth. Interpretation overlooks and obliterates this aspect of appearances in its search for hidden meaning. This is why interpretation is so characteristically opposed to seduction, and why every interpretive discourse is so unappealing. The havoc interpretation wreaks in the domain of appearances is incalculable, and its privileged quest for hidden meanings may be profoundly mistaken. For we needn't search in some beyond, in a *hinterwelt*, or in an unconscious, to find what diverts discourse. What actually displaces it, "seduces" it in the literal sense, and makes it seductive, is its very appearance: the aleatory, meaningless, or ritualistic and meticulous, circulation of signs on the surface; its inflections, and its nuances. All of this effaces the content value (*teneur*) of meaning, and this is seductive. The meaning of an interpretative discourse, by contrast, has never seduced anyone. *Every interpretive discourse (discours de sens) wants to get beyond appearances*; this is its illusion and fraud. But getting beyond appearances is an impossible task: inevitably every discourse is revealed in its own appearance, and is hence subject to the stakes imposed by seduction, and consequently to *its own failure as discourse*. Perhaps every discourse is secretly tempted by this failure and by having its objectives put into question, changing its truth effects into surface effects which act like a mirror absorbing and engulfing meaning. This is what happens initially when a discourse *seduces itself*; the original way in which it absorbs meaning and empties itself of meaning in order better to fascinate others: the primitive seduction of language.

Every discourse is complicit in this abduction of meaning, in this seductive maneuver of interpretation; if one discourse did not do this, then others would take its place. All appearances conspire to combat meaning, to uproot meaning, whether intentional or not, and to convert it into a game, according to some other rules of the game, arbitrary ones this time, to some other elusive ritual, more adventurous and more seductive than the mastery of meaning. Discourse must struggle not so much against the secrets of the unconscious as against the superficial abyss of its own appearance. And if it must overcome something, it is not fantasies and hallucinations, which are full of meaning and counter-meaning, but rather the brilliant surface of nonsense and all the play that it makes possible. Only recently have we been able to eliminate the dangers of seduction, whose domain is the sacred horizon of appearances, in order to substitute for it "serious" problematics; problematics of the unconscious and problematics of interpretation. But nothing can guarantee that this substitution, or the obsession with latent discourse initiated by psychoanalysis, which is the equivalent of generalizing to all levels the violence and terrorism of interpretation, is itself not fragile and ephemeral. No one knows whether this strategy, in which we have eliminated or sought to eliminate all deduction, is not itself a very fragile simulation model, one that only pretends to be an invulnerable structure in order to hide the effects of the alternative, the effects of seduction which have begun to threaten it. The worst thing for psychoanalysis, after all, is in fact that the unconscious seduces. It seduces with dreams. It seduces by its concept. It deduces when "the

id speaks" and when it desires to speak. Everywhere there is a double
structure in place. Everywhere there is a parallel structure in which
signs from the unconscious connive with their exchange – a conniving
that devours the other, the "work" of the unconscious, and the pure
and simple processes of transference and counter-transference. The
whole edifice of psychoanalysis is crumbling from having seduced
itself and from seducing others in the process. Let us become analysts
for a short moment, and let us say that this is the return of Freud's
primary repression, *the repression of seduction*, a repression which is
at the origin of the emergence of psychoanalysis as a "science."

The writings of Freud unfold between two polar positions,
positions that radically challenge his intermediate construct. These
poles are seduction and the death instinct. In *L'Échange symbolique et
la mort* I have previously argued that the death instinct is a reversion
to an earlier topical or economic model of psychoanalysis.[1] Concerning seduction, which through some hidden attraction connects with
the other pole, we should say that it remains something of a lost
object of psychoanalysis.

> It is traditional to look upon Freud's dropping of the seduction theory
> in 1897 as a decisive step in the foundation of psycho-analytic theory,
> and in the bringing to the fore of such conceptions as unconscious
> fantasy, psychical reality, spontaneous infantile sexuality and so on.[2]

Seduction, as the primeval form, finds itself relegated to a condition of
"primal fantasy." Consequently it is treated, according to a logic that
is no longer its own, as residue, vestige, and smokescreen within a
logic and structure henceforth triumphant over psychical and sexual
reality. Rather than demoting seduction to the status of a normal
phase in development, we must see it as an event which is crucial
and full of consequences. As we know, seduction will eventually
disappear from psychoanalytic discourse, or reappear only to be
buried and forgotten again, in a logical repetition of the founding
act of denegation by the master himself. Seduction is not simply
dismissed as a secondary element in comparison to more significant
ones, such as infant sexuality, repression, the Oedipus complex, etc. It
is rather denounced as a dangerous form, which could potentially be
fatal to the development and coherence of the future system.

It is exactly the same with Saussure as with Freud. Saussure also
began in *Anagrams* by identifying a form of language, or of
the abolition of language; a meticulous and ritualistic form of the
deconstruction of meaning and value. He then ended all of this in
order to turn to the construction of linguistics. Was this change of

focus due to some apparent failure to achieve real knowledge or rather was it the abandonment of the *anagrammatic challenge* in favor of a *constructive*, lasting and scientific analysis of the mode of production of meaning, an avoidance of its possible extermination? It doesn't matter in any case. Linguistics emerged out of this irrevocable change of direction, and it becomes the fundamental rule and axiom for all who continue Saussure's work. We cannot return to what has been destroyed. And forgetting the original murder is part of the logical and triumphant development of a science. All of the energy of mourning and of the dead object will be transferred to a simulated resurrection in the activities of the living. Yet we should mention that in the end Saussure – he at least – sensed the failure of this linguistic enterprise. He left dangling a sense of uncertainty, one that provided a glimpse into a weakness, a possible flaw of his remarkable mechanics of substitution. But his successors, satisfied with managing a discipline, lacked such scruples, scruples that might reveal hints of the violent and premature burying of the *Anagrams*. They could no longer imagine the abyss of language, the abyss of the seduction of language, nor conceive of a radically different process of the absorption of meaning, rather than of its production. The linguistic sarcophagus was well sealed, relying on the veil of the signifier.

Likewise the veil of psychoanalysis, the veil of hidden meaning, and of a *hidden* surplus of meaning, preyed upon seduction to the detriment of the superficial abyss of appearances; and to the detriment of the absorptive surface, the panic-inducing surface of the exchange and competition of signs established by seduction (hysteria being only a "symptomatic" manifestation, one that is already contaminated by the symptom's latent structure and is therefore prepsychoanalytic, and hence debased. This is why it has been able to serve as the "matrix of conversion" for psychoanalysis). Freud also abolished seduction in order to replace it with an eminently operational mechanics of *interpretation*, and an eminently sexual mechanics of repression, one which offers all the characteristics of objectivity and coherence (if we disregard all of the internal distortions of psychoanalysis, whether personal or theoretical: how can such a perfect coherence be frustrated; how does every challenge and every seduction buried within a rigorous discourse manage to reemerge, like the living-dead? – but then, claim the well meaning, this means that psychoanalysis is alive. Freud, in any case, broke with seduction and took the side of interpretation (until the last version of his metapsychology, where most explicitly, the break is made). But everything that was repressed in this admirable taking of sides reemerged in the conflicts and vicissitudes of the history of psychoanalysis. It is reenacted in the course of every cure (never will we hear the end of hysteria!) It is a delight to see seduction sweep through psychoanalysis in the works of Lacan. In the hallucinatory form of the play of signifiers, Lacanian psychoanalysis, with exigencies of rigor and form so favored by Freud, marks the death of psychoanalysis, just as assuredly as its institutional trivialization.

The Lacanian seduction is certainly an imposture, but in its own way it corrects, repairs and expiates Freud's original imposture: the foreclosure of the seduction/form to the benefit of a science which is not one. Lacan's discourse, promoting a seductive version of psychoanalysis, in a sense avenges that foreclosed seduction, but in a form that is itself contaminated by psychoanalysis; that is to say, always under the bar of the Law (of the Symbolic). This is a specious form of seduction. It always operates under the bar of the law and in the effigy of the Master who rules with the Word over hysterical masses incapable of sensual gratification...

After all, it is the death of psychoanalysis that is at issue with Lacan, a death brought about by the triumphant, yet posthumous, resurgence of what was initially denied. Is this not the fulfillment of a destiny? Psychoanalysis will at least have had the opportunity of finishing with a Great Imposture after beginning with a Great Denial.

We should be excited and comforted by the fact that the most remarkable system of meaning and interpretation ever erected is collapsing under the weight and the play of its own signs, signs that have become the disguises of unrestrained seduction, of unrestrained terms, once full of meaning, in an exchange that is complicit and devoid of meaning (even in therapy). This is a sign, at least, that we will be spared the truth (and a reason why only imposters rule). And what would appear to be the failure of psychoanalysis is merely the temptation, as in every great system of meaning, to lose itself in its own image at the risk of losing all meaning. This is clearly the rebirth from its own ashes of primitive seduction and the revenge of appearances. Well then, where is the imposture? Having refused the form of seduction from the outset, perhaps psychoanalysis was simply an illusion, the illusion of truth, the illusion of interpretation, which the Lacanian illusion of seduction refutes and corrects. Thus a cycle is completed, perhaps giving other interrogative and seductive forms a chance to emerge.

It was the same with God and with the Revolution. Iconoclasts were under the illusion that by destroying appearances God's truth would shine forth. Since there was no truth to God, which perhaps they secretly knew, their failure resulted from the same premise as that of the idolaters of images: *we can only live with the idea of an altered truth.* This is the only way to live in truth. The alternative is unbearable (precisely because *truth does not exist*). We must not wish to destroy appearances (the seduction of images). This project must fail if we are to prevent the absence of truth from exploding in our faces, or the absence of God, or of the Revolution. The Revolution is alive only in the fact that everyone is opposed to it, especially that mimetic and parodic double, Stalinism. Stalinism is immortal because it will always be there to hide the fact that the Revolution, the truth of the Revolution, doesn't exist. It thus restores hope. "The people," says Rivarol, "did not want the Revolution, they only wanted the spectacle." This is the only way to preserve the seduction of Revolution, rather than nullifying it in its truth.

"We don't believe that truth remains truth after it is unveiled." (Nietzsche)

The trompe-l'oeil or the enchanted simulation[3]

Disenchanted simulation: porn, more real than the real, and the height of simulation.

Enchanted simulation: the trompe-l'oeil, more false than the false, and the secret of appearances.

No fables, no narratives, no compositions. No scenes, no theater, no action. The trompe-l'oeil forgets all this and circumvents it by the slight figuration of certain objects. They figure in the great works of all times, but here they appear alone, as if they had abolished the discourse of painting. As a result, they are no longer "represented," no longer objects, no longer specific objects. They are the anti-representation of the social, religious and artistic, blank and empty signs which are the expression of anti-formality. The detritus of social life, they react to it and parody its theatricality: which is why they are scattered, juxtaposed in the randomness of their appearance. Even this is meaningful: *these objects are not objects*. They do not describe a familiar reality, like a still life. They describe the void and absence found in every representational hierarchy which organizes the elements of a painting, as it does the political realm.

These are not mere stand-ins which have been displaced from the principal scene, but reappearances that haunt the emptiness of a scene. This seduction is not an aesthetic one, that of a painting and of a likeness, but an acute and metaphysical seduction, one derived from the nullification of the real. The unreal inversion of these haunted and metaphysical objects contrasts completely with the representative space of the Renaissance.

Their insignificance is offensive. Only objects without referents, out of context – like these old newspapers, these old books, these old nails, these old boards, these scraps of food – only destitute and isolated objects, ghostly in their deinscription from all discourse, could portray the mood of a lost reality, like a previous life that haunts an individual and his or her self-awareness. "The trompe-l'oeil tends to substitute the inflexible opacity of Presence for the transparent and allusive image that the art lover expects."[4] Simulacra without perspective, "trompe-l'oeil" images appear suddenly, with sidereal accuracy, as if stripped of the aura of meaning and bathed in empty ether. Pure appearances, the irony is their excess of reality.

Nature is not represented in the trompe-l'oeil. There are no landscapes, no skies, no lines of flight or natural light; no faces either; neither psychology nor historicity. Everything here is artefact. A vertical backdrop creates, out of pure signs, objects isolated from their referential context.

Translucidity, suspense, fragility, obsolescence: thus the insistence on writing, the insistence of the letter (fringed on the edges), of the mirror and the watch – these are the lost and distant signs of a transcendence that vanished into the quotidian. The reflection of a worn plank whose knots and rings marked the flow of time, like a clock without hands that leaves us to guess the time: these are things which have already transpired, a time which has already occurred. Only anachrony stands out, the involuted image of time and space.

There are no fruits here, no meats or flowers, no baskets or bouquets, nor any of the elements of (still) life. Nature is carnal, a carnal arrangement on a horizontal plane, on a ground or a table. Even though it sometimes plays with distortion, with the undefined boundaries of objects and the ambiguity of their use, it always retains the gravity of real things. It is always underscored by the horizontal. Whereas the trompe-l'oeil functions in weightlessness, figured against a vertical background, everything here is in suspense, objects as well as time, even light and perspective. While still life works with classical shapes and shades, the shadows of the trompe-l'oeil do not have the depth that a *real* source of light provides: like the obsolescence of objects, they are the sign of a (s)light vertigo, the vertigo of a previous life, of an appearance prior to reality.

This mysterious light without origin, whose oblique rays are no longer real, is like a shallow pool of water, a stagnant pool, soft to the touch like a natural death. Things here no longer have a shadow (a substance). The sun that shines upon them is very different. It is a much brighter star, without an atmosphere or with an ether that doesn't refract. Perhaps death illuminates things directly, and this is all the shadow means? This shadow does not move with the sun; it does not elongate at sunset; it does not budge; it is an inflexible band. Not a result of chiaroscuro, nor a complicated dialectic of shade and light (for these are still painterly effects), but simply the result of the transparency of objects to a black sun.

We sense that these objects are approaching the black hole from where reality, the real world, and normal time emerge. The forward decentering effect, and the advancement of the reflection of objects at the subject's encounter, is the appearance, in the form of insignificant objects, of the double which creates the effect of seduction and exhilaration that is characteristic of the trompe-l'oeil: a tactile vertigo that recounts the subject's insane desire to grasp its own image, and then vanish. For reality is gripping only when we have lost our identity, or when it reappears as our hallucinated death.

A weak physical desire to grasp things, but a desire which is itself suspended and therefore metaphysical, the objects of the trompe-l'oeil have the same remarkable vivacity as when the child discovers his or her own image, like an instant hallucination prior to perception.

If there is a miracle in the trompe-l'oeil, it is never achieved through realism, like the grapes of Zeuxis which are so real that birds came to peck at them. This is absurd. Nor is a miracle achieved from a surplus of reality but, on the contrary, from the sudden break in reality and from the vertigo of being engulfed in it. The *surreal* familiarity of objects is the expression of this disappearance of the scene of the real. When the hierarchical organization of space that privileges the eye and vision, this perspective simulation – for it is merely a simulacrum – disintegrates, something else emerges; this we express as a kind of *touch*, for lack of a better term, a tactile hyperpresence of things, "as if we could grasp them." But this tactile fantasy has nothing to do with our sense of touch: it is a metaphor for "seizure," the annihilation of the scene and space of representation. As a result, this seizure rebounds on the surrounding world we call "real," revealing to us that "reality" is nothing but a staged world, objectified according to rules of depth, that is to say, the *principle* upon which paintings, sculptures, and the architecture of a period are defined, but only a principle; a simulacrum which the experimental hypersimulation of the trompe-l'oeil undermines.

The trompe-l'oeil does not attempt to confuse itself with the real. Fully aware of play and artifice, it produces a simulacrum by mimicking the third dimension, questioning the reality of the third dimension, and by mimicking and surpassing the effect of the real, radically questioning the principle of reality.

Release from the real is achieved *by the very excess of its appearances*. Objects resemble too much what they are, and this resemblance is like a second state, their true depth. It is the irony of excess reality, through *allegorical* resemblance, and diagonal lighting.

Depth is thereby inverted: in contrast to the whole space of the Renaissance, organized according to a receding line of flight, the perspective effect of the trompe-l'oeil is in a sense a forward projection. Instead of fleeing panoramically before the scrutinizing eye (the privilege of the panoptic eye), objects here "fool" the eye (*"trompent" l'oeil*) by some sort of internal depth: not by creating the illusion of a real world, but by eluding the privileged position of the gaze. The eye, instead of being the source of structured space, is merely the internal point of flight for the convergence of objects. Another universe whirls forward, an opaque mirror placed before the eye, with nothing behind it – *no horizon*, no horizontality. This is specifically the realm of appearances where there is nothing to see, where things see you. Things do not flee from you, they stand before you in a light that comes from elsewhere, and with shadows that never quite give them a true third dimension. Because this dimension, that of perspective, is also still the bad faith of the sign in relation to reality. And because of bad faith, all of art since the Renaissance has been rot.

Unlike aesthetic pleasure, the trompe-l'oeil produces a disturbing unfamiliarity, casts a strange light on a brand new, Western reality that triumphantly emerged out of the Renaissance: its *ironic simulacrum*. This is what surrealism was to the functionalist revolution of the twentieth century, since surrealism is also simply the ironic delirium of the principle of functionality. Surrealism, like the trompe-l'oeil, is not really a part of art or art history. Surrealism and the trompe-l'oeil have a metaphysical dimension. Aspects of style are not their concern. They disrupt at the very point of impact with reality or functionality, and therefore with consciousness. They aim to reverse and to revert. They undermine the world's certainty. This is why their pleasure and seduction is radical, even if minor, for they derive from an extreme *surprise* within appearances, from a life prior to the mode of production of the real world.

Today the trompe-l'oeil is no longer within the realm of painting. Like stucco, its contemporary, it can do anything, mimic anything, parody anything. In the sixteenth century, it became the prototype of the malevolent use of appearances, a game of fantastic proportions which eventually eliminated the boundaries between painting, sculpture and architecture. In the murals and ceilings of the Renaissance and baroque periods, painting and sculpture converge. In the murals or streets in the trompe-l'oeil of Los Angeles, architecture is deceived and defeated by illusion; the seduction of space by the signs of space. We have said so much about its production, is it not the time to discuss the seduction of space?

And of political space as well, such as the studiolos of the Duke of Urbino, and Frederigo da Montefeltre, in the ducal palace of Urbino and Gubbio: minute sanctuaries of trompe-l'oeil at the heart of the immense space of a palace. This is the triumph of an informed architectural perspective, of a space deployed according to the rules. The studiolo is a reverse microcosm: cut off from the rest of the structure, without windows, literally without space, since *here space is actualized in simulation*. If the palace as a whole constitutes the architectural act par excellence, the manifest discourse of art (and power), then what do we make of the miniscule studiolo cell that adjoins the chapel like yet another sacred place, but one a bit magical? It is not very clear what is happening here in the organization of space, and consequently of the entire representational system that orders the palace and the republic.

Truly private (privatissime) space was the prerogative of the Prince, just as incest and transgression were the exclusive right of kings. A complete reversal of the rules of the game is in effect here, one which would ironically lead us to think that, through the allegory of the trompe-l'oeil, the external space of the palace and beyond it to the city, as well as the political space, the actual locus of power, *would perhaps be nothing more than a perspective effect*. Such a dangerous secret, such a radical hypothesis, the Prince must keep to himself, within himself, in strict secrecy: *for it is in fact the secret of his power.*

Since Machiavelli politicians have perhaps always known that the mastery of a *simulated* space is the source of power, that the political is not a *real* activity or space, but a simulation model, whose manifestations are simply achieved effects. *The very secret of appearances* can be found in this blind spot in the palace, this secluded place of architecture and public life, which in a sense governs the whole, not by direct determination, but by a kind of internal reversion or abrogation of the rule secretly performed, as in primitive societies; a hole in reality or an ironic transfiguration, an exact simulacrum hidden at the heart of reality, which reality depends on in all of its operations.

Thus the pope, the grand inquisitor, and the great Jesuits or theologians all knew that God did not exist; this was their secret and their strength. Similarly Montefeltre's studiolo in trompe-l'oeil is an inverse secret of nonexistence at the heart of reality: the secret of the ever-possible profound reversibility of "real" space, including political space; the commanding secret of the political which has since been completely lost in the masses' illusion of the "reality."

The secret and the challenge

The secret: the seductive and initiatory quality of that which cannot be said because it is meaningless, and of that which is not said even though it gets around. Hence I know the other's secret but do not reveal it, and he knows I know it but does not let it be acknowledged: the intensity between the two is simply the secret of the secret. This complicity has nothing to do with some hidden information. Besides, even if the partners wished to reveal the secret they could not, since there is nothing to say... Everything that can be revealed lies outside the secret. For it is not a hidden signified, nor the key to something; it circulates through and traverses everything that can be said, just as seduction flows beneath the obscenity of speech. It is the opposite of communication and yet shares something with it. Only at the cost of remaining unspoken does it maintain power, just as seduction functions from never being spoken or desired.

The hidden or the repressed has a tendency to manifest itself, whereas the secret does not do so at all. It is an introductory and implosive form: we enter it, but are unable to exit. The secret is never revealed, never communicated, never even "secreted."[5] It derives its strength from this allusive and ritual power of exchange.

Thus in Kierkegaard's *Diary of a Seducer*, seduction takes the form of an enigma to be resolved. The young girl is an enigma, and in order to seduce her one must become an enigma for her; it is an *enigmatic duel*, and seduction resolves it *without disclosing the secret*. If the secret were disclosed, the revelation would be sexuality. The true meaning of the story, if it had one, would be about sex – but in fact there isn't one. There is nothing in the place where meaning should be, where sex should occur, in the place where words designate, and where others think it to be. And this nothing of the secret, this unsignified of seduction circulates, flows beneath words and meaning, faster than meaning: it is what affects you before utterances reach you, in the time it takes for them to vanish. Seduction beneath discourse is invisible; from sign to sign, it remains a secret circulation.

This is exactly the opposite of the psychological relation: to share another's secrets is not to share in their fantasies and desires, nor is it to share an unspoken being. When "it" (the id) speaks, it is in fact not seductive. Everything derived from expressive energy, repression, or the unconscious; everything that wishes to speak and everywhere the ego must appear – all of this belongs to the *exoteric* order, and contradicts the *esoteric* form of secrecy and seduction.

Yet the unconscious, the "adventure" of the unconscious appears to be the last ambitious attempt to fabricate secrets in a society without secrets. The unconscious would then be our secret, our mystery in a confessional and transparent society. But it really isn't a secret, for it is merely psychological. It does not exist in itself, since the unconscious was created at the same time as psychoanalysis; that is, together with the procedures to assimilate it and the techniques to abandon the secret to its deep structures.

But perhaps something is taking revenge on all interpretations and in a subtle way is able to disrupt its process? Something which decidedly does not wish to be mentioned and which, being an enigma, enigmatically possesses its own resolution, and therefore only aspires to remain in secret and in the *joy* of secrecy.

Despite all efforts to uncover it, to betray it, to make it signify, language returns to its secret seduction. We always return to our own insoluble pleasures.

Seduction does not have its moment, nor is there a time *for* seduction, but it has a rhythm, without which it would not happen. Unlike an instrumental strategy, which proceeds by intermediate phases, seduction operates instantaneously, in a single movement, and is always its own end.

No cycle comes to a halt in seduction. You can seduce this one in order to seduce the other, but also seduce the other for fun. The illusion (*leurre*)[6] that leads from one to the other is subtle. Is it seducing, or being seduced, that is seductive? Yet being seduced is still the best way of seducing. It is an endless strophe. There is no active or passive in seduction, no subject or object, or even interior or exterior: it plays on both sides of the border with no border separating the sides. No one can seduce another if they have not been seduced themselves.

Since seduction never stops at the truth of signs, but operates by deception and secrecy, it inaugurates a mode of circulation which is also secretive and ritualistic, a kind of immediate initiation that plays only by its own rules.

To be seduced is to be diverted from one's truth. To seduce is to divert the other from his truth. This truth then becomes the secret that escapes him.[7]

Seduction is directly reversible, and this reversibility is constituted by the challenge it implies and the secret in which it is absorbed.

This is the power of attraction and distraction, the power of absorption and fascination, the power of collapse not only of sex but of the real in general, and the power of defiance. It is never an economy of sex and speech, but an escalation of charm and violence, an instantaneous passion, a moment when sex can occur. But seduction can just as easily exhaust itself in the process of defiance and death, and in the radical indetermination that distinguishes it from an instinct. While indeterminate in relation to its object, instincts are determined as force and as origin. The passion of seduction is without substance and without origin: it is not through some libidinal investment, through some energy of desire that it acquires intensity, but through the pure form of gaming and bluffing.

Likewise, the challenge, also a dual form, exhausts itself instantaneously, and derives its intensity from this immediate reversion. Also bewitching, like a meaningless discourse, to which, *for this absurd reason*, we cannot help but respond. Why do we answer a challenge? This is the same mysterious question as: what is it that seduces?

What could be more seductive than a challenge? To challenge or seduce is always to drive the other mad, but in a mutual vertigo: madness from the vertiginous absence that unites them, and from their mutual involvement. Such is the inevitability of the challenge, and consequently the reason why we cannot help but respond to it: for it inaugurates a kind of mad relation, quite different from communication and exchange; a dual relation transacted by meaningless signs, but connected by a fundamental rule, and its secret observance. The challenge terminates all contracts, all exchanges regulated by law (the law of nature or the law of value) and substitutes for it a highly conventional and ritualized *pact*. An unremitting obligation to respond and to outdo, governed by a fundamental rule of the game, and proceeding according to its own rhythm. Contrary to the law which is always written in stone, in the heart, or in the sky, this fundamental rule never needs to be stated; *it must never be stated*. It is immediate, immanent, and inevitable (whereas the law is transcendental and explicit).

There could never be a seduction contract, nor a challenge contract. For seduction or challenge to exist all contractual relations must be nullified in favor of a dual relation. A relation that is comprised of secret signs removed from the exchange, and which obtain their intensity from a formal division and from an immediate reverberation. Likewise, the enchantment of seduction puts an end to every libidinal economy, every sexual and psychological contract, substituting in its place a staggering openness of possible responses. It is never an investment but a risk; never a contract but a pact; never individual but dual; never psychological but ritual; never natural but artificial. It is no one's strategy, but a destiny.

Challenge and seduction are extremely similar. And yet is there not a difference? The challenge consists in drawing the other within your area of strength, which is also his or her strength, given that there can be an unlimited escalation. Whereas the strategy(?) of seduction consists in drawing the other within your area of weakness, which will also be his or hers. A calculated failure: an incalculable failure: a challenge to the other to be taken in. Weakness or failure: is not the panther's scent a weakness, an abyss that other animals dizzily approach? In fact, the panther with the mythical scent is actually the epicenter of death, and from this weakness subtle fragrances emerge.

To seduce is to weaken. To seduce is to falter. We seduce with weakness, never with strong powers and strong signs. In seduction we enact this weakness, and through it seduction derives its power.

We seduce with our death, with our vulnerability, and with the void that haunts us. The secret is to know how to make use of death, in the absence of a gaze, in the absence of a gesture, in the absence of knowledge, or in the absence of meaning.

Psychoanalysis proclaims: "assume passivity, assume weakness;" but turns them into forms of resignation and acceptance, in terms still almost religious, in order to promote the development of a resilient, balanced psyche. Seduction, however, makes use of weakness, makes a game of it, with its own rules.

Everything is seduction and nothing but seduction.

They wanted us to believe that everything was production. The leitmotiv of world transformation, the play of productive forces is to regulate the flow of things. Seduction is merely an immoral, frivolous, superficial, and superfluous process: one within the realm of signs and appearances; one that is devoted to pleasure and to the usufruct of useless bodies. What if everything, contrary to appearances – in fact according to the secret rule of appearances – operated by (the principle of) seduction?

> the moment of seduction
> the suspense of seduction
> the risk of seduction
> the accident of seduction
> the delirium of seduction
> the pause of seduction

Production merely accumulates and is never diverted from its end. It replaces all illusions with just one: its own, which has become the reality principle. Production, like the Revolution, puts an end to the epidemic of appearances. But seduction is inevitable. No one alive escapes it – not even the dead through their names and their remembrance. They are dead only when echoes no longer reach them from this world to seduce them, and when rituals no longer defy them to exist.

To us, only those who can no longer produce are dead. In reality, only those who do not wish to seduce, nor be seduced, are dead.

But seduction takes hold of them anyway, as it takes hold of all production and finally annihilates it.

Because the void, an absence hollowed out at any point by the backfiring of any sign, the meaninglessness that is the sudden charm of seduction, is also what waits, but without illusion, for production to reach its limits. Everything returns to the void, including our words and our gestures. But some, before they disappeared, had the time, anticipating their demise, to exercise a seduction others will never know. The secret of seduction is in this evocation and reevocation of the other, in movements whose slowness and suspense are poetic, like a slow motion film of a fall or an explosion, because something has had, before fulfilling itself, the time to be missed and this is, if there is such a thing, the perfection of "desire."

Seduction, it is destiny

Are we to understand that this diffuse form of seduction, without charm, without stakes, this specter of seduction that haunts our circuits without secrets, our fantasies without affect, our contact network without contacts, that this is the pure form? As if the modern form of the happening with its participation and expressiveness, when the stage and the magic of the stage have disappeared, would be the pure form of theater? Or if the hypothetical and hyperreal mode of intervention in reality – acting pictures, land-art, body-art[8] – in which the object, the frame and the scene of illusion have disappeared, would be the pure form of painting and of art?

We do in fact live among pure forms, in radical obscenity, which is to say visible and undifferentiated, among figures that were previously secret and distinct. The same is true of the social, which rules today also in its pure form, that is, obscene and empty. The same for seduction, which in its actual form, has lost all risk, suspense, and magic to take the form of a faint and undifferentiated obscenity.

Need we refer to Walter Benjamin's[9] genealogy of the work of art
and its destiny? Primarily the work of art has the status of *ritual*
object, related to the ancestral form of the cult. Next it takes the
cultural and *aesthetic* form, a system with less obligations, which still
retains a singular quality, no longer immanent as in the ritual object,
but transcendental and individualized. And the aesthetic form in turn
gives way to the *political* form, where the work as such disappears in
the inevitable destiny of mechanical reproduction. While in the
ritual form originality was unknown (within the sacred there is little
concern for the aesthetic originality of cult objects); it is again lost in
the political form, which has become entirely the multiplication of
objects without an original. This is the form of maximal circulation
and minimal intensity.

Thus, seduction had its ritual phase (dual, magical, agonistic); its
aesthetic phase (reflected in the "aesthetic strategy" of the seducer,
whose sphere of influence approaches that of the feminine and of
sexuality, of the ironic and the diabolic – it is then that it takes on
the meaning it has for us: diversion, strategy, (possibly cursed) gaming, and appearances); and finally its "political" phase (taking up
Benjamin's term, here a bit ambiguous), the phase of the complete
disappearance of the original of seduction, of its ritual and its aesthetic form, in favor of an unlimited distribution where seduction
becomes *the informal form of the political*, the demultiplied framework of elusive politics, which is devoted to the endless reproduction
of a form without content. (This informal form in inseparable from its
technical nature, which is that of networks, just as the political
form of the object is inseparable from the techniques of serial reproduction.) As it was the case for the object, this "political" form
corresponds to the maximum diffusion and the minimum intensity
of seduction.

Is this the destiny of seduction? Or can we, against this involutional
destiny, take on the challenge of *seduction as destiny*? Production as
destiny, or seduction as destiny? Is this the destiny of appearances as
opposed to the truths of deep structure? In any case we live in non-
sense, and if simulation is its disenchanted form, seduction is its
enchanted form.

Anatomy is not destiny, nor is politics: seduction is destiny. It is
what remains of destiny, of risk, of magic, of predestination and
vertigo, and also of quiet efficiency in a world of visible efficiency
and of stability.

The world is naked, the king is naked, things are clear. All of
production, and truth itself, aim to uncover things, and the unbearable
"truth" of sex is a recent result of this. Luckily this is insignificant, and

seduction still retains, from truth itself, the most sibylline answer, which is that "perhaps we only wish to uncover truth because it is so difficult to imagine it naked."

NOTES

1   Jean Baudrillard, *L'Échange symbolique et la mort* (Paris: Gallimard, 1976). This book has been translated in part(s): *Simulations*, trans. P. Foss, P. Patton, and P. Beitchman, (New York: Semiotext(e), 1983) is a translation of *Simulacres et simulations* (Paris: Galilée, 1981) pp. 9–68 and *L'Échange symbolique et la mort*, pp. 77–117; also "The structural law of value and the order of the simulacra," in *The Structural Allegory*, ed. J. Fekete and trans. Charles Levin (Minneapolis: University of Minnesota Press, 1984), contains selections from *L'Échange symbolique et la mort* some of which have been reproduced and supplemented in the present volume (chapter 6). [Trans.]

2   Jean Laplanche and J.-B. Pontalis, *The Language of Psychoanalysis*, trans. Donald Nicholson-Smith (New York: Norton, 1973) p. 405.

3   *Trompe-l'oeil* means literally a painting which at a distance offers the illusion (*leurre*) of reality. Figuratively: a false appearance. On the *trompe-l'oeil* within the frame of representation see Michel Foucault, *This is not a Pipe* (Berkeley: University of California Press, 1983). [Trans.]

4   From Pierre Charpentrat, "Le trompe-l'oeil," *Nouvelle reveu de psychanalyse* 11 (Autumn, 1971) 161. [Trans.]

5   Zempleny, *Nouvelle Revue de Psychanalyse* 14.

6   *Leurre* is a seductive word whose polyphony resonates throughout this text, at times in the guise of "illusion," other times as "deception," and always as "lure." Although the word "lure" does not appear in this English version it is always present beneath (*il court sous*) the surface of the text. The reader should be(a)ware. [Trans.]

7   Vincent Descombes, *L'inconscient malgr lui* (Paris: Minuit, 1977). [Trans.]

8   Expressions are all in English in the original. [Trans.]

9   Walter Benjamin, "The work of art in the age of mechanical reproduction," *Illuminations*, trans. Harry Zohn, ed. Hannah Arendt (New York: Schocken, 1969) pp. 217–52. [Trans.]

7

Simulacra and Simulations

The simulacrum is never that which conceals the truth – it is
the truth which conceals that there is none.
The simulacrum is true.

Ecclesiastes

If we were able to take as the finest allegory of simulation the Borges
tale where the cartographers of the Empire draw up a map so detailed
that it ends up exactly covering the territory (but where, with the
decline of the Empire this map becomes frayed and finally ruined, a
few shreds still discernible in the deserts – the metaphysical beauty of
this ruined abstraction, bearing witness to an imperial pride and
rotting like a carcass, returning to the substance of the soil, rather
as an aging double ends up being confused with the real thing), this
fable would then have come full circle for us, and now has nothing
but the discrete charm of second-order simulacra.[1]

Abstraction today is no longer that of the map, the double, the
mirror or the concept. Simulation is no longer that of a territory, a
referential being or a substance. It is the generation by models of a
real without origin or reality: a hyperreal. The territory no longer
precedes the map, nor survives it. Henceforth, it is the map that
precedes the territory – *precession of simulacra* – it is the map
that engenders the territory and if we were to revive the fable today,
it would be the territory whose shreds are slowly rotting across the
map. It is the real, and not the map, whose vestiges subsist here and
there, in the deserts which are no longer those of the Empire, but our
own. *The desert of the real itself.*

In fact, even inverted, the fable is useless. Perhaps only the allegory
of the Empire remains. For it is with the same imperialism that

present-day simulators try to make the real, all the real, coincide with their simulation models. But it is no longer a question of either maps or territory. Something has disappeared: the sovereign difference between them that was the abstraction's charm. For it is the difference which forms the poetry of the map and the charm of the territory, the magic of the concept and the charm of the real. This representational imaginary, which both culminates in and is engulfed by the cartographer's mad project of an ideal coextensivity between the map and the territory, disappears with simulation, whose operation is nuclear and genetic, and no longer specular and discursive. With it goes all of metaphysics. No more mirror of being and appearances, of the real and its concept; no more imaginary coextensivity: rather, genetic miniaturization is the dimension of simulation. The real is produced from miniaturized units, from matrices, memory banks and command models – and with these it can be reproduced an indefinite number of times. It no longer has to be rational, since it is no longer measured against some ideal or negative instance. It is nothing more than operational. In fact, since it is no longer enveloped by an imaginary, it is no longer real at all. It is a hyperreal: the product of an irradiating synthesis of combinatory models in a hyperspace without atmosphere.

In this passage to a space whose curvature is no longer that of the real, nor of truth, the age of simulation thus begins with a liquidation of all referentials – worse: by their artificial resurrection in systems of signs, which are a more ductile material than meaning, in that they lend themselves to all systems of equivalence, all binary oppositions and all combinatory algebra. It is no longer a question of imitation, nor of reduplication, nor even of parody. It is rather a question of substituting signs of the real for the real itself; that is, an operation to deter every real process by its operational double, a metastable, programmatic, perfect descriptive machine which provides all the signs of the real and short-circuits all its vicissitudes. Never again will the real have to be produced: this is the vital function of the model in a system of death, or rather of anticipated resurrection which no longer leaves any chance even in the event of death. A hyperreal henceforth sheltered from the imaginary, and from any distinction between the real and the imaginary, leaving room only for the orbital recurrence of models and the simulated generation of difference.

The divine irreference of images

To dissimulate is to feign not to have what one has. To simulate is to feign to have what one hasn't. One implies a presence, the other an absence. But the matter is more complicated, since to simulate is not simply to feign: "Someone who feigns an illness can simply go to bed and pretend he is ill. Someone who simulates an illness produces in himself some of the symptoms" (Littre). Thus, feigning or dissimulating leaves the reality principle intact: the difference is always clear, it is only masked; whereas simulation threatens the difference between "true" and "false," between "real" and "imaginary". Since the simulator produces "true" symptoms, is he or she ill or not? The simulator cannot be treated objectively either as ill, or as not ill. Psychology and medicine stop at this point, before a thereafter undiscoverable truth of the illness. For if any symptom can be "produced," and can no longer be accepted as a fact of nature, then every illness may be considered as simulatable and simulated, and medicine loses its meaning since it only knows how to treat "true" illnesses by their objective causes. Psychosomatics evolves in a dubious way on the edge of the illness principle. As for psychoanalysis, it transfers the symptom from the organic to the unconscious order: once again, the latter is held to be real, more real than the former; but why should simulation stop at the portals of the unconscious? Why couldn't the "work" of the unconscious be "produced" in the same way as any other symptom in classical medicine? Dreams already are.

The alienist, of course, claims that "for each form of the mental alienation there is a particular order in the succession of symptoms, of which the simulator is unaware and in the absence of which the alienist is unlikely to be deceived." This (which dates from 1865) in order to save at all cost the truth principle, and to escape the specter raised by simulation: namely that truth, reference and objective causes have ceased to exist. What can medicine do with something which floats on either side of illness, on either side of health, or with the reduplication of illness in a discourse that is no longer true or false? What can psychoanalysis do with the reduplication of the discourse of the unconscious in a discourse of simulation that can never be unmasked, since it isn't false either?[2]

What can the army do with simulators? Traditionally, following a direct principle of identification, it unmasks and punishes them. Today, it can reform an excellent simulator as though he were equivalent to a "real" homosexual, heart-case or lunatic. Even military psychology retreats from the Cartesian clarities and hesitates to draw the distinction between true and false, between the "produced" symptom and the authentic symptom. "If he acts crazy so well, then he must be mad." Nor is it mistaken: in the sense that all lunatics are simulators, and this lack of distinction is the worst form of subversion. Against it, classical reason armed itself with all its categories.

But it is this today which again outflanks them, submerging the truth principle.

Outside of medicine and the army, favored terrains of simulation, the affair goes back to religion and the simulacrum of divinity: "I forbade any simulacrum in the temples because the divinity that breathes life into nature cannot be represented." Indeed it can. But what becomes of the divinity when it reveals itself in icons, when it is multiplied in simulacra? Does it remain the supreme authority, simply incarnated in images as a visible theology? Or is it volatilized into simulacra which alone deploy their pomp and power of fascination – the visible machinery of icons being substituted for the pure and intelligible Idea of God? This is precisely what was feared by the Iconoclasts, whose millennial quarrel is still with us today.[3] Their rage to destroy images rose precisely because they sensed this omnipotence of simulacra, this facility they have of erasing God from the consciousnesses of people, and the overwhelming, destructive truth which they suggest: that ultimately there has never been any God; that only simulacra exist; indeed that God himself has only ever been his own simulacrum. Had they been able to believe that images only occulted or masked the Platonic idea of God, there would have been no reason to destroy them. One can live with the idea of a distorted truth. But their metaphysical despair came from the idea that the images concealed nothing at all, and that in fact they were not images, such as the original model would have made them, but actually perfect simulacra forever radiant with their own fascination. But this death of the divine referential has to be exorcised at all cost.

It can be seen that the iconoclasts, who are often accused of despising and denying images, were in fact the ones who accorded them their actual worth, unlike the iconolaters, who saw in them only reflections and were content to venerate God at one remove. But the converse can also be said, namely that the iconolaters possessed the most modern and adventurous minds, since, underneath the idea of the apparition of God in the mirror of images, they already enacted his death and his disappearance in the epiphany of his representations (which they perhaps knew no longer represented anything, and that they were purely a game, but that this was precisely the greatest game – knowing also that it is dangerous to unmask images, since they dissimulate the fact that there is nothing behind them).

This was the approach of the Jesuits, who based their politics on the virtual disappearance of God and on the worldly and spectacular manipulation of consciences – the evanescence of God in the epiphany of power – the end of transcendence, which no longer serves as alibi for a strategy completely free of influences and signs. Behind the baroque of images hides the grey eminence of politics.

Thus perhaps at stake has always been the murderous capacity of images: murderers of the real; murderers of their own model as the Byzantine icons could murder the divine identity. To this murderous capacity is opposed the dialectical capacity of representations as a visible and intelligible mediation of the real. All of Western faith and good faith was engaged in this wager on representation: that a sign could refer to the depth of meaning, that a sign could *exchange* for meaning and that something could guarantee this exchange – God, of course. But what if God himself can be simulated, that is to say, reduced to the signs which attest his existence? Then the whole system becomes weightless; it is no longer anything but a gigantic simulacrum: not unreal, but a simulacrum, never again exchanging for what is real, but exchanging in itself, in an uninterrupted circuit without reference or circumference.

So it is with simulation, insofar as it is opposed to representation. Representation starts from the principle that the sign and the real are equivalent (even if this equivalence is Utopian, it is a fundamental axiom). Conversely, simulation starts from the Utopia of this principle of equivalence, *from the radical negation of the sign as value*, from the sign as reversion and death sentence of every reference. Whereas representation tries to absorb simulation by interpreting it as false representation, simulation envelops the whole edifice of representation as itself a simulacrum.

These would be the successive phases of the image:

1 It is the reflection of a basic reality.
2 It masks and perverts a basic reality.
3 It masks the *absence* of a basic reality.
4 It bears no relation to any reality whatever: it is its own pure simulacrum.

In the first case, the image is a *good* appearance: the representation is of the order of sacrament. In the second, it is an *evil* appearance: of the order of malefice. In the third, it *plays at being* an appearance: it is of the order of sorcery. In the fourth, it is no longer in the order of appearance at all, but of simulation.

The transition from signs which dissimulate something to signs which dissimulate that there is nothing, marks the decisive turning point. The first implies a theology of truth and secrecy (to which the notion of ideology still belongs). The second inaugurates an age of simulacra and simulation, in which there is no longer any God to recognize his own, nor any last judgement to separate truth from false, the real from its artificial resurrection, since everything is already dead and risen in advance.

When the real is no longer what it used to be, nostalgia assumes its full meaning. There is a proliferation of myths of origin and signs of reality; of second-hand truth, objectivity and authenticity. There is an escalation of the true, of the lived experience; a resurrection of the figurative where the object and substance have disappeared. And there is a panic-stricken production of the real and the referential, above and parallel to the panic of material production. This is how simulation appears in the phase that concerns us: a strategy of the real, neo-real and hyperreal, whose universal double is a strategy of deterrence.

Hyperreal and imaginary

Disneyland is a perfect model of all the entangled orders of simulation. To begin with it is a play of illusions and phantasms: pirates, the frontier, future world, etc. This imaginary world is supposed to be what makes the operation successful. But, what draws the crowds is undoubtedly much more the social microcosm, the miniaturized and *religious* revelling in real America, in its delights and drawbacks. You park outside, queue up inside, and are totally abandoned at the exit. In this imaginary world the only phantasmagoria is in the inherent warmth and affection of the crowd, and in that sufficiently excessive number of gadgets used there to specifically maintain the multitudinous affect. The contrast with the absolute solitude of the parking lot – a veritable concentration camp – is total. Or rather: inside, a whole range of gadgets magnetize the crowd into direct flows; outside, solitude is directed onto a single gadget: the automobile. By an extraordinary coincidence (one that undoubtedly belongs to the peculiar enchantment of this universe), this deep-frozen infantile world happens to have been conceived and realized by a man who is himself now cryogenized; Walt Disney, who awaits his resurrection at minus 180 degrees centigrade.

The objective profile of the United States, then, may be traced throughout Disneyland, even down to the morphology of individuals and the crowd. All its values are exalted here, in miniature and comic-strip form. Embalmed and pacified. Whence the possibility of an ideological analysis of Disneyland (L. Marin does it well in *Utopies, jeux d'espaces*): digest of the American way of life, panegyric to

American values, idealized transposition of a contradictory reality. To be sure. But this conceals something else, and that "ideological" blanket exactly serves to cover over a *third-order simulation*: Disneyland is there to conceal the fact that it is the "real" country, all of "real" America, which *is* Disneyland (just as prisons are there to conceal the fact that it is the social in its entirety, in its banal omnipresence, which is carceral). Disneyland is presented as imaginary in order to make us believe that the rest is real, when in fact all of Los Angeles and the America surrounding it are no longer real, but of the order of the hyperreal and of simulation. It is no longer a question of a false representation of reality (ideology), but of concealing the fact that the real is no longer real, and thus of saving the reality principle.

The Disneyland imaginary is neither true nor false: it is a deterrence machine set up in order to rejuvenate in reverse the fiction of the real. Whence the debility, the infantile degeneration of this imaginary. It is meant to be an infantile world, in order to make us believe that the adults are elsewhere, in the "real" world, and to conceal the fact that real childishness is everywhere, particularly among those adults who go there to act the child in order to foster illusions of their real childishness.

Moreover, Disneyland is not the only one. Enchanted Village, Magic Mountain, Marine World: Los Angeles is encircled by these "imaginary stations" which feed reality, reality-energy, to a town whose mystery is precisely that it is nothing more than a network of endless, unreal circulation: a town of fabulous proportions, but without space or dimensions. As much as electrical and nuclear power stations, as much as film studios, this town, which is nothing more than an immense script and a perpetual motion picture, needs this old imaginary made up of childhood signals and faked phantasms for its sympathetic nervous system.

Political incantation

Watergate. Same scenario as Disneyland (an imaginary effect concealing that reality no more exists outside than inside the bounds of the artificial perimeter): though here it is a scandal-effect concealing that there is no difference between the facts and their denunciation (identical methods are employed by the CIA and the *Washington Post* journalists). Same operation, though this time tending towards scandal as a means to regenerate a moral and political principle, towards the imaginary as a means to regenerate a reality principle in distress.

The denunciation of scandal always pays homage to the law. And Watergate above all succeeded in imposing the idea that Watergate *was* a scandal – in this sense it was an extraordinary operation of intoxication: the reinjection of a large dose of political morality on a global scale. It could be said along with Bourdieu that: "The specific character of every relation of force is to dissimulate itself as such, and to acquire all its force only because it is so dissimulated"; understood as follows: capital, which is immoral and unscrupulous, can only function behind a moral superstructure, and whoever regenerates this public morality (by indignation, denunciation, etc.) spontaneously furthers the order of capital, as did the *Washington Post* journalists.

But this is still only the formula of ideology, and when Bourdieu enunciates it, he takes "relation of force" to mean the *truth* of capitalist domination, and he *denounces* this relation of force as itself a *scandal*: he therefore occupies the same deterministic and moralistic position as the *Washington Post* journalists. He does the same job of purging and reviving moral order, an order of truth wherein the genuine symbolic violence of the social order is engendered, well beyond all relations of force, which are only elements of its indifferent and shifting configuration in the moral and political consciousness of people.

All that capital asks of us is to receive it as rational or to combat it in the name of rationality, to receive it as moral or to combat it in the name of morality. For they are *identical*, meaning *they can be read another way*: before, the task was to dissimulate scandal; today, the task is to conceal the fact that there is none.

Watergate is not a scandal: this is what must be said at all cost, for this is what everyone is concerned to conceal, this dissimulation masking a strengthening of morality, a moral panic as we approach the primal (mise-en-)scene of capital: its instantaneous cruelty; its incomprehensible ferocity; its fundamental immorality – these are what are scandalous, unaccountable for in that system of moral and economic equivalence which remains the axiom of leftist thought, from Enlightenment theory to communism. Capital doesn't give a damn about the idea of the contract which is imputed to it: it is a monstrous unprincipled undertaking, nothing more. Rather, it is "enlightened" thought which seeks to control capital by imposing rules on it. And all that recrimination which replaced revolutionary thought today comes down to reproaching capital for not following the rules of the game. "Power is unjust; its justice is a class justice;

capital exploits us; etc." – as if capital were linked by a contract to the society it rules. It is the left which holds out the mirror of equivalence, hoping that capital will fall for this phantasmagoria of the social contract and fulfill its obligation towards the whole of society (at the same time, no need for revolution: it is enough that capital accept the rational formula of exchange).

Capital in fact has never been linked by a contract to the society it dominates. It is a sorcery of the social relation, it is *a challenge to society* and should be responded to as such. It is not a scandal to be denounced according to moral and economic rationality, but a challenge to take up according to symbolic law.

Moebius: spiraling negativity

Hence Watergate was only a trap set by the system to catch its adversaries – a simulation of scandal to regenerative ends. This is embodied by the character called "Deep Throat," who was said to be a Republican grey eminence manipulating the leftist journalists in order to get rid of Nixon – and why not? All hypotheses are possible, although this one is superfluous: the work of the Right is done very well, and spontaneously, by the Left on its own. Besides, it would be naive to see an embittered good conscience at work here. For the Right itself also spontaneously does the work of the Left. All the hypotheses of manipulation are reversible in an endless whirligig. For manipulation is a floating causality where positivity and negativity engender and overlap with one another; where there is no longer any active or passive. It is by putting an *arbitrary* stop to this revolving causality that a principle of political reality can be saved. It is by the *simulation* of a conventional, restricted perspective field, where the premises and consequences of any act or event are calculable, that a political credibility can be maintained (including, of course, "object-ive" analysis, struggle, etc.) But if the entire cycle of any act or event is envisaged in a system where linear continuity and dialectical polarity no longer exist, in a field *unhinged by simulation*, then all determina-tion evaporates, every act terminates at the end of the cycle having benefited everyone and been scattered in all directions.

Is any given bombing in Italy the work of leftist extremists; or of extreme right-wing provocation; or staged by centrists to bring every terrorist extreme into disrepute and to shore up its own failing power; or again, is it a police-inspired scenario in order to appeal to calls for public security? All this is equally true, and the search for proof –

indeed the objectivity of the fact – does not check this vertigo of interpretation. We are in a logic of simulation which has nothing to do with a logic of facts and an order of reasons. Simulation is characterized by a *precession of the model*, of all models around the merest fact – the models come first, and their orbital (like the bomb) circulation constitutes the genuine magnetic field of events. Facts no longer have any trajectory of their own, they arise at the intersection of the models; a single fact may even be engendered by all the models at once. This anticipation, this precession, this short-circuit, this confusion of the fact with its model (no more divergence of meaning, no more dialectical polarity, no more negative electricity or implosion of poles) is what each time allows for all the possible interpretations, even the most contradictory – all are true, in the sense that their truth is exchangeable, in the image of the models from which they proceed, in a generalized cycle.

The communists attack the socialist party as though they wanted to shatter the union of the Left. They sanction the idea that their reticence stems from a more radical political exigency. In fact, it is because they don't want power. But do they not want it at this conjuncture because it is unfavorable for the Left in general, or because it is unfavorable for them within the union of the Left – or do they not want it by definition? When Berlinguer declares, "We mustn't be frightened of seeing the communists seize power in Italy," this means simultaneously:

1   That there is nothing to fear, since the communists, if they come to power, will change nothing in its fundamental capitalist mechanism.
2   That there isn't any risk of their ever coming to power (for the reason that they don't want to); and even if they do take it up, they will only ever wield it by proxy.
3   That in fact power, genuine power, no longer exists, and hence there is no risk of anybody seizing it or taking it over.
4   But more: I, Berlinguer, am not frightened of seeing the communists seize power in Italy – which might appear evident, but not so evident, since:
5   It can also mean the contrary (no need for psychoanalysis here): *I am frightened* of seeing the communists seize power (and with good reason, even for a communist).

All the above is simultaneously true. This is the secret of a discourse that is no longer only ambiguous, as political discourses can be, but that conveys the impossibility of a determinate position of power, the impossibility of a determinate position of discourse. And this logic belongs to neither party. It traverses all discourses without their wanting it.

Who will unravel this imbroglio? The Gordian knot can at least be cut. As for the Moebius strip, if it is split in two, it results in an additional spiral without there being any possibility of resolving its surfaces (here the reversible continuity of hypotheses). Hades of simulation, which is no longer one of torture, but of the subtle, maleficent, elusive twisting of meaning[4] – where even those condemned at Burgos are still a gift from Franco to Western democracy, which finds in them the occasion to regenerate its own flagging humanism, and whose indignant protestation consolidates in return Franco's regime by uniting the Spanish masses against foreign intervention? Where is the truth in all that, when such collusions admirably knit together without their authors even knowing it?

The conjunction of the system and its extreme alternative like two ends of a curved mirror, the "vicious" curvature of a political space henceforth magnetized, circularized, reversibilized from right to left, a torsion that is like the evil demon of commutation, the whole system, the infinity of capital folded back over its own surface: transfinite? And isn't it the same with desire and libidinal space? The conjunction of desire and value, of desire and capital. The conjunction of desire and the law; the ultimate joy and metamorphosis of the law (which is why it is so well received at the moment): only capital takes pleasure, Lyotard said, before coming to think that *we* take pleasure in capital. Overwhelming versatility of desire in Deleuze: an enigmatic reversal which brings this desire that is "revolutionary by itself, and as if involuntarily, in wanting what it wants," to want its own repression and to invest paranoid and fascist systems? A malign torsion which reduces this revolution of desire to the same fundamental ambiguity as the other, historical revolution.

All the referentials intermingle their discourses in a circular, Moebian compulsion. Not so long ago sex and work were savagely opposed terms: today both are dissolved into the same type of demand. Formerly the discourse on history took its force from opposing itself to the one on nature, the discourse on desire to the one on power: today they exchange their signifiers and their scenarios.

It would take too long to run through the whole range of operational negativity, of all those scenarios of deterrence which, like Watergate, try to revive a moribund principle by simulated scandal, phantasm, murder – a sort of hormonal treatment by negativity and crisis. It is always a question of proving the real by the imaginary; proving truth by scandal; proving the law by transgression; proving work by the strike; proving the system by crisis and capital by revolution; and for that matter proving ethnology by the dispossession of its object (the Tasaday). Without counting: proving theater by anti-theater; proving art by anti-art; proving pedagogy by anti-pedagogy; proving psychiatry by anti-psychiatry, etc., etc.

Everything is metamorphosed into its inverse in order to be perpetuated in its purged form. Every form of power, every situation speaks of itself by denial, in order to attempt to escape, by simulation of death, its real agony. Power can stage its own murder to rediscover a glimmer of existence and legitimacy. Thus with the American presidents: the Kennedys are murdered because they still have a political dimension. Others – Johnson, Nixon, Ford – only had a right to puppet attempts, to simulated murders. But they nevertheless needed that aura of an artificial menace to conceal that they were nothing other than mannequins of power. In olden days the king (also the god) had to die – that was his strength. Today he does his miserable utmost to pretend to die, so as to preserve the *blessing* of power. But even this is gone.

To seek new blood in its own death, to renew the cycle by the mirror of crisis, negativity and anti-power: this is the only alibi of every power, of every institution attempting to break the vicious circle of its irresponsibility and its fundamental nonexistence, of its déjà-vu and its déjà-mort.

Strategy of the real

Of the same order as the impossibility of rediscovering an absolute level of the real, is the impossibility of staging an illusion. Illusion is no longer possible, because the real is no longer possible. It is the whole *political* problem of the parody, of hypersimulation or offensive simulation, which is posed here.

For example: it would be interesting to see whether the repressive apparatus would not react more violently to a simulated hold up than to a real one? For a real hold up only upsets the order of things, the right of property, whereas a simulated hold up interferes with the very principle of reality. Transgression and violence are less serious, for they only contest the *distribution* of the real. Simulation is infinitely more dangerous since it always suggests, over and above its object, that *law and order themselves might really be nothing more than a simulation.*

But the difficulty is in proportion to the peril. How to feign a violation and put it to the test? Go and simulate a theft in a large department store: how do you convince the security guards that it is a simulated theft? There is no "objective" difference: the same gestures and the same signs exist as for a real theft; in fact the signs incline neither to one side nor the other. As far as the established order is concerned, they are always of the order of the real.

Go and organize a fake hold up. Be sure to check that your weapons are harmless, and take the most trustworthy hostage, so that no life is in danger (otherwise you risk committing an offence). Demand ransom, and arrange it so that the operation creates the greatest commotion possible. In brief, stay close to the "truth," so as to test the reaction of the apparatus to a perfect simulation. But you won't succeed: the web of artificial signs will be inextricably mixed up with real elements (a police officer will really shoot on sight; a bank customer will faint and die of a heart attack; they will really turn the phoney ransom over to you). In brief, you will unwittingly find yourself immediately in the real, one of whose functions is precisely to devour every attempt at simulation, to reduce everything to some reality: that's exactly how the established order is, well before institutions and justice come into play.

In this impossibility of isolating the process of simulation must be seen the whole thrust of an order that can only see and understand in terms of some reality, because it can function nowhere else. The simulation of an offence, if it is patent, will either be punished more lightly (because it has no "consequences") or be punished as an offence to public office (for example, if one triggered off a police operation "for nothing") – but *never as simulation*, since it is precisely as such that no equivalence with the real is possible, and hence no repression either. The challenge of simulation is irreceivable by power. How can you punish the simulation of virtue? Yet as such it is as serious as the simulation of crime. Parody makes obedience and transgression equivalent, and that is the most serious crime, since it *cancels out the difference upon which the law is based.* The established order can do nothing against it, for the law is a second-order simulacrum whereas simulation is a third-order simulacrum, beyond true and false, beyond equivalences, beyond the rational distinctions upon which function all power and the entire social stratum. Hence, *failing the real*, it is here that we must aim at order.

This is why order always opts for the real. In a state of uncertainty, it always prefers this assumption (thus in the army they would rather take the simulator as a true madman). But this becomes more and more difficult, for it is practically impossible to isolate the process of simulation; through the force of inertia of the real which surrounds us, the inverse is also true (and this very reversibility forms part of the apparatus of simulation and of power's impotency): namely, *it is now impossible to isolate the process of the real*, or to prove the real.

Thus all hold ups, hijacks and the like are now as it were simulation hold ups, in the sense that they are inscribed in advance in the decoding and orchestration rituals of the media, anticipated in their mode of presentation and possible consequences. In brief, where they function as a set of signs dedicated exclusively to their recurrence as signs, and no longer to their "real" goal at all. But this does not make them inoffensive. On the contrary, it is as hyperreal events, no longer having any particular contents or aims, but indefinitely refracted by each other (for that matter like so-called historical events: strikes, demonstrations, crises, etc.[5]), that they are precisely unverifiable by an order which can only exert itself on the real and the rational, on ends and means: a referential order which can only dominate referentials, a determinate power which can only dominate a determined world, but which can do nothing about that indefinite recurrence of simulation, about that weightless nebula no longer obeying the law of gravitation of the real – power itself eventually breaking apart in this space and becoming a simulation of power (disconnected from its aims and objectives, and dedicated to *power effects* and mass simulation).

The only weapon of power, its only strategy against this defection, is to reinject realness and referentiality everywhere, in order to convince us of the reality of the social, of the gravity of the economy and the finalities of production. For that purpose it prefers the discourse of crisis, but also – why not? – the discourse of desire. "Take your desires for reality!" can be understood as the ultimate slogan of power, for in a nonreferential world even the confusion of the reality principle with the desire principle is less dangerous than contagious hyperreality. One remains among principles, and there power is always right.

Hyperreality and simulation are deterrents of every principle and of every objective; they turn against power this deterrence which is so well utilized for a long time itself. For, finally, it was capital which was the first to feed throughout its history on the destruction of every referential, of every human goal, which shattered every ideal distinction between true and false, good and evil, in order to establish a radical law of equivalence and exchange, the iron law of its power. It was the first to practice deterrence, abstraction, disconnection, deterritorialization, etc.; and if it was capital which fostered reality, the reality principle, it was also the first to liquidate it in the extermination of every use value, of every real equivalence, of production and wealth, in the very sensation we have of the unreality of the stakes and the omnipotence of manipulation. Now, it is this very logic which is today hardened even more *against* it. And when it wants to fight this catastrophic spiral by secreting one last glimmer of reality, on which to found one last glimmer of power, it only multiplies the *signs* and accelerates the play of simulation.

As long as it was historically threatened by the real, power risked deterrence and simulation, disintegrating every contradiction by means of the production of equivalent signs. When it is threatened today by simulation (the threat of vanishing in the play of signs), power risks the real, risks crisis, it gambles on remanufacturing artificial, social, economic, political stakes. This is a question of life or death for it. But it is too late.

Whence the characteristic hysteria of our time: the hysteria of production and reproduction of the real. The other production, that of goods and commodities, that of *la belle epoque* of political economy, no longer makes any sense of its own, and has not for some time. What society seeks through production, and overproduction, is the restoration of the real which escapes it. That is why *contemporary "material" production is itself hyperreal*. It retains all the features, the whole discourse of traditional production, but it is nothing more than its scaled-down refraction (thus the hyperrealists fasten in a striking resemblance a real from which has fled all meaning and charm, all the profundity and energy of representation). Thus the hyperrealism of simulation is expressed everywhere by the real's striking resemblance to itself.

Power, too, for some time now produces nothing but signs of its resemblance. And at the same time, another figure of power comes into play: that of a collective demand for *signs* of power – a holy union which forms around the disappearance of power. Everybody belongs to it more or less in fear of the collapse of the political. And in the end the game of power comes down to nothing more than the *critical* obsession with power: an obsession with its death; an obsession with its survival which becomes greater the more it disappears. When it has totally disappeared, logically we will be under the total spell of power – a haunting memory already foreshadowed everywhere, manifesting at one and the same time the satisfaction of having got rid of it (nobody wants it any more, everybody unloads it on others) and grieving its loss. Melancholy for societies without power: this has already given rise to fascism, that overdose of a powerful referential in a society which cannot terminate its mourning.

But we are still in the same boat: none of our societies know how to manage their mourning for the real, for power, for the *social itself*, which is implicated in this same breakdown. And it is by an artificial revitalization of all this that we try to escape it. *Undoubtedly this will even end up in socialism.* By an unforeseen twist of events and an irony which no longer belongs to history, it is through the death of the social that socialism will emerge – as it is through the death of God that religions emerge. A twisted coming, a perverse event, an unintelligible reversion to the logic of reason. As is the fact that power is no longer present except to conceal that there is none. A simulation which can go on indefinitely, since – unlike "true" power which is, or was, a structure, a strategy, a relation of force, a stake – this is nothing but the object of a social *demand*, and hence subject to the law of supply and demand, rather than to violence and death. Completely expunged from the *political* dimension, it is dependent, like any other commodity, on production and mass consumption. Its spark has disappeared; only the fiction of a political universe is saved.

Likewise with work. The spark of production, the violence of its stake no longer exists. Everybody still produces, and more and more, but work has subtly become something else: a need (as Marx ideally envisaged it, but not at all in the same sense), the object of a social "demand," like leisure, to which it is equivalent in the general run of life's options. A demand exactly proportional to the loss of stake in the work process.[6] The same change in fortune as for power: the *scenario* of work is there to conceal the fact that the work-real, the production-real, has disappeared. And for that matter so has the strike-real too, which is no longer a stoppage of work, but its alternative pole in the ritual scansion of the social calendar. It is as if everyone has "occupied" their work place or work post, after declaring the strike, and resumed production, as is the custom in a "self-managed" job, in exactly the same terms as before, by declaring themselves (and virtually being) in a state of permanent strike.

This isn't a science-fiction dream: everywhere it is a question of a doubling of the work process. And of a double or locum for the strike process – strikes which are incorporated like obsolescence in objects, like crises in production. Then there are no longer any strikes or work, but both simultaneously, that is to say something else entirely: a wizardry of work, a trompe-l'oeil, a scenodrama (not to say melodrama) of production, collective dramaturgy upon the empty stage of the social.

It is no longer a question of the *ideology* of work – of the traditional ethic that obscures the "real" labour process and the "objective" process of exploitation – but of the scenario of work. Likewise, it is no longer a question of the ideology of power, but of the *scenario* of power. Ideology only corresponds to a betrayal of reality by signs;

simulation corresponds to a short-circuit of reality and to its reduplication by signs. It is always the aim of ideological analysis to restore the objective process; it is always a false problem to want to restore the truth beneath the simulacrum.

This is ultimately why power is so in accord with ideological discourses and discourses on ideology, for these are all discourses of *truth* – always good, even and especially if they are revolutionary, to counter the mortal blows of simulation.

NOTES

1 Counterfeit and reproduction imply always an anguish, a disquieting foreignness: the uneasiness before the photograph, considered like a witch's trick – and more generally before any technical apparatus, which is always an apparatus of reproduction, is related by Benjamin to the uneasiness before the mirror-image. There is already sorcery at work in the mirror. But how much more so when this image can be detached from the mirror and be transported, stocked, reproduced at will (cf. *The Student of Prague*, where the devil detaches the image of the student from the mirror and harrasses him to death by the intermediary of this image). All reproduction implies therefore a kind of black magic, from the fact of being seduced by one's own image in the water, like Narcissus, to being haunted by the double and, who knows, to the mortal turning back of this vast technical apparatus secreted today by man as his own image (the narcissistic mirage of technique, McLuhan) and that returns to him, cancelled and distorted – endless reproduction of himself and his power to the limits of the world. Reproduction is diabolical in its very essence; it makes something fundamental vacillate. This has hardly changed for us: simulation (that we describe here as the operation of the code) is still and always the place of a gigantic enterprise of manipulation, of control and of death, just like the imitative object (primitive statuette, image of photo) always had as objective an operation of black image.

2 There is furthermore in Monod's book a flagrant contradiction, which reflects the ambiguity of all current science. His discourse concerns the code, that is the third-order simulacra, but it does so still according to "scientific" schemes of the second-order – objectiveness, "scientific" ethic of knowledge, science's principle of truth and transcendence. All things incompatible with the indeterminable models of the third-order.

3 "It's the feeble 'definition' of TV which condemns its spectator to rearranging the few points retained into a kind of *abstract work*. He participates suddenly in the creation of a reality that was only just presented to him in dots: the television watcher is in the position of an individual who is asked to project his own fantasies on inkblots that are not supposed to represent anything." TV as perpetual Rorschach test. And furthermore: "The TV image requires each instant that we 'close' the

spaces in the mesh by a convulsive sensuous participation that is profoundly kinetic and tactile."
4   "The Medium is the Message" is the very slogan of the political economy
of the sign, when it enters into the third-order simulation – the distinction
between the medium and the message characterizes instead signification
of the second-order.
5   The entire current "psychological" situation is characterized by this short-
circuit.

Doesn't emancipation of children and teenagers, once the initial phase
of revolt is passed and once there has been established the *principle* of the
right to emancipation, seem like the *real* emancipation of parents. And
the young (students, high-schoolers, adolescents) seem to sense it in their
always more insistent demand (though still as paradoxical) for the presence and advice of parents or of teachers. Alone at last, free and responsible, it seemed to them suddenly that other people possibly have
absconded with their true liberty. Therefore, there is no question of
"leaving them be." They're going to hassle them, not with any emotional
or material spontaneous demand, but with an exigency that has been
premeditated and corrected by an implicit oedipal knowledge. Hyperde-
pendence (much greater than before) distored by irony and refusal, *parody of libidinous original mechanisms.* Demand without content, without
referent, unjustified, but for all that all the more severe – naked demand
with no possible answer. The contents of knowledge (teaching) or of
affective relations, the pedagogical or familial referent having been
eliminated in the act of emancipation, there remains only a demand
linked to the empty form of the institution – perverse demand, and for
that reason all the more obstinate. "Transferable" desire (that is to say
non-referential, un-referential), desire that has been fed by lack, by the
place left vacant, "liberated," desire captured in its own vertiginous
image, desire of desire, as pure form, hyperreal. Deprived of symbolic
substance, it doubles back upon itself, draws its energy from its own
reflection and its disappointment with itself. This is literally today the
"demand," and it is obvious that unlike the "classical" objective or
transferable relations this one here is insoluble and interminable.

Simulated Oedipus.

François Richard: "Students asked to be seduced either bodily or verb-
ally. But also they are aware of this and they play the game, ironically.
'Give us your knowledge, your presence, you have the word, speak, you
are there for that.' Contestation certainly, but not only: the more authority is contested, vilified, the greater the need for authority as such. They
play at Oedipus also, to deny it all the more vehemently. The 'teach,' he's
Daddy, they say; it's fun, you play at incest, malaise, the untouchable, at
being a tease – in order to de-sexualize finally." Like one under analysis
who asks for Oedipus back again, who tells the "oedipal" stories, who has
the "analytical" dreams to satisfy the supposed request of the analyst, or
to resist him? In the same way the student goes through his oedipal

number, his seduction number, gets chummy, close, approaches, dominates – but this isn't desire, it's simulation. Oedipal psychodrama of
simulation (neither less real nor less dramatic for all that). Very different
from the real libidinal stakes of knowledge and power or even of a real
mourning for the absence of same (as could have happened after 1968 in
the universities). Now we've reached the phase of desperate reproduction,
and where the stakes are nil, the simulacrum is maximal – exacerbated
and parodied simulation at one and the same time – as interminable as
psychoanalysis and for the same reasons.

The interminable psychoanalysis.

There is a whole chapter to add to the history of transference and
countertransference: that of their liquidation by simulation, of the impossible psychoanalysis because it is itself, from now on, that produces and
reproduces the unconscious as its institutional substance. Psychoanalysis
dies also of the exchange of the *signs* of the unconscious. Just as revolution dies of the exchange of the critical signs of political economy. This
short-circuit was well known to Freud in the form of the gift of the
analytic dream, or with the "uninformed" patients, in the form of
the gift of their analytic knowledge. But this was still interpreted as
resistance, as detour, and did not put fundamentally into question either
the process of analysis or the principle of transference. It is another thing
entirely when the unconscious itself, the discourse of the unconscious
becomes unfindable – according to the same scenario of simulative anticipation that we have seen at work on all levels with the machines of the
third order. The analysis then can no longer end, it becomes logically and
historically interminable, since it stabilizes on a puppet-substance of
reproduction, an unconscious programmed on demand – an impossible-
to-break-through point around which the whole analysis is rearranged.
The messages of the unconscious have been short-circuited by the psychoanalysis "medium." This is libidinal hyperrealism. To the famous
categories of the real, the symbolic and the imaginary, it is going to
be necessary to add the hyperreal, which captures and obstructs the
functioning of the three orders.

6   Athenian democracy, much more advanced than our own, had reached
the point where the vote was considered as payment for a service, after all
other repressive solutions had been tried and found wanting in order to
insure a quorum.

8

Fatal Strategies

Ecstasy and inertia

Things have found a way to elude the dialectic of meaning, a dialectic which bored them: they did this by infinite proliferation, by potentializing themselves, by outmatching their essence, by going to extremes, and by obscenity which henceforth has become their immanent purpose and insane justification.

We can imagine obtaining the same effects by going in the inverse order, attaining another insanity, one that also is victorious. And when insanity is victorious in every way, we have the principle of Evil.

The universe is not dialectical: it moves toward the extremes, and not toward equilibrium; it is devoted to a radical antagonism, and not to reconciliation or to synthesis. And it is the same with the principle of Evil. It is expressed in the cunning genius of the object, in the ecstatic form of the pure object, and in its victorious strategy over the subject.

This victory operates by subtle forms of radicalizing hidden qualities, and by combating obscenity with its own weapons. To the more true than true we will oppose the more false than false. We will not oppose the beautiful and the ugly; we will seek what is more ugly than the ugly: the monstrous. We will not oppose the visible to the hidden; we will seek what is more hidden than the hidden: the secret.

We will not seek change, nor oppose the fixed and the mobile; we will seek what is more mobile than the mobile: metamorphosis... We will not distinguish the true from the false; we will seek what is more false than the false: illusion and appearance...

In this ascent to extremes, while we may need to oppose it in a radical way, we may perhaps need to accumulate the effects of obscenity and seduction.

We will seek something faster than communication: the challenge, the duel. Communication is too slow; it is an effect of slowness; it proceeds through contact and speech. The look is much faster; it is the medium of the media, the quickest. Everything must occur instantaneously. We never communicate. In the to and fro of communication the speed of the look, of light, and of seduction is already lost.

But also, against the acceleration of networks and circuits, we will seek slowness; not the nostalgic slowness of the mind, but an insurmountable immobility, that is slower than the slow: inertia and silence. Inertia is insurmountable even with effort, as is silence even in a dialogue. There is a secret here as well.

Just as the model is more real than the real (being the quintessence of the significant aspects of a situation), acquiring thus a vertiginous impression of truth, the amazing aspect of fashion is that it is more beautiful than the beautiful: it is fascinating. Its seductive capacity is independent of all judgements. It exceeds the aesthetic form in the ecstatic form of unconditional metamorphosis.

Whereas the aesthetic form always implies a moral distinction between the beautiful and the ugly, the ecstatic form is immoral. If there is a secret to fashion, beyond the sheer pleasures of art and taste, it is this immorality, the sovereignty of ephemeral models, the fragile and total passion which excludes all feelings, and the arbitrary, superficial and regulated metamorphosis, which excludes all desire (unless in fact this is desire).

If in fact this is desire, we can imagine that in the social, in the political, and in every domain other than the ornamental, desire would also show a preference for immoral forms, which are equally affected by the potential denial of all value judgments and more dedicated to the ecstatic destiny that wrenches things from their "subjective" quality, leaving them solely to the attraction of the redoubled trait, of the reduplicated definition, and that wrenches them from their "objective" causes, leaving them solely to the power of their unbridled effects.

Every characteristic thus elevated to the superlative power, caught in an intensifying spiral – more true than the true, more beautiful than the beautiful, more real than the real – is assured a vertiginous effect that is independent of all content or specific quality, and which presently has the tendency of being our only passion. The passion of intensification, of escalation, of mounting power, of ecstasy, of whatever quality so long as, having ceased to be relative to its opposite (the true to the false, the beautiful to the ugly, the real to the imaginary), it becomes superlative, positively sublime as if it had absorbed the energy of its opposite. Imagine something beautiful that has absorbed all the energy of the ugly: you have fashion ... Imagine truth having absorbed all the energy of the false: you have simulation ...

Seduction is itself vertiginous, being the effect not of some simple attraction, but of an attraction that is redoubled in a sort of challenge to or fatality of its essence: "I am not beautiful, I am worse," proclaimed Marie Duval.

We have become completely absorbed by models, completely absorbed by fashion, completely absorbed by simulation: Roger Caillois was perhaps correct in his terminology, and our whole culture is in the process of shifting from games of competition and expression to games of risk and vertigo. Uncertainty, even about fundamentals, drives us to a vertiginous overmultiplication of formal qualities. Hence we move to the form of ecstasy. Ecstasy is that quality specific to each body that spirals in on itself until it has lost all meaning, and thus radiates as pure and empty form. Fashion is the ecstasy of the beautiful: the pure and empty form of a spiraling aesthetics. Simulation is the ecstasy of the real. To prove this, all you need do is watch television, where real events follow one another in a perfectly ecstatic relation, that is to say through vertiginous and stereotyped traits, unreal and recurrent, which allow for continuous and uninterrupted juxtapositions. Ecstatic: such is the object of advertising, and such is the consumer in the eyes of advertising. Advertising is the spiraling of use value and exchange value to the point of annulment, into the pure and empty form of a lack ...

But we need to go further: anti-pedagogy is the ecstatic form, that is to say, the pure and empty form of pedagogy. The anti-theater is the ecstatic form of theater: no more stage, no more content; theater in the streets, without actors, theater for everyone by everyone, which, to a certain extent, would merge with the exact unfolding of our lives, lives without illusion. Where is the power of illusion if theater delights merely in mimicking our daily life and in transfiguring our work place? Yet it is in this manner that art looks to escape itself, to deny itself. The more art tries to realize itself, the more it hyperrealizes itself, the more it transcends itself to find its own empty essence. There is vertigo here as well, a vertigo *mise-en-abyme* and stupefied. Nothing has been more effective in stupefying the "creative" act, in making it shine in its pure and inane form, than Duchamp's unexpected exhibition of a wine rack in an art gallery. The ecstasy of a prosaic object transfers the pictorial act into its ecstatic form – which henceforth without an object will spiral in on itself and in a sense disappear, but not without exercising over us a definite fascination. Art, today, merely practises the magic of disappearance.

Imagine something good that would shine forth from all the power of Evil: that's God, a perverse god who in defiance created the world, enjoining it to destroy itself...

What is also fascinating is the surpassing of the social, the irruption of the more social than the social: the masses. Here as well we have a social that has absorbed all the inverse energies of the antisocial, or inertia, of resistance, and of silence. With the masses, the logic of the social is at its extreme: the point where its finalities are inverted and where it reaches its point of inertia and extermination, but where at the same time it verges on ecstasy. The masses are the ecstasy of the social, the ecstatic form of the social, the mirror where the social is reflected in its total immanence.

The real does not concede anything to the benefit of the imaginary: it concedes only to the benefit of the more real than real (the hyperreal) and to the more true than true. This is simulation.

Presence is not effaced by a void, but by a redoubling of presence that effaces the opposition between presence and absence. Nor is a void effaced by fullness, but rather by repletion and saturation, by a plenitude greater than fullness. This is the reaction of the body by obesity, of sex by obscenity, an abreaction to a void.

Motion does not disappear so much in immobility as it does in speed and acceleration, in what is more mobile than movement, so to speak, and which transports it to extremes while depriving it of meaning.

Sexuality does not vanish in sublimation, repression and morality. It vanishes more effectively in what is more sexual than sex: pornography. The hypersexual is the contemporary of the hyperreal.

More generally, visible things do not terminate in obscurity and in silence; they vanish into what is more visible than the visible: obscenity.

An example of this ex-centricity of things, of this drift into excrescence, is the irruption of randomness, indeterminancy, and relativity within our system. The reaction to this new state of things has not been a resigned abandonment of traditional values, but rather a crazy overdetermination, an exacerbation, of these values of reference, function, finality, and causality. Perhaps nature is, in fact, horrified by the void, for it is in the void, and in order to avoid it, that plethoric, hypertrophic, and saturated systems emerge. Some-thing redundant always settles in the place where there is no longer any-thing.

Determinacy does not withdraw to the benefit of indeterminacy, but to the benefit of a hyperdeterminacy: the redundancy of determinacy in a void.

Finality does not disappear in favor of the aleatory, but rather in favor of hyperfinality, of a hyperfunctionality: more functional than the functional, more final than the final – the hypertelic (*hypertélie*).

Having been plunged into an in-ordinate uncertainty by randomness, we have responded by an excess of causality and teleology. Hypertelic growth is not an accident in the evolution of certain species, it is the challenge of telos as a response to increasing indeterminacy. In a system where things are increasingly left to chance, telos turns into delirium, and develops entities that know all too well how to exceed their own ends, to the point of invading the entire system.

This is true of the behavior of the cancerous cell (hypervitality in a single direction), of the hyperspecialization of objects and people, of the operationalism of the smallest detail, and of the hypersignification of the slightest sign: the leitmotiv of our daily lives. But this is also the chancroid secret of every obese and cancerous system: those of communication, of information, of production, of destruction – each having long since exceeded the limits of functionality, and use value, in order to enter the phantasmic escalation of finalities.

The hysteria of causality, the inverse of the hysteria of finalities, which corresponds to the simultaneous effacement of origins and causes, is the obsessive search for origins, for responsibility, for reference; an attempt to extinguish phenomena in infinitesimal causes. But it is also the genesis and genetics complex, which on various accounts are represented by psychoanalytic palingenesis (the whole psyche hypostatized in prime infancy, every sign a symptom); and biogenetics (all probabilities saturated by the fatal ordering of molecules); and the hypertrophying of historical research, the delirium of explaining everything, of ascribing everything, of referencing everything... All this becomes a fantastic burden – references living one off the other and at the other's expense. Here again we have an excrescent interpretive system developing without any relation to its objective. All of this is a consequence of a forward flight in the face of the haemorrhaging of objective causes.

Inertial phenomena are accelerating. Arrested forms proliferate, and growth is immobilized in excrescence. This is the form of the hypertelic, that which goes beyond its own ends: the crustacean that strays far from the ocean unable to return (to what secret end?); or the increasing gigantism of Easter Island statues.

Tentacular, protuberant, excrescent, hypertelic: this is the inertial destiny of a saturated world. The denial of its own end in hyper-finality; is this not also the mechanism of cancer? The revenge of growth in excrescence. The revenge and summons of speed in inertia. The masses are also caught in this gigantic process of inertia by acceleration. The masses are this excrescent process, which precipitates all growth towards ruin. It is the circuit that is short-circuited by a monstrous finality.

Exxon: the American government requests a complete report on the multinational's activities throughout the world. The result is twelve 1,000 page volumes, whose reading alone, not to mention the analysis, would exceed a few years' work. Where is the information?

Should we initiate an information dietetics? Should we thin out the obese, the obese systems, and create institutions to uninform?

The incredible destructive stockpiling of strategic weapons is only equaled by the worldwide demographic overgrowth. As paradoxical as it may seem, both are of the same nature and correspond to the same logic of excrescence and inertia. A triumphant anomaly: no principle of justice or of proportion can temper either one; they incite one another. And worse, there isn't even so much as Promethean defiance here, no excessive passion or pride. It appears simply that the species has crossed a particular mysterious point, where it has become impossible to turn back, to decelerate, or to slow down.

> A tormenting thought: as of a certain point, history was no longer *real*. Without noticing it, all mankind suddenly left reality: everything happening since then was supposedly not true; but we supposedly didn't notice. Our task would now be to find that point, and as long as we didn't have it, we would be forced to abide in our present destruction. (Elias Canetti)[1]

Dead point:[2] the neutral point where every system crosses the subtle limit of reversibility, contradiction, and reevaluation, in order to be completely absorbed in noncontradiction, in desperate self-contemplation, and in ecstasy...

Here begins the pataphysics of systems. Even though logical overcoming, or escalation, always takes the form of a catastrophe in slow motion, it does not only present inconveniences. This is also the case for systems of destruction and for strategic arms. Beyond the limit of the forces of destruction, the stage for war is abolished. There is no longer any practical correlation between the potential for destruction and its purpose, and referring to it becomes ridiculous. The warfare system dissuades itself, and this is the paradoxically beneficial aspect of deterrence (*dissuasion*): there is no longer any space for warfare. Hence we must hope that nuclear escalation and the arms race will persist. This is the cost of pure warfare;[3] that is, of the pure and empty form, of the hyperreal and eternally dissuasive form of warfare, where for the first time we can congratulate ourselves on the absence of events. Like the real, warfare will no longer have any place – except precisely if the nuclear powers are successful in de-escalation and manage to define new spaces for warfare. If military power, at the cost of de-escalating this marvelously practical madness to the second power, reestablishes a setting for warfare, a confined space that is in fact human, then weapons will regain their use value and their exchange value: it will again be possible *to exchange warfare*. In its orbital and ecstatic form warfare has become an impossible exchange, and this orbitalness protects us.

What can we say about Canetti's desire to locate this blind spot beyond which "things have ceased to be real," where history has ceased to exist, without us realizing it, and where, lacking such insight, we can only persevere in our current destruction?

Supposing we could locate such a point, what would we do? What miracle would make history true again? What miracle would allow us to go back in time so that we may prepare ourselves for its disappearance? For this point is also the end of linear time, and all the marvelous inventions of science fiction for "going back in time" are useless if time already no longer exists.

What precautions should we have taken to avoid this historical collapse, this coma, this volitalization of the real? Have we made an error? Has the human race made some error, violated some secret, committed some fatal imprudence? It is as vain to ask such questions as it is to ponder on the mysterious reasons why a woman has left you: nothing could have changed in any case. The terrifying aspect of such an event is that, beyond a certain point, every effort to exorcise it only serves to precipitate it: no premonition has ever been of any use; each event confirms and legitimates the one that preceded it. It is the naivety of attributing a cause to each event which allows us to think that the event need not have occurred: the pure, noncausal event unfolds inescapably; however, this event can never be duplicated, whereas a causal process can always be repeated. Which is precisely why it is no longer an event.

Canetti's wish is therefore pious, if his hypothesis is truly radical. The point to which he refers is, by definition, impossible to recover, because if we could do so it would mean the return of time. The point at which we could reverse the process of dispersion of time and history escapes us – which is why in the first place we crossed it without realizing it, and doing so of course without wishing to.

Besides, the point Canetti seeks may not even exist. It only exists if we can prove that previously there has actually been history – which becomes impossible once this point has been traversed. Outside the realm of history, history itself can no longer reflect, nor even prove its own coherence. This is why we call upon every previous epoch, every way of life, all modes of self-historicizing and of narrating oneself with the support of proof and documentation (everything becomes documentary): we sense that in our era which is that of the end of history all of this is invalidated.

We can neither go back in time, nor accept this situation. Some have cheerfully resolved this dilemma: they have discovered the anti-Canetti point, a deceleration that would allow us to reenter history, the real, and the social, like a stray satellite in hyperspace reentering the Earth's atmosphere. A false sense of the radical misled us into centrifugal spaces; a vital jolt returns us to reality. Once this obsessive fear of the unreality of history, in the sudden collapse of time and the real, has been warded off, everything again becomes real and meaningful.

Maybe they're right. Perhaps it was necessary to stop this haemorrhaging of value. Enough terrorist radicalism, enough simulacra; we need the resurgence of morality, of faith, and of meaning. Down with fatalistic (*crépusculaires*) analyses!

Beyond this point there are only events (and theories) without consequences. Precisely because events absorb their own meaning, nothing is refracted, nothing is presaged.

Beyond this point there are only catastrophes.

Perfect is the event or the language that assumes, and is able to stage, its own mode of disappearance, thus acquiring the maximal energy of appearances. The catastrophe is the maximal raw event, here again more event-like than the event – but an event without consequences and which leaves the world hanging.

When history is no longer meaningful, once the point of inertia is crossed, every event becomes a catastrophe, becomes a pure event, without consequences (but therein lies its power).

The event without consequences is like Musil's man without qualities, like [Deleuze and Guattari's] body without organs, like [Bergson's] time without memory.

When light is harnessed and engulfed by its own source, there occurs a brutal involution of time into the event itself. This is a catastrophe in the literal sense: an inflection or curvature that makes the origin of a thing coincide with its end, and re-turns the end onto the origin in order to annul it, leaving behind an event without precedent and without consequences – the pure event.

This is also the catastrophe of meaning: the event without con-sequences is identified by the fact that every cause can be indifferently assigned to it, without being able to choose among them . . . Its origin is unintelligible, and so is its destination. We can neither reverse the course of time, nor the course of meaning.

Today every event is virtually without consequences, it is open to all possible interpretations, none of which can fix meaning: the equiprobability of every cause and of every consequence – a multiple and aleatory ascription.

If the wavelengths of meaning, and of historical memory and time around the event are shrinking, if the wavelengths of causality around the effect are fading, it is because light is slowing down (and, today, the event has truly become a wave: it does not simply travel "on a wavelength," it is a wave which is undecipherable in terms of language or meaning; it is only, and instantaneously, decipherable in terms of color, tactility, ambience, in terms of sensory effects). Somewhere a gravitational effect causes the light of event(s), the light that transports meaning beyond the event itself, the carrier of messages, to slow down to a halt; like the light of politics and history that we now so weakly perceive, or the light of celestial bodies we now only receive as faint simulacra.

We must be able to grasp the catastrophe that awaits us in the slowing of light: the slower light becomes, the less it escapes its source; thus things and events tend not to release their meaning, tend to slow down their emanation, to harness that which was previously refracted in order to absorb it in a black hole.

Science fiction has always been attracted by speeds exceeding the speed of light. Light traveling below such a speed, however, would be much more bizarre.

The speed of light protects the reality of things by guaranteeing that the images we have of them are contemporaneous. The plausibility of a causal universe would disappear with some appreciable change in this speed. All things would interfere in total disaster. This is the extent to which this speed is our referent, our God, and for us represents the absolute. If the speed of light becomes relative, then no more transcendence, no more God to recognize his own, and the universe lapses into indeterminacy.

This is happening today with electronic media, where information is beginning to circulate everywhere at the speed of light. There is no longer any absolute with which to measure the rest. But beneath this acceleration something is beginning to slow down absolutely. Perhaps it is we who are beginning to slow down absolutely.

What if light slowed to "human" speeds? If it bathed us in a flux of slow motion images, to the point of being slower than our own movements?

We would thus need to generalize the example of the light that reaches us from stars long since extinct – their images taking light-years to reach us. If light was infinitely slower, a host of things, closer to home, would already have been subject to the fate of these stars: we would see them, they would be there, yet already no longer there. Would this not also be the case for a reality in which the image of a thing still appears, but is no longer there? An analogy with mental objects, and the ether of the mind.

Or, assuming that light travels very slowly, bodies could approach us faster than their image, and what would happen then? We would be struck without ever seeing the obstacles approaching. In fact we can imagine a universe, the opposite of our own, where all bodies move much slower than the speed of light, a universe where bodies would travel at phenomenal speeds, but light would travel very slowly. It would be total chaos, no longer regulated by the simultaneity of optical messages.

The speed of light, like the wind, would be variable, there would be moments of stillness when no image would reach us from the effected zones.

Like perfume, light would vary according to different bodies, scarcely diffusing beyond the immediate environment, a field of optical messages fading at a distance. The images of bodies would scarcely propagate beyond a luminous territory, outside of which they would no longer exist.

Or again, light traveling at the speed of continental drifts, like continental plates sliding on one another creating seismic movements that would distort every image and our perception of space.

Can we imagine the slow refraction of faces and gestures, like the strokes of a swimmer in heavy water? How could we look someone in the eye, how would we seduce them if we are not sure that they are still there? What if cinematographic slow motion seized the whole universe? There is comical excitement in the accelerated, as it transcends meaning by explosion; but there is poetic enchantment in the decelerated, as it destroys meaning by implosion.

Ever since acceleration has become our common condition, suspense and slow motion are the current forms of the tragic. Time is no longer present in its normal unfolding, ever since it has become distended and enlarged to the floating dimension of reality. It is no longer illuminated by a will; nor is space any longer defined by movement. Since we have lost a historical destiny, it is necessary that a kind of predestination reintervene to provide some sense of the tragic. This predestination can be seen in suspense and in slow motion. It is these which suspend the unfolding of form to such an extent that meaning no longer crystallizes. Or, in the discourse of meaning, it is the slow emergence of another meaning that comes to implode into the first one. So slow that light would curl up on itself and even come to a halt; it would initiate a total suspension of the universe.

This play of systems around the point of inertia is modeled on the form of catastrophe inherent to the era of simulation; the seismic form. The form that lacks a ground, in the form of a fault and of failure, of dehiscence and of fractal objects, where immense plates, entire sections, slide under one another and produce intense surface tremors. No longer in the form of a devouring fire in the sky that strikes us down, a generative lightning that was (at) once punishment and purification, and which regenerated the earth. Nor is it in the form of a deluge, which is more of a maternal catastrophe at the point of the origin of the world. These are the great legendary and mythical forms that haunt us. The most recent one is in the form of an explosion, culminating in the obsession over nuclear catastrophe (but conversely, it has fueled the myth of the Big Bang, of the explosion as the origin of the universe). The seismic form is even more recent: it demonstrates the extent to which the forms of catastrophe take the shape of their culture. Cities are distinguished by the forms of catastrophe they have assumed, which is the animating aspect of their charm. New York is King Kong, or the blackout, or the vertical bombardment, the Towering Inferno. Los Angeles is the horizontal fault line, with California breaking off and sliding into the Pacific: the earthquake. This form is today much more immediate and evocative: of the same nature as fission and instantaneous propagation; of the same nature as the undulatory, the spasmodic and radical mutations. The sky is no longer falling on your head; it is the terrain that is sliding. We are in a fissile universe; a universe of erratic icebergs and horizontal drifts. Interstitial collapse: this is the effect of the seismic rupture that awaits us, and of mental seismic ruptures as well. The dehiscence of the most tightly closed things; the shaking of things that tighten up, and that contract on their emptiness. For at bottom the ground never existed, only a cracked epidermis. Nor was there ever depth, which we know undergoes fusion. Seismic movements tell us this; they are the requiem of the infrastructure. We can no longer observe the stars or the sky; we must now observe the subterranean deities that threaten a collapse into the void.

We also dream of harnessing this energy, but this is sheer madness. We might as well harness the energy of automobile accidents, or of dogs that have been run over, or of all things that collapse. (A new hypothesis: if things have a greater tendency to disappear and to collapse, perhaps the principal source of future energy will be accidents and catastrophes). One thing is certain, even if we are never able to harness seismic energy, the symbolic wave of an earthquake will most likely never subside: symbolic energy, so to speak, which is to say the power of fascination and derision at such an event, is incomparable to any material destruction.

It is this energy, this rupturing symbolic energy, that we in fact strive to harness in such an insane project, or in a more immediate one, in the anticipation of seismic movements by various evacuation scenarios. The scandal is that experts have calculated that a state of emergency declared on the basis of a prediction of seismic activity would trigger off a panic whose consequences would be more disastrous than the catastrophe itself. Here again we are fully in the midst of derision: in the absence of a real catastrophe it is quite possible to trigger one off by simulation, equivalent to the former, and which can be substituted for it. One wonders if this is not what fuels the fantasies of the "experts" – which is exactly the case within the nuclear domain: isn't every system of prevention and deterrence a virtual locus of catastrophe? Designed to thwart catastrophe, it materializes all of its consequences in the immediate present. Since we cannot count on chance to bring about a catastrophe, we must find an equivalent programmed into the defense system.

It is thus evident that a country or government sophisticated enough to predict earthquakes and prevent their consequences would constitute a much greater danger to the community and the species than the seismic activity itself. The *Terremotati* of southern Italy have violently attacked the Italian government for its negligence (the media arrived before the emergency assistance, an obvious sign of our current hierarchy of priorities). They quite justifiably blamed the political order for the catastrophe (to the extent that it claims to guard the general welfare of the population). But never could it imagine a system capable of complete prevention of catastrophes: everyone would in fact have to prefer catastrophe, which at least, with its miseries, corresponds to the prophetic oracle of a violent end. At least it satisfies the political order's underlying exigency for derision. The same is true for terrorism: what would become of a country capable of annihilating terrorism at its source (Germany)? It would have to implement the same level of terrorism; it would have to generalize terror at all levels. If this is the cost of security, does the whole world in its heart of hearts dream of it?

Pompeii. Everything in this city is metaphysical, including its dream-like geometry, not a geometry of space, but a mental geometry, one of labyrinths – the freezing of time even more poignant in the midday heat.

The tactile presence of these ruins, their suspense, their revolving shadows, their everydayness, is magnificent for the psyche. It is the conjunction of the banality of a stroll and the immanence of another time, of another instant, unique, a time of catastrophe. The deadly, but extinguished, presence of Vesuvius gives the deserted streets the charm of a hallucination – the illusion of being here and now, on the verge of eruption – and it is resuscitated, by a miracle of nostalgia, two thousand years later in the immanence of a previous life.

Few places leave such an impression of strange disturbance (it is no surprise that Jansen and Freud have located here the psychic function of Gradiva). It is the very warmth of death that we sense here, brought to life in the fossilized and fugitive signs of everyday existence: wheel tracks in the rock; the signs of wear in the curb; the petrified wood of a half opened door; the pleat of a toga on a body buried in ashes. No history, like the one which gives prestige to monuments, can intervene between these things and ourselves. They are materialized here, at once, in the very heat where death seized them.

Neither monumentality nor beauty are essential to Pompeii – as are the fatal intimacy of things and the fascination in their simultaneity, like the perfect simulacrum of our own death.

Pompeii is a sort of trompe-l'oeil, a sort of primitive scene: the same vertigo with one dimension missing: time; the same hallucination with an added dimension: the transparency of the smallest detail, like the clear vision of trees completely submerged at the bottom of an artificial lake, which you glide over in stride. This is the mental effect of catastrophe: stopping things before they come to an end, and holding them suspended in their apparition.

Pompeii again destroyed by an earthquake. What kind of catastrophe so unrelentlessly pursues ruins? What is a ruin that needs to be demolished and buried again? The sadistic irony of catastrophe is that it secretly awaits for things, even ruins, to regain their beauty and meaning only to destroy them once again. It is intent upon destroying the illusion of eternity, but it also plays with that illusion, since it fixates things in an alternate eternity. This fixation-paralysis, the shattering of a presence swarming with life in a catastrophic instant, is what gave Pompeii its charm. The first catastrophe, Vesuvius, was a success. The last seismic movement is much more problematic. It appears to obey the rule of the doubling of events in an effect of parody: the pathetic repetition of the great original. The accomplishment of a great destiny with a little help from a wretched divinity. But it has perhaps another meaning; it comes as a warning that this is no longer the era of great collapses, of resurrections, or of games of death and eternity, but the era of little fractionized events, of smooth and effective annihilation, by progressive slippage, an era henceforth without a future, since the traces themselves erase this new destiny. This inaugurates the horizontal era of events without consequences; the last act was staged by nature itself in a glimmer of parody.

Toward a principle of evil

Do these fatal strategies exist? It does not appear that I have described them, nor even touched upon them. The power of the real over the imagination is so great that such a hypothesis appears to be no more than a dream. Where do you get the stories you tell about the object? Objectivity is the opposite of fatality. The object is real, and the real is subject to laws, and that is that.

There it is: faced with a delirious world, only the ultimatum of realism will do. Which means that if you wish to escape the world's insanity, you must sacrifice all of its charm as well. By increasing its delirium, the world has raised the stakes of the sacrifice, blackmailed by reality. Today, in order to survive, illusion no longer works; one must draw nearer to the nullity of the real.

There is perhaps one, and only one, fatal strategy: theory. And undoubtedly the only difference between a banal theory and a fatal theory is that in the former the subject always believes itself to be more clever than the object, while in the latter the object is always taken to be more clever, more cynical, more ingenious than the subject, which it awaits at every turn. The metamorphoses, tactics, and strategies of the object exceed the subject's understanding. The object is neither the subject's double nor his or her repression; neither the subject's fantasy nor hallucination; neither the subject's mirror nor reflection: but it has its own strategy. It withholds one of the rules of the game which is inaccessible to the subject, not because it is deeply mysterious, but because it is endlessly ironic.

An objective irony watches over us, it is the object's fulfillment without regard for the subject, nor for its alienation. In the alienation phase, subjective irony is triumphant. Here the subject constitutes an unsolvable challenge to the blind world that surrounds him.

Subjective irony, ironic subjectivity, is the finest manifestation of a universe of prohibition, of Law and of desire. The subject's power derives from a promise of fulfillment, whereas the realm of the object is characterized by what is fulfilled, and for that reason it is a realm we can not escape.

We confuse the fatal with the resurgence of the repressed (desire as that which is inescapable), but the order of fatality is antithetical to that of repression. It is not desire that we cannot escape, but the ironic presence of the object, its indifference, and its indifferent interconnections, its challenge, its seduction, its violation of the symbolic order (therefore of the subject's unconscious as well, if it had one). In short, it is the principle of Evil we cannot escape.

The object disobeys our metaphysics, which has always attempted to distill the Good and filter Evil. The object is translucent to Evil. This is why it appears, maliciously and diabolically, to be so voluntarily cooperative, and to bend willingly, like nature, to whatever law we may impose, thus violating all legislation. When I refer to the object, and to its fundamental duplicity, I am referring to all of us and to our social and political order. The whole problem of voluntary servitude is to be reexamined in this light, not to resolve it, but to anticipate the enigma; obedience is, in effect, a banal strategy, which need not be explained, for it secretly contains, every obedience secretly contains, a disobedience fatal to the symbolic order.

Herein lies the principle of Evil, not in some mystical agency or transcendence, but as a concealment of the symbolic order, the abduction, rape, concealment and ironic corruption of the symbolic order. It is in this way that the object is translucent to the principle of Evil: as opposed to the subject, it is a bad conductor of the symbolic order, yet a good conductor of the fatal, that is, of pure objectivity, sovereign and irreconcilable, immanent and enigmatic.

Moreover, Evil is not what is interesting; it is the spiraling of the worst that is interesting. The principle of Evil is indeed reflected in the subject's misfortune, in his or her mirror, but the object desires to be worst, it claims the worst. This represents a more radical negativity, which means, if all things eventually violate the symbolic order, that everything will have been diverted at its origin.

Prior to being produced, the world was seduced. A strange precession, which today still weighs heavily on all reality. The world was contradicted at its origin: it is therefore impossible ever to verify it. Negativity, whether historical or subjective, is nothing: the original diversion is truly diabolical, even in thought.

The vertigo of simulation, the Luciferian rapture in the eccentricity of the origin and the end, contrasts with the Utopia of the Last

Judgement, the complement of original baptism. Which is why gods can only live and hide in the inhuman, in objects and beasts, in the realm of silence and objective stupefaction, and not in the human realm, that of language and subjective stupefaction. A human-god is an absurdity. A god who throws off the ironic mask of the inhuman, who abandons the bestial metaphor and the objective metamorphosis where, in silence, it embodied the principle of Evil, providing itself a soul and a face, simultaneously assumes the hypocrisy of human psychology.

We must be just as respectful of the inhuman as certain cultures, which we have therefore labeled fatalistic. We condemn them without further recourse because they obtained their commandments on the side of the inhuman, from the stars or the animal god, from constellations or a divinity without image. A divinity without image – what a grand idea. Nothing could be more opposed to our modern and technical iconolatry.

Metaphysics allows only the good radiations to filter through; it wants to make the world a mirror of the subject (having himself or herself passed the mirror stage), a world of forms distinct from its double, from its shadow, from its image: that is the principle of Good. Here the object is always the fetish, the false, the *feticho*, the factitious, the delusion – all that embodies the abominable integration of a thing and its magical and artificial double, and which no religion of the transparent or of the mirror will ever come to resolve: this is the principle of Evil.

When I speak of the object and of its fatal strategies I am speaking of a person and of his or her inhuman strategies. For example, a human being can find a much deeper boredom while on vacation than in daily life – boredom intensified by the fact that it contains all the elements of happiness and recreation. The important point is that vacation is predestined to boredom, along with the bitter and triumphant premonition of being unable to escape it. How can one imagine that people would repudiate their everyday life in search of an alternative? On the contrary, they make it their destiny: by intensifying it in the appearances of the contrary; by submerging themselves to the point of ecstasy; and by fixating monotony in an even greater one. Super-banality is the equivalent of fatality.

If we do not understand this, we will understand nothing of this collective stupefaction, even though it is a grand act of transcendence. I am not joking: people are not looking to amuse themselves, they seek a fatal diversion. No matter how boring, the important thing is to increase boredom; such an increase is salvation, it is ecstasy. It can be the ecstatic amplification of just about anything. It may be the increase of oppression or abjection that acts as the liberating ecstasy of abjection, just as the absolute commodity is the liberating form of commodity. This is the only solution to the problem of "voluntary servitude," and moreover, this is the only form of liberation: the amplification of negative conditions. All forms that tend to advertise a miraculous freedom are nothing but revolutionary homilies. The logic of liberation, essentially, is heard only by a few, and for the most part, a fatal logic prevails.

This will to spectacle and illusion, in contrast to every will to knowledge and power, is another form of fundamental cynicism. It is alive in the hearts of people, but haunts just as well the processes of events. In the raw event, in objective information, and in the most secret acts and thoughts, there is something like a drive to revert to the spectacle, or to climax on stage instead of producing oneself originally. To manifest one's being is necessary; to be enraptured is absolutely vital.

Things only occur under these extreme circumstances; that is, not under the constraint of representation, but through the magic of their effect – only here do they appear ingenious, and offer themselves the luxury of existence. Although we maintain that nature is indifferent, and it is certainly so to the passions and enterprises of people, perhaps it isn't when it makes a spectacle of itself in natural catastrophes. Catastrophe is a parable(?), which is there to signify this passion of passions, a simulating passion, a seductive passion, a diverting passion, where things are only meaningful when transfigured by illusion, by derision, by a staging that is in no way representational; only meaningful in their exceptional form, in their eccentricity, in the will to scorn their causes and extinguish themselves in their effects, and particularly in their form of disappearance. Moralists of all times have strictly condemned this exceptional form, because things here cynically divert from their origin and their end, in a distant echo of the original sin.

Nevertheless, this eccentricity is what protects us from the real, and from its disastrous consequences. The fact that things extinguish themselves in the spectacle, in a magical and artificial fetishization, is a distortion serious thinkers will always combat, under the Utopian banner of expunging the world in order to deliver it exact, intact, and authentic on the day of the Last Judgement. But this is perhaps the lesser evil, since God knows where the unleashing of meaning will lead when it refuses to produce itself as appearance.

Even revolution can take place only if there is the possibility of spectacle; what people of goodwill deplore is that the media has put an end to the real event. But if we take the example of the nuclear threat, it may be that its distillation in the simulated panic of our daily life, in the spectacular obsessions and thrills that feed our fear, and not the balance of terror (there is no strategic guarantee in deterrence, nor is there, in fact, any instinct of self-preservation), is what protects us from nuclear confrontation. What protects us is that in nuclear war the event is likely to eliminate the possibility of the spectacle. *This is why it will not take place.* For humanity can accept physical annihilation, but cannot agree to sacrifice the spectacle (unless it can find a spectator in another world). The drive to spectacle is more powerful than the instinct of preservation, and it is on the former that we must rely.[4]

If the morality of things is in their sacrosanct use value, then long live the immorality of the atom and of weapons so that even they are subject to the ultimate and cynical terms of the spectacle! Hail the secret rule of the game whereby all things disobey the symbolic law! What will save us is neither the rational principle nor use value, but the immoral principle of the spectacle, the ironic principle of Evil.

To become absorbed in this second outcome is a sort of passion, a sort of fatal will. Likewise, no life can be conceived without the existence of a second chance. A purpose in life can only be ascertained by the strong certainty of a necessary return, sooner or later, of certain moments or faces that once appeared, like the resurrection of bodies, but without a Last Judgement. They will return, they have only temporarily disappeared from the horizon of our life, whose trajectory, specifically diverted by these events, curves sufficiently, and unconsciously, to provide them the opportunity for a second existence, or a final return. Only then will they have truly lived. Only then will they have been won or lost.

From a certain time, these second events constitute the very guidelines of life, where things thus no longer occur by chance. It is the first event that occurs by chance, having no meaning in itself and losing itself in the banal night of experience. Only by redoubling itself does it become an actual event, thereby attaining the character of a day of reckoning – like a sign that would only be valid redoubled by its ascendant. The sign itself is indifferent; redoubled it becomes ineluctable.

Once certain life events have had their second chance, when the cycle has returned them once, and only once, then that life is completed. If a life is not given the opportunity of a second chance, it is finished before it has begun.

The fatal is there somewhere. In this sense, ancient heresies were right. Everyone has the right to a second birth, the real one, and everyone is predestined, not by astral decree, but rather by an internal predestination, one that is immanent in our own lives: the necessary return of certain events. This is why, once chance is abolished, the Last Judgement is unnecessary.

This is why the theory of predestination is infinitely superior to the theory of the freedom of the soul. Since, if one eliminates from life only that which is destined, but not predestined, everything that occurs only once is accidental, whereas that which is accomplished a second time becomes fatal. Predestination provides life with the intensity of these second events, which appear to have the depth of a previous life.

A first encounter has neither form nor meaning, it is always tainted by misunderstanding and banality. Fatality only comes after, by the present undertakings of a previous life. And, in this instance, there is a kind of will and energy, which no one knows anything about, and which is not the resurgence of a hidden order, not at all. It is in the full light of day that certain things come to their designated dead end.

If the stars would rise and set in any order, even the sky would be meaningless. Their recurrent trajectory makes the sky eventful. And the recurrence of certain fatal episodes makes life eventful.

Consequently, if the object is ingenious, if the object is fatal, what is to be done?

Does the ironic art of disappearance succeed the art of survival? The subject has always dreamed of disappearance: it is the converse of his or her dream of totalization; yet the one has never been able to suppress the other, quite the opposite. This failure currently arouses more subtle passions.

Is the insistent desire of fatal strategies thus at the heart of banal strategies?

Nothing can insure us against fatality, much less provide us with a strategy. Also, the conjunction of the two terms is paradoxical: how can there be fate if there is strategy? But precisely: the enigma is that fate is at the heart of every strategy; this is what emerges as a fatal strategy at the heart of the most banal strategies. It is the object whose fate would be a strategy – like the rule of some other game. In fact, the object mocks the laws we decorate it with. It agrees to appear in our calculations as a sarcastic variable and to let the equations verify themselves. But no one knows the rules of the game, the conditions under which one accepts to play, and these may change all of a sudden.

No one knows what a strategy is. There are not enough means in the world to have the ends at our disposal. Thus no one is capable of articulating a final process. God himself is forced to tinker (*bricoler*). What is interesting is the inexorable logical process that emerges whereby the object plays the very game we want it to play, and in a way it doubles the ante. By outbidding the strategic constraints we have imposed on it, the object institutes a strategy without finality, a "dynamic" strategy that thwarts the subject's strategy; a fatal strategy since the subject succumbs to the transgression of his own objectives.

We are accomplice to the object's excess of finality (it may be the excess of meaning, and thus the inability to decipher a single word, which is so effective at signaling us). Every strategy we invent is in the hope that it will unfold unexpectedly. We invent the real in the hope of seeing it unfold as a great ruse. From every object we seek a blind response that will disrupt our projects. From strategy we expect control, but from seduction we hope for surprise.

Seduction is fatal. It is the effect of a sovereign object which recreates within us the original disturbance and seeks to surprise us. Fatality in turn is seductive, like the discovery of an unknown rule of the game. Discovering a rule of the game is wonderful and it compensates in advance for the most bitter losses.

Hence the phenomenon of wit. If I seek a fatal progression in language I confront the witticism, which is itself the dénouement of language that is immanent in language (this is the fatal: the same sign overseeing the crystallization and the solution of a life, the intricacies and the dénouement of an event). In language that has become pure object, irony (in Freud's *Jokes and their Relation to the Unconscious*) is the objective form of this dénouement. As in *Jokes*, redoubling and outbidding are always a spiritual form of dénouement.

Everything must unfold in the fatal and spiritual mode, just as everything was entangled in the beginning by an original diversion.

Even predestination is a form of the ironic diversion of fate, but then so too is chance. What is the point of turning chance into an objective process, since it is an ironic process? Of course it exists, but in contrast to everything scientific; it exists as the irony of risk, even at the level of the molecule. And of course fatality exists as well, simultaneously – there is no paradox here. The difference is that the irony of fate is greater than the irony of chance, which makes it more tragic and more seductive.

It is true that there is an obscure and difficult side to this: to pass on the side of the object, to take the side of the object. One must look for another rule, another axiomatic: there is nothing mystical here, no otherworldly delirium of a subjectivity entrapped and fleeing forward in a descriptive paroxysm. Simply to outline this other logic, to unfold these other strategies, to leave the field open for objective irony is also a challenge, possibly absurd, and one which runs the risk of what it describes – but the risk is to be taken: hypothesizing the fatal strategy can only be fatal as well.

If there is morality, it is also caught in the eccentric cycle of its effects, it is itself hypermorality, just as the real is hyperreal. This is no longer moral stasis, but moral ecstasy. It is in itself a special effect.

Lévi-Strauss once claimed that the symbolic order had withdrawn to the benefit of history. Today, says Canetti, even history has retreated. What is left then but to pass over to the side of the object, to its affected and eccentric effects, to its fatal effects (fatality is merely the absolute freedom of effects). Semiorrhage.

These days when all critical radicalism has become pointless, when all negativity is resolved in a world that pretends to be fulfilled, when critical thought has found in socialism a secondary home, when the effect of desire has long since gone, what is left but to return things to their enigmatic ground zero? The enigma has been inverted however: previously it was the Sphinx who put to man the question about man, one which Oedipus is thought to have resolved, one which all of us thought we resolved. Today it is man who puts to the Sphinx, to the inhuman, the question of the inhuman, of the fatal, of the world's indifference to our endeavors and to objective laws. The object (the Sphinx) is more subtle and does not answer. But, by disobeying laws and thwarting desire, it must answer secretly to some enigma. What is left but to go over to the side of this enigma?

Everything finally boils down to this: let us for one time hypothesize that there is a fatal and enigmatic bias in the order of things.

In any case there is something stupid about our present situation. There is something stupid in the raw event, to which destiny, if it exists, cannot help but be sensitive. There is something stupid in the current forms of truth and objectivity, from which a superior irony must give us leave. Everything is expiated in one way or another. Everything proceeds in one way or another. Truth only complicates things.

And if the Last Judgement consists, as everyone knows, in saving and eternalizing one moment of life, and only one, for each of us, with whom do we share this ironic end?

NOTES

"*Les Stratégies Fatales*": In both British English (*OED*) and French (Larousse) the words fatality (*fatalité*) and fatal (*fatale*) mean primarily predestined and inevitable, and secondarily dreaded, doomed, and disastrous. In American English the order is inverted so that fatal(ity) is primarily deadly (in fact, destined is considered an obsolete definition for fatal in the *American Heritage Dictionary*), whereas fateful and fated have retained inevitability as a primary meaning, and death and disaster as a secondary. Needless to say Baudrillard makes (ample) use (play) of both meanings. But I believe that while these strategies are disastrous (governed by cunning genius and the principle of Evil) they are primarily inevitable, destined (*amor fati*). I was thus tempted (seduced) to entitle this chapter "Fateful Strategies" but current usage (of Baudrillard), and a certain awkwardness is responsible for the present rendition (a fatal strategy perhaps). Nevertheless, where it seemed clear that inevitability/destiny was the overriding meaning in context I translated *fatalité* as fate (fatality otherwise). Since clarity is elusive (*leurre*) the reader should keep the dual (duel?) meaning in mind. [Trans.]

1   Elias Canetti, *The Human Province*, trans. Joachim Neugroschel (New York: Seabury, 1978) p. 69; original edition, 1973.
2   "Dead point" was originally in English.
3   Cf. the works of Paul Virilio.
4   Of course this is no longer the same spectacle situationists denounced as the height of alienation and the ultimate strategy of capital. It would instead be the opposite, for it is the case here of the victorious strategy of the object, its mode of diversion, and not of being diverted. This is much closer to the enchantment (*féerie*) of commodities described by Baudelaire.

9

The Masses: The Implosion of the Social in the Media

Up to now there have been two great versions of the analysis of the media (as indeed that of the masses), one optimistic and one pessimistic. The optimistic one has assumed two major tonalities, very different from one another. There is the technological optimism of Marshall McLuhan: for him the electronic media inaugurate a generalized planetary communication and should conduct us, by the mental effect alone of new technologies, beyond the atomizing rationality of the Gutenberg galaxy to the global village, to the new electronic tribalism – an achieved transparency of information and communication. The other version, more traditional, is that of dialectical optimism inspired by progressivist and Marxist thought: the media constitute a new, gigantic productive force and obey the dialectic of productive forces. Momentarily alienated and submitted to the law of capitalism, their intensive development can only eventually explode this monopoly. "For the first time in history," writes Hans Enzensberger, "the media make possible a mass participation in a productive process at once social and socialized, a participation whose practical means are in the hands of the masses themselves."[1] These two positions more or less, the one technological, the other ideological, inspire the whole analysis and the present practice of the media.[2]

It is more particularly to the optimism of Enzensberger that I formerly opposed a resolutely pessimist vision in "Requiem for the Media." In that I described the mass media as a "speech without response." What characterizes the mass media is that they are opposed to mediation, intransitive, that they fabricate noncommunication – if one accepts the definition of communication as an exchange, as the reciprocal space of speech and response, and thus of *responsibility*. In other words, if one defines it as anything other than the simple emission/reception of information. Now the whole present architecture of the media is founded on this last definition: they are what finally forbids response, what renders impossible any process of exchange (except in the shape of a simulation of a response, which is itself integrated into the process of emission, and this changes nothing in the unilaterality of communication). That is their true abstraction. And it is in this abstraction that is founded the system of social control and power. To understand properly the term *response*, one must appreciate it in a meaning at once strong, symbolic, and primitive: power belongs to him who gives and to whom no return can be made. To give, and to do it in such a way that no return can be made, is to break exchange to one's own profit and to institute a monopoly: the social process is out of balance. To make a return, on the contrary, is to break this power relationship and to restore on the basis of an antagonistic reciprocity the circuit of symbolic exchange. The same applies in the sphere of the media: there speech occurs in such a way that there is no possibility of a return. The restitution of this possibility of response entails upsetting the whole present structure; even better (as started to occur in 1968 and the 70s), it entails an "antimedia" struggle.

In reality, even if I did not share the technological optimism of McLuhan, I always recognized and considered as a gain the true revolution which he brought about in media analysis (this has been mostly ignored in France). On the other hand, though I also did not share the dialectical hopes of Enzensberger, I was not truly pessimistic, since I believed in a possible subversion of the code of the media and in the possibility of an alternate speech and a radical reciprocity of symbolic exchange.

Today all that has changed. I would no longer interpret in the same way the forced silence of the masses in the mass media. I would no longer see in it a sign of passivity and of alienation, but to the contrary an original strategy, an original response in the form of a challenge; and on the basis of this reversal I suggest to you a vision of things which is no longer optimistic or pessimistic, but ironic and antagonistic.

I will take the example of opinion polls, which are themselves a mass medium. It is said that opinion polls constitute a manipulation of democracy. This is certainly no more the case than that publicity is a manipulation of need and of consumption. It too produces demand (or so it claims) and invokes needs just as opinion polls produce answers and induce future behavior. All this would be serious if there were an objective truth of needs, an objective truth of public opinion. It is obvious that here we need to exercise extreme care. The influence of publicity, of opinion polls, of all the media, and of information in general would be dramatic if we were certain that there exists in opposition to it an authentic human nature, an authentic essence of the social, with its needs, its own will, its own values, its finalities. For this would set up the problem of its radical alienation. And indeed it is in this form that traditional critiques are expressed.

Now the matter is at once less serious and more serious than this. The uncertainty which surrounds the social and political effect of opinion polls (do they or do they not manipulate opinion?), like that which surrounds the real economic efficacy of publicity, will never be completely relieved – and it is just as well! This results from the fact that there is a compound, a mixture of two heterogeneous systems whose data cannot be transferred from one to the other. An operational system which is statistical, information-based, and simulational is projected onto a traditional values system, onto a system of representation, will, and opinion. This collage, this collusion between the two, gives rise to an indefinite and useless polemic. We should agree neither with those who praise the beneficial use of the media, nor with those who scream about manipulation, for the simple reason that there is no relationship between a system of meaning and a system of simulation. Publicity and opinion polls would be incapable, even if they wished and claimed to do so, of alienating the will or the opinion of anybody at all, for the reason that they do not act in the time–space of will and of representation where judgement is formed. For the same reason, though reversed, it is quite impossible for them to throw any light at all on public opinion or individual will, since they do not act in a public space, on the stage of a public space. They are strangers to it, and indeed they wish to dismantle it. Publicity and opinion polls and the media in general can only be imagined; they only exist on the basis of a disappearance, the disappearance from the public space, from the scene of politics, of public opinion in a form at once theatrical and representative as it was enacted in earlier epochs. Thus we can be reassured: they cannot destroy it. But we should not have any illusions: they cannot restore it either.

It is this lack of relationship between the two systems which today plunges us into a state of stupor. That is what I said: stupor. To be more objective one would have to say: a radical uncertainty as to our own desire, our own choice, our own opinion, our own will. This is the clearest result of the whole media environment, of the information which makes demands on us from all sides and which is as good as blackmail.

We will never know if an advertisement or opinion poll has had a real influence on individual or collective wills, but we will never know either what would have happened if there had been no opinion poll or advertisement.

The situation no longer permits us to isolate reality or human nature as a fundamental variable. The result is therefore not to provide any additional information or to shed any light on reality, but on the contrary, because we will never in future be able to separate reality from its statistical, simulative projection in the media, a state of suspense and of definitive uncertainty about reality. And I repeat: it is a question here of a completely new species of uncertainty, which results not from the *lack* of information but from information itself and even from an *excess* of information. It is information itself which produces uncertainty, and so this uncertainty, unlike the traditional uncertainty which could always be resolved, is irreparable.

This is our destiny: subject to opinion polls, information, publicity, statistics; constantly confronted with the anticipated statistical verification of our behavior, and absorbed by this permanent refraction of our least movements, we are no longer confronted with our own will. We are no longer even alienated, because for that it is necessary for the subject to be divided in itself, confronted with the other, to be contradictory. Now, where there is no other, the scene of the other, like that of politics and of society, has disappeared. Each individual is forced despite himself or herself into the undivided coherency of statistics. There is in this a positive absorption into the transparency of computers, which is something worse than alienation.

There is an obscenity in the functioning and the omnipresence of opinion polls as in that of publicity. Not because they might betray the secret of an opinion, the intimacy of a will, or because they might violate some unwritten law of the private being, but because they exhibit this redundancy of the social, this sort of continual voyeurism of the group in relation to itself: it must at all times know what it wants, know what it thinks, be told about its least needs, its least quivers, *see* itself continually on the videoscreen of statistics, constantly watch its own temperature chart, in a sort of hypochondriacal madness. The social becomes obsessed with itself; through this auto-information, this permanent autointoxication, it becomes its own vice, its own perversion. This is the real obscenity. Through this feedback, this incessant anticipated accounting, the social loses its own scene. It no longer enacts itself; it has no more time to enact itself; it no longer occupies a particular space, public or political; it becomes confused with its own control screen. Overinformed, it develops ingrowing obesity. For everything which loses its *scene* (like the obese body) becomes for that very reason *ob-scene*.

The silence of the masses is also in a sense obscene. For the masses are also made of this useless hyperinformation which claims to enlighten them, when all it does is clutter up the space of the representable and annul itself in a silent equivalence. And we cannot do much against this obscene circularity of the masses and of information. The two phenomena fit one another: the masses have no opinion and information does not inform them. Both of them, lacking a scene where the meaning of the social can be enacted, continue to feed one another monstrously – as the speed with which information revolves increases continually the weight of the masses as such, and not their self-awareness.

So if one takes opinion polls, and the uncertainty which they induce about the principle of social reality, and the type of obscenity, of statistical pornography to which they attract us – if we take all that seriously, if we confront all that with the claimed finalities of information and of the social itself, then it all seems very dramatic. But there is another way of taking things. It does not shed much more credit on opinion polls, but it restores a sort of status to them, in terms of derision and of play. In effect we can consider the indecisiveness of their results, the uncertainty of their effects, and their unconscious humor, which is rather similar to that of meteorology (for example, the possibility of verifying at the same time contradictory facts or tendencies); or again the casual way in which everybody uses them, disagreeing with them privately and especially if they verify exactly one's own behavior (no one accepts a perfect statistical evaluation of his chances). That is the real problem of the credibility accorded to them.

Statistics, as an objective computation of probabilities, obviously eliminate any elective chance and any personal destiny. That is why, deep down, none of us believes in them, any more than the gambler believes in chance, but only in Luck (with a capital, the equivalent of Grace, not with lower case, which is the equivalent of probability). An amusing example of this obstinate denial of statistical chance is given by this news item: "If this will reassure you, we have calculated that, of every 50 people who catch the metro twice a day for 60 years, only one is in danger of being attacked. Now there is no reason why it should be *you!*" The beauty of statistics is never in their objectivity but in their involuntary humor.

So if one takes opinion polls in this way, one can conceive that they could work for the masses themselves as a game, as a spectacle, as a means of deriding both the social and the political. The fact that

opinion polls do their best to destroy the political as will and representation, the political as meaning, precisely through the effect of
simulation and uncertainty – this fact can only give pleasure to the
ironic unconscious of the masses (and to our individual political
unconscious, if I may use this expression), whose deepest drive
remains the symbolic murder of the political class, the symbolic
murder of political *reality*, and this murder is produced by opinion
polls in their own way. That is why I wrote in *Silent Majorities* that
the masses, which have always provided an alibi for political representation, take their revenge by allowing themselves the theatrical
representation of the political scene.[3] The people have become *public*.
They even allow themselves the luxury of enjoying day by day, as in a
home cinema, the fluctuations of their own opinion in the daily reading of the opinion polls.

It is only to this extent that they believe in them, that we all believe
in them, as we believe in a game of malicious foretelling, a double or
quits on the green baize of the political scene. It is, paradoxically, as a
game that the opinion polls recover a sort of legitimacy. A game of the
undecidable; a game of chance; a game of the undecidability of the
political scene, of the equifinality of all tendencies; a game of truth
effects in the circularity of questions and answers. Perhaps we can see
here the apparition of one of these collective forms of game which
Caillois called *aléa*[4] – an irruption into the polls themselves of a ludic,
aleatory process, and ironic mirror for the use of the masses (and we
all belong to the masses) of a political scene which is caught in its own
trap (for the politicians are the only ones to believe in the polls, along
with the pollsters obviously, as the only ones to believe in publicity are
the publicity agents).

In this regard, one may restore to them a sort of positive meaning:
they would be part of a contemporary cultural mutation, part of the
era of simulation.

In view of this type of consequence, we are forced to congratulate
ourselves on the very failure of polls, and on the distortions which
make them undecidable and chancy. Far from regretting this, we must
consider that there is a sort of fate or evil genius (the evil genius of the
social itself?) which throws this too beautiful machine out of gear and
prevents it from achieving the objectives which it claims. We must
also ask if these distortions, far from being the consequence of a bad
angle of refraction of information onto an inert and opaque matter,
are not rather the consequence of an offensive resistance of the social
itself to its investigation, the shape taken by an occult duel between
the pollsters and the object polled, between information and the
people who receive it?

This is fundamental: people are always supposed to be willing partners in the game of truth, in the game of information. It is agreed that the object can always be persuaded of its truth; it is inconceivable that the object of the investigation, the object of the poll, should not adopt, generally speaking, the strategy of the subject of the analysis, of the pollster. There may certainly be some difficulties (for instance, the object does not understand the question; it's not its business; it's undecided; it replies in terms of the interviewer and not of the question, and so on), but it is admitted that the poll analyst is capable of rectifying what is basically only a lack of adaptation to the analytic apparatus. The hypothesis is never suggested that all this, far from being a marginal, archaic residue, is the effect of an offensive (not defensive) counterstrategy by the object; that, all in all, there exists somewhere an original, positive, possibly victorious strategy of the object opposed to the strategy of the subject (in this case, the pollster or any other producer of messages).

This is what one could call the evil genius of the object, the evil genius of the masses, the evil genius of the social itself, constantly producing failure in the truth of the social and in its analysis, and for that reason unacceptable, and even unimaginable, to the tenants of this analysis.

To reflect the other's desire, to reflect its demand like a mirror, even to anticipate it: it is hard to imagine what powers of deception, of absorption, of deviation – in a word, of subtle revenge – there is in this type of response. This is the way the masses escape as reality, in this very mirror, in those simulative devices which are designed to capture them. Or again, the way in which events themselves disappear behind the television screen, or the more general screen of information (for it is true that events have no probable existence except on this deflective screen, which is no longer a mirror). While the mirror and screen of alienation was a mode of production (the imaginary subject), this new screen is simply its mode of disappearance. But disappearance is a very complex mode: the object, the individual, is not only condemned to disappearance, but *disappearance is also its strategy*; it is its way of response to this device for capture, for networking, and for forced identification. To this *cathodic* surface of recording, the individual or the mass reply by a *parodic* behavior of disappearance. What are they; what do they do; what do they become behind this screen? They turn themselves into an impenetrable and meaningless surface, which is a method of disappearing. They eclipse themselves; they melt into the superficial screen in such a way that their reality and that of their movement, just like that of particles of matter, may be radically questioned without making any fundamental change to the probabilistic analysis of their behavior. In fact, behind this "objective" fortification of networks and models which believe they can capture them, and where the whole population of analysts and expert observers believe that they capture them, there passes a wave of derision, of reversal, and of parody which is the active exploitation, the parodic enactment by the object itself of its mode of disappearance.

There is and there always will be major difficulties in analyzing the media and the whole sphere of information through the traditional categories of the philosophy of the subject: will, representation, choice, liberty, deliberation, knowledge, and desire. For it is quite obvious that they are absolutely contradicted by the media; that the subject is absolutely alienated in its sovereignty. There is a distortion of principle between the sphere of information, and the moral law which still dominates us and whose decree is: you shall know yourself, you shall know what is your will and your desire. In this respect the media and even technics and science teach us nothing at all; they have rather restricted the limits of will and representation; they have muddled the cards and deprived any subject of the disposal of his or her own body, desire, choice, and liberty.

But this idea of alienation has probably never been anything but a philosopher's ideal perspective for the use of hypothetical masses. It has probably never expressed anything but the alienation of the philosopher himself; in other words, the one who *thinks himself or herself other*. On this subject Hegel is very clear in his judgement of the *Aufklärer*, of the *philosophe* of the Enlightenment, the one who denounces the "empire of error" and despises it.

Reason wants to enlighten the superstitious mass by revealing trickery. It seeks to make it understand that it is *itself*, the mass, which enables the despot to live and not the despot which makes it live, as it believes when it obeys him. For the demystifier, credulous consciousness is mistaken *about itself*.

> The Enlightenment speaks as if juggling priests had, by sleight of hand, spirited away the being of consciousness for which they substituted something absolutely *foreign* and *other*; and, at the same time, the Enlightenment says that this foreign thing is a being of consciousness, which believes in consciousness, which trusts it, which seeks to please it.[5]

There is obviously a contradiction, says Hegel: one cannot confide oneself to an other than oneself and be mistaken about oneself, since when one confides in another, one demonstrates the certainty that one is safe with the other; in consequence, consciousness, which is said to be mystified, knows very well where it is safe and where it is not. Thus there is no need to correct a mistake which only exists in the *Aufklärer* himself. It is not *consciousness*, concludes Hegel, which takes itself for another, but it is the *Aufklärer* who takes himself for another, another than this common man whom he endeavors to make aware of his own stupidity. "When the question is asked if it is allowable to deceive a people, one must reply that the question is worthless, because it is impossible to deceive a people about itself."[6]

So it is enough to reverse the idea of a mass alienated by the media to evaluate how much the whole universe of the media, and perhaps the whole technical universe, is the result of a secret strategy of this mass which is claimed to be alienated, *of a secret form of the refusal of will*, of an in-voluntary challenge to everything which was demanded of the subject by philosophy – that is to say, to all rationality of choice and to all exercise of will, of knowledge, and of liberty.

In one way it would be no longer a question of revolution but of massive *devolution*, of a massive delegation of the power of desire, of choice, of responsibility, a delegation to apparatuses either political or intellectual, either technical or operational, to whom has devolved the duty of taking care of all of these things. A massive devolition, a massive desisting from will, but not through alienation or voluntary servitude (whose mystery, which is the modern enigma of politics, is unchanged since La Boétie because the problem is put in terms of the consent of the subject to his own slavery, which fact no philosophy will ever be able to explain). We might argue that there exists another philosophy of lack of will, a sort of radical antimetaphysics whose secret is that the masses are deeply aware that they do not have to make a decision about themselves and the world; that they do not have to wish; that they do not have to know; that they do not have to desire.

The deepest desire is perhaps to give the responsibility for one's desire to someone else. A strategy of ironic investment in the other, in the others; a strategy toward others not of appropriation but, on the contrary, of expulsion, of philosophers and people in power, an expulsion of the obligation of being responsible, of enduring philosophical, moral, and political categories. Clerks are there for that, so are professionals, the representative holders of concept and desire. Publicity, information, technics, the whole intellectual and political class are there to tell us what we want, to tell the masses what they want – and basically we thoroughly enjoy this massive transfer of responsibility because perhaps, very simply, it is not easy to want what we want; because perhaps, very simply, it is not very interesting to know what we want to decide, to desire. Who has imposed all this on us, even the need to desire, unless it be the philosophers?

Choice is a strange imperative. Any philosophy which assigns man to the exercise of his will can only plunge him in despair. For if nothing is more flattering to consciousness than to know what it wants, on the contrary nothing is more seductive to the other consciousness (the unconscious?) – the obscure and vital one which makes happiness depend on the despair of will – than not to know what it wants, to be relieved of choice and diverted from its own objective will. It is much better to rely on some insignificant or powerful instance than to be dependent on one's own will or the necessity of choice. Beau Brummel had a servant for that purpose. Before a splendid landscape dotted with beautiful lakes, he turns toward his valet to ask him: "Which lake do I prefer?"

Even publicity would find an advantage in discarding the weak hypothesis of personal will and desire. Not only do people certainly not want to be *told* what they wish, but they certainly do not want to *know* it, and it is not even sure that they want to *wish* at all. Faced with such inducements, it is their evil genius who tells them not to want anything and to rely finally on the apparatus of publicity or of information to "persuade" them, to construct a choice for them (or to rely on the political class to order things) – just as Brummel did with his servant.

Whom does this trap close on? The mass knows that it knows nothing, and it does not want to know. The mass knows that it can do nothing, and it does not want to achieve anything. It is violently reproached with this mark of stupidity and passivity. But not at all: the mass is very snobbish; it acts as Brummel did and delegates in a sovereign manner the faculty of choice to someone else by a sort of game of irresponsibility, of ironic challenge, of sovereign lack of will, of secret ruse. All the mediators (people of the media, politicians, intellectuals, all the heirs of the *philosophes* of the Enlightenment in contempt for the masses) are really only adapted to this purpose: to manage by delegation, by procuration, this tedious matter of power and of will, to unburden the masses of this transcendence for their greater pleasure and to turn it into a show for their benefit. *Vicarious*: this would be, to repeat Thorstein Veblen's concept, the status of these so-called privileged classes, whose will would be, in a way, diverted against themselves, toward the secret ends of the very masses whom they despise.

We live all that, subjectively, in the most paradoxical mode, since in us, in everyone, this mass coexists with the intelligent and voluntary being who condemns it and despises it. Nobody knows what is truly opposed to consciousness, unless it may be the repressive unconscious which psychoanalysis has imposed on us. But our true unconscious is perhaps in this ironic power of nonparticipation of nondesire, of nonknowledge, of silence, of absorption of all powers, of *expulsion* of all powers of all wills, of all knowledge, of all meaning onto representatives surrounded by a halo of derision. Our unconscious would not then consist of drives, of *pulsions*, whose destiny is sad repression; it would not be repressed at all; it would be made of this joyful *expulsion* of all the encumbering superstructures of being and of will.

We have always had a sad vision of the masses (alienated), a sad vision of the unconscious (repressed). On all our philosophy weighs this sad correlation. Even if only for a change, it would be interesting to conceive the mass, the object-mass, as the repository of a finally delusive, illusive, and allusive strategy, the correlative of an ironic, joyful, and seductive unconscious.

About the media you can sustain two opposing hypotheses: they are the strategy of power, which finds in them the means of mystifying the masses and of imposing its own truth. Or else they are the strategic territory of the ruse of the masses, who exercise in them their concrete power of the refusal of truth, of the denial of reality. Now the media are nothing else than a marvellous instrument for destabilizing the real and the true, all historical or political truth (there is thus no possible political strategy of the media: it is a contradiction in terms). And the addiction that we have for the media, the impossibility of doing without them, is a deep result of this phenomenon: it is not a result of a desire for culture, communication, and information, but of this perversion of truth and falsehood, of this destruction of meaning in the operation of the medium. The desire for a show, the desire for simulation, which is at the same time a desire for dissimulation. This is a vital reaction. It is a spontaneous, total resistance to the ultimatum of historical and political reason.

It is essential today to evaluate this double challenge: the challenge to meaning by the masses and their silence (which is not at all a passive resistance), and the challenge to meaning which comes from the media and their fascination. All the marginal alternative endeavors to resuscitate meaning are secondary to this.

Obviously there is a paradox in the inextricable entanglement of the masses and the media: is it the media that neutralize meaning and that produce the "formless" (or informed) mass; or is it the mass which victoriously resists the media by diverting or by absorbing without reply all the messages which they produce? Are the mass media on the side of power in the manipulation of the masses, or are they on the side of the masses in the liquidation of meaning, in the violence done to meaning? Is it the media that fascinate the masses, or is it the masses who divert the media into showmanship? The media toss around sense and nonsense; they manipulate in every sense at once. No one can control this process: the media are the vehicle for the simulation which belongs to the system and for the simulation which destroys the system, according to a circular logic, exactly like a Möbius strip – and it is just as well. There is no alternative to this, no logical resolution. Only a logical *exacerbation* and a catastrophic resolution. That is to say, this process has no return.

In conclusion, however, I must make one reservation. Our relationship to this system is an insoluble "double bind" – exactly that of children in their relationship to the demands of the adult world. They are at the same time told to constitute themselves as autonomous subjects, responsible, free, and conscious, and to constitute themselves as submissive objects, inert, obedient, and conformist. The child resists on all levels, and to these contradictory demands he or she replies by a double strategy. When we ask the child to be object, he or she opposes all the practices of disobedience, of revolt, of emancipation; in short, the strategy of a subject. When we ask the child to be subject, he or she opposes just as obstinately and successfully a resistance as object; that is to say, exactly the opposite: infantilism, hyperconformity, total dependence, passivity, idiocy. Neither of the two strategies has more objective value than the other. Subject resistance is today given a unilateral value and considered to be positive – in the same way as in the political sphere only the practices of liberation, of emancipation, of expression, of self-constitution as a political subject are considered worthwhile and subversive. This is to take no account of the equal and probably superior impact of all the practices of the object, the renunciation of the position of subject and of meaning – exactly the practices of the mass – which we bury with the disdainful terms *alienation* and *passivity*. The liberating practices correspond to *one* of the aspects of the system, to the constant ultimatum we are given to constitute ourselves as pure objects; but they do not correspond at all to the other demand to constitute ourselves as subjects, to liberate, to express ourselves at any price, to vote, to produce, to decide, to speak, to participate, to play the game: blackmail and ultimatum just as serious as the other, probably more serious today. To a system whose argument is oppression and repression, the strategic resistance is to demand the liberating rights of the subject. But this seems rather to reflect an earlier phase of the system; and even if we are still confronted with it, it is no longer a strategic territory: the present argument of the system is to maximize speech, to maximize the production of meaning, of participation. And so the strategic resistance is that of the refusal of meaning and the refusal of speech; or of the hyperconformist simulation of the very mechanisms of the system, which is another form of refusal by overacceptance. It is the actual strategy of the masses. This strategy does not exclude the other, but it is the winning one today, because it is the most adapted to the present phase of the system.

NOTES

1 Hans Magnus Enzensberger, "Constituents of a Theory of the Media," *New Left Review* 64 (1970) 13–36.
2 Armand Mattelart, *De l'usage des média en temps de crise* (Paris, 1979).
3 Jean Baudrillard, *A l'ombre des majorités silencieuses* (Paris, 1978).
4 Roger Caillois, *Man, Play and Games*, trans. Meyer Barash (London, 1962), ch. 8.
5 Georg Wilhelm Friedrich Hegel, *Phänomenologie des Geistes*, ed. Johannes Hoffmeister, trans. M. M. (Hamburg, 1952) pp. 391–2.
6 Hegel, ibid., p. 392.

10

Cool Memories

Male eroticism in advertising is always ridiculous. Those who argue for it as the equivalent of the 'erotic prostitution' of the female body on the public stage have no understanding of the mental play of images. The success of the erotic hallucination of the feminine (even for women) comes from the translucidity of those arses, their perfection as objects of idolatry. Only the feminine lends itself to this hallucination. The masculine is never transparent, it cannot be hallucinated. Once it appears, with its ponderousness, its affectation, the magic of the object is gone. The masculine performs poorly on the stage of illusion: whatever thinks it is a subject is always exposed to ridicule by the play of appearances.

All it can do is disappear.

If we consider the superiority of the human species, the size of its brain, its powers of thinking, language, and organization, we can say this: were there the slightest possibility that another rival or superior species might appear, on earth or elsewhere, man would use every means at his disposal to destroy it. Humans won't tolerate any other species – not even a superhuman one: they see themselves as the climax and culmination of the earthly enterprise, and they keep a vigorous check on any new intrusion in the cosmological process. Now there is no reason why this process should come to a halt with the human species, but, by universalizing itself (though only over a few thousand years) that species has more or less fixed it that an end be put to the occurrence of the world, assuming for itself all the possibilities of further evolution, reserving for itself a monopoly of natural and artificial species.

This is not the ferocity of wild and predatory animal species, for these are part of cycles, and are located within constantly reversible hierarchies: neither their appearance nor their disappearance ever puts an end to the process. Only man invents a hierarchy against which there is no possible appeal, in which he is the keystone. This is a sort of ferocity raised to the second power, a disastrous pretension.

The ferocity of man as a species is reflected in the ferocity of humanism as a way of thinking: his claim to universal transcendence and his intolerance of other types of thought is the very model of a superior racism.

Whilst they are hardly to be seen in real life these days, the most intense passions continue to figure in our dreams. Are these then a reserve of fresh and timeless energy, running beneath the stages of life (and perhaps reaching beyond the mishap that is death)? Or is this freshness not merely the hallucination of a jaded desire? In other words: are there two lines to our lives, the one of a non-biological, immemorial youth, which we experience in dreams, and the other an organic line of life and death, of duration and of remembrance, with which we identify our pale and mortal existence? Could there be two fundamental sequences and no relation between them? Or is the first simply the projection of the second, its hallucinatory discourse, as, deep down, psychoanalysis argues?

I am for the first hypothesis: we have two existences, each of which is wholly original and independent of the other (it is not a case of a psychological splitting). Neither existence can be used to interpret the other – which is why psychoanalysis is futile.

There is certainly some interplay between body and mind. The weaker the body, the more apparent the organic wretchedness or obsolescence of that machine, the freer and the more adventurous one's thinking becomes. It too partakes of that sort of timeless youth which has nothing whatever to do with being in the prime of life. Thinking lives on neither health nor vitality, but on lucidity and pride, and the decaying of the body stimulates that lucidity and that pride.

There is nothing worse than this obligation to research, to seek out references and documentation that has taken up residence in the realm of thought and which is the mental and obsessional equivalent of hygiene. In the 'intellectual field', as it is so aptly called, one has to plough the furrow of the concept. It is true that we no longer have a culture of leisure, in which thought and writing were violent and pleasurable. And our leisure now is no more than the charnel-house where dead time is born.

The anxiety specific to leisure and the Coast. Too many forms of natural beauty artificially brought together. Too many villas, too many flowers. Villegiatura, nomenklatura: the same struggle. The same artificial privilege, whether it be that of the political bureaucracy or the luxuriance of lifestyle. Nature putrefied by leisure, purged of all barbarity, sickeningly comfortable – one day perhaps this dream climate, this heatwave of luxury will explode into one last forest fire.

The book must break up so as to resemble the ever increasing number of extreme situations. It must break up to resemble the flashes of holograms. It must roll around on itself like the snake on the mountains of the heavens. It must turn all the figures of style on their head. It must fade away as it is being read. It must laugh in its sleep. It must turn in its grave.

If there is a species which is more maltreated than children, then it must be their toys, which they handle in an incredibly off-hand manner (how long will it be before someone starts a society for the protection of battered and maltreated objects?). Toys are thus the end point in that long chain in which all the conditions of despotic high-handedness are in play which enchain beings one to another, from one species to another – from cruel divinities to their sacrificial victims, from masters to slaves, from adults to children, and from children to their objects. This is actually the only strong symbolic chain, the one through which a victim of the whim of a superior power passes it on to an inferior species, the whole process ending with someone taking it out on a powerless simulacrum, like a toy – and beginning no doubt with an all-powerful simulacrum, like the masked divinities which men themselves invent to justify this wretched chain.

The mind's real power (what else can we call it?) is its ability to distinguish a particular nerve, fibre or infinitesimal articulation of the body and invest or disinvest it at will (a sudden thought produces pain in an unknown muscle, or makes a particular line of the face smile, but not some other). The mind can exert itself upon a particular fraction of the body which cannot be located anatomically, as it can on a particular particle of language which cannot be located linguistically, or a particular fraction of time which cannot be located chronologically.

We end up doing everything for reasons of mental hygiene. Thinking out of mental hygiene, to keep in good shape intellectually. Screwing out of mental hygiene, to keep in good shape sexually. Socializing out of mental hygiene to keep in good shape operationally. All our activities are attuned to this hygienic objective. The modern person, condemned to obsolescence like a piece of military hardware, must nonetheless remain in a functioning state. Why? For no reason. For his mental health. Isn't the production system just a vast apparatus that we keep going for the sake of the workers' mental health?

Beautiful as the sensual panorama of discrimination
Beautiful as the sensual illusion of the orifices of the body
Beautiful as the aesthetic division of the work of households
Beautiful as the succession of phases of the light of day

The proximity of bodies in the dark, the tactile promiscuity of objects, the confusion of desires in dreams – these are the fundamental qualities, and they are qualities of the night.

A study of the differential resistance of the skin of the buttocks of the two sexes to blood pressure – there's a fine subject for research in a sterile and functional future.

On the truth of things, three hypotheses:

- That things are as they are makes them true (this is the empirical version).
- That they cannot be other than as they are does not prevent them from being true (though it is not really clear why: this is the confused and paradoxical version).
- That they cannot but be as they are is what prevents them from being true. The necessity of being such takes from them the ring of truth (this is the negative and subtle version).

The seal of secrecy is a fine metaphor. The secret is in fact that which is sealed, that which circulates beneath the seal of appearances and not beneath the sign of communication (not even beneath the opposite sign of the unsaid and silence). The secret is what has no need of being said and is therefore the most obvious of things and shines forth in full daylight, needing no other form of expression.

One way of dying is to make your death alter the state of things in such a way that you no longer have any reason to be a part of it. Thus death can have the effect of a prophetic disappearance. Such were the deaths of Barthes and Lacan, I believe: the world has taken another direction since, in which these subtle figures would no longer have had any meaning. The death of Sartre, by contrast, left the world unchanged and seems an ineluctable, but insignificant event. Before dying, he was already to live in a world that was no longer his own.

So far as existence is concerned, as Ajar[1] would say, it needs to be taken in charge by someone. No one can be expected to bear the responsibility for their own life. This Christian and modern idea is a vain and arrogant proposition. Moreover, it is a groundless utopian notion. The individual would have to be able to transform himself into the vestal, or the slave, of his identity, control all his circuits and all the circuits of the world which meet in his genes, nerves and thoughts. An unprecedented state of servitude. Who would wish to have salvation at such a price?

It is so much more human to put one's fate, one's desire, one's will into the hands of another. Circulation of responsibilities, declension of wills, perpetual transfer of forms. Apart from this subtle path, which is attested to by a great many cultures, there is only the totalitarian path of a collective assumption.

The old form of voluntary servitude was that of free men using that freedom paradoxically to turn themselves into serfs. The new voluntary servitude is that of men obeying the demand that they be free.

What you look for in travel is neither discovery nor exchange, but a gentle deterritorialization, being taken in charge by the journey itself, and therefore by absence. In the metallic vectors which transcend the meridians, the oceans and the poles, absence takes on a carnal quality. The secrecy of hiding away in one's private life gives way to annihilation by latitude and longitude. But in the end the body wearies of not knowing where it is, whilst the mind is excited by that absence, as if by a lively, subtle quality that is its own. The body is woven of too many ties of blood and flesh. It resists this disfiguring of familiar space in the anamorphosis of travel.

All things considered, what we look for in other people is perhaps the same gentle deterritorialization we look for in travel. The temptation of exile in the desire of another and of journey across that desire come to be substituted for one's own desire and for discovery. Often looks and amorous gestures already have the distance of exile, language expatriates itself into words which are afraid to mean, the body is like a hologram, gentle on the eyes and soft to the touch, and can thus easily be striated in all directions by desire like an aerial space. We move circumspectly within our emotions, passing from one to another, on a mental planet made up of convolutions. And we bring back the same transparent memories from our excesses and passions as we do from our travels.

The more advanced life-simulation technology becomes, the more the question of the soul intervenes, perversely, as an accident. Everything becomes transformed into a pure, incessant production of accidents. From the moment we leave the world of substance and come to live in that of accident, perversion becomes normal and constitutive.

She disliked the fact that men would always want to take a woman there-and-then, without delay... One day, she gets her own back. She does not take the lift, but goes up the stairs instead and undresses floor by floor – her sweater, her skirt, her shoes, her watch, finally, just outside the door, her knickers; then she rings the bell. When I open the door she is standing there completely naked, like a dream, with her raincoat over her arm. The most beautiful present she could give me (but also, what artifice there is in immodesty!).

What she did not say was that she wanted to be undressed slowly with all the ceremonial that should go into unveiling a perfect body, which would only finally be penetrated with extreme politeness, almost out of consideration for the difference between the sexes, a delicate seduction which women dream of as intensely as men dream of the opposite.

Right from the start our relationship had gone astray over this divergence. Sometimes she had imposed her dream of sensual attentiveness. This time, she was giving herself to me – far beyond my own wildest dreams. At least she was pretending to. For, renouncing the game of femininity, she it was once again who was overturning the rules.

They say other species have stopped short, and that only the human species, the humanoid branch, has made its definitive breakthrough. In fact while all the others persevered in their specific forms and ended up disappearing genetically, thus leaving evolution to run its course, only the human species succeeded in surpassing itself in the simulacrum of itself – in disappearing genetically to resuscitate artificially. By perpetuating itself in a world of clones and electronic prostheses (perfect in so far as they will have eliminated every potential species, including humanity), man will thus, in a definitive act, have wiped out the natural genesis of things.

Contact with the men who wield power and authority still leaves an intangible sense of repulsion. It's very like being in close proximity to faecal matter, the faecal embodiment of something unmentionable and you wonder what it is made of and where it acquired its historically sacred character. Why this feeling of loathing for the politician? Is it the impression of being artificially subjected to a will that is even more stupid than your own and which, by its very function, has to be crude? How can the decision-making function be performed without simplifying the mechanisms of thought?

Political charisma is precisely not that gracious charisma which emanates from the irresistible power of a pure object, such as the power of a woman, but an ungracious will which derives its power and its glory from voluntary servitude. This is true of all institutions, the military, the clerical, the medical, and more recently the psychoanalytic, but it is particularly so in politics which remains the most striking hallucination of all the weaknesses of the will.

One may justify the existence of men in power in many different ways. Yet power remains a pernicious thing for what justifies it is inexpiable.

Fragility, which belongs to the realm of appearances, is to be preferred to the fractal which is merely the quality of a mathematical object.

It is exciting to hear one of your fondest ideas formulated in one fell swoop, better than you could have done it yourself. You feel no intellectual jealousy at seeing yourself outstripped in this way. You only feel jealous when you are overtaken by your shadow.

Two bodies side by side, which are not asleep and know it: a strange kind of communication sets in between them, formed of respect for simulated sleep, and yet it needs to betray itself by some furtive sign – a breathing pattern which is not that of real sleep or movements which are not those of a dreaming body. Neither, however, wants to break the spell. It is a conspiracy in the dark, an emotional conspiracy filled with delicious tension.

There has been much discussion of the uninterpretable answer to the question: 'are you lying?' But ask someone next to you, very softly so as not to wake him: 'are you asleep?' If he replies that he is, then that makes him a liar. But he can reply by pretending to be asleep, which is not actually lying, but pretending to lie. There is a big difference, since this is a lovers' game. The question itself is a lovers' game because it assumes the partner is not asleep while making every effort not to wake him. Besides, these are the same questions: do you love me? are you lying to me? are you asleep? And the reply – yes, I love you, yes, I'm lying, yes, I'm asleep – is equally paradoxical. But it is not untruthful. It simply comes from another world which is not the truth of the first. 'Yes, I'm asleep. Yes, I'm lying. Yes, I love you' all these answers reflect a marvellous somnambulism and, all in all, a very clear grasp of the relations we establish with reality when we are sleeping, lying or in love.

NOTE

1   The novelist Romain Gary's alter-ego. [Trans.]

11

The Gulf War Did Not Take Place

The Gulf War will not take place

From the beginning, we knew that this war would never happen. After the hot war (the violence of conflict), after the cold war (the balance of terror), here comes the dead war – the unfrozen cold war – which leaves us to grapple with the corpse of war and the necessity of dealing with this decomposing corpse which nobody from the Gulf has managed to revive. America, Saddam Hussein and the Gulf powers are fighting over the corpse of war.

War has entered into a definitive crisis. It is too late for the (hot) WW III: this has already taken place, distilled down the years into the Cold War. There will be no other. It might have been supposed that the defection of the Eastern Bloc would have opened up new spaces of freedom for war by unlocking deterrence. Nothing of the sort, since deterrence has not come to an end, on the contrary. In the past it functioned as reciprocal deterrence between the two blocs on the basis of a virtual excess of the means of destruction. Today it functions all the more effectively as self-deterrence, total self-deterrence up to and including the self-dissolution of the Eastern Bloc, the profound self-deterrence of American power and of Western power in general, paralysed by its own strength and incapable of assuming it in the form of relations of force.

This is why the Gulf War will not take place. It is neither reassuring nor comforting that it has become bogged in interminable suspense. In this sense, the gravity of the non-event in the Gulf is even greater than the event of war: it corresponds to the highly toxic period which affects a rotting corpse and which can cause nausea and powerless stupor. Here again, our symbolic defences are weak: the mastery of the end of war escapes us and we live all this in a uniform shameful indifference, just like the hostages.

Non-war is characterised by that degenerate form of war which includes hostage manipulation and negotiation. Hostages and black-mail are the purest products of deterrence. The hostage has taken the place of the warrior. He has become the principal actor, the simulacral protagonist, or rather, in his pure inaction, the protagoniser of non-war. The warriors bury themselves in the desert leaving only hostages to occupy the stage, including all of us as information hostages on the world media stage. The hostage is the phantom actor, the extra who occupies the powerless stage of war. Today, it is the hostage at the strategic site, tomorrow the hostage as Christmas present, as exchange value and liquidity. Fantastic degradation of that which was the very figure of impossible exchange. With Saddam Hussein, even that strong value has weakened and become the symbol of weak war. Saddam has made himself the capitalist of hostage value; after the market in slaves and proletarians, the vulgar merchant of the hostage market. Taking the place of the warrior's challenge, hostage value has become synonymous with the debility of war. We are all hostages of media intoxication, induced to believe in the war just as we were once led to believe in the revolution in Romania, and con-fined to the simulacrum of war as though confined to quarters. We are already all strategic hostages *in situ*; our site is the screen on which we are virtually bombarded day by day, even while serving as exchange value. In this sense, the grotesque vaudeville played by Saddam Hussein is a diversion, at once a diversion of both war and international terrorism. His soft terrorism will at least have put an end to the hard terrorism of Palestinians and others, thereby showing him to be in this as in many other respects the perfect accomplice of the West.

This impossibility of proceeding to the act, this absence of strategy, implies the triumph of blackmail as strategy (in the case of Iran, there was still a challenge; with Saddam there is only blackmail). Saddam Hussein's abjection lies in his having vulgarised everything: religious challenge has become fake holywar, the sacrificial hostage a commer-cial hostage, the violent refusal of the West a nationalistic scam and war an impossible comedy. But we have helped him to do this. By allowing him to believe that he had won the war against Iran, we drove him towards the mirage of a victory against the West – this mercenary's revolt is indeed the only ironic and pleasing trait of this whole story.

We are in neither a logic of war nor a logic of peace but in a logic of deterrence which has wound its way inexorably through forty years of cold war to a denouement in our current events; a logic of weak events, to which belong those in Eastern Europe as well as the Gulf War. Peripeteias of an anorexic history or an anorexic war which can no longer devour the enemy because it is incapable of conceiving the enemy as worthy of being challenged or annihilated – and God knows Saddam Hussein is worthy of neither challenge nor annihilation – and thus devours itself. It is the de-intensified state of war, that of the right to war under the green light of the UN and with an abundance of precautions and concessions. It is the bellicose equivalent of safe sex: make war like love with a condom! On the Richter scale, the Gulf War would not even reach two or three. The build-up is unreal, as though the fiction of an earthquake were created by manipulating the measuring instruments. It is neither the strong form nor the degree zero of war, but the weak or phthisical degree, the asymptotic form which allows a brush with war but no encounter, the transparent degree which allows war to be seen from the depths of the darkroom.

We should have been suspicious about the disappearance of the declaration of war, the disappearance of the symbolic passage to the act, which already presaged the disappearance of the end of hostilities, then of the distinction between winners and losers (the winner readily becomes the hostage of the loser: the Stockholm syndrome), then of operations themselves. Since it never began, this war is therefore interminable. By dint of dreaming of pure war, of an orbital war purged of all local and political peripeteias, we have fallen into soft war, into the virtual impossibility of war which translates into the paltry fantasia where adversaries compete in de-escalation, as though the irruption or the event of war had become obscene and insupportable, no longer sustainable, like every real event moreover. Everything is therefore transposed into the virtual, and we are confronted with a virtual apocalypse, a hegemony ultimately much more dangerous than real apocalypse.

The most widespread belief is in a logical progression from virtual to actual, according to which no available weapon will not one day be used and such a concentration of force cannot but lead to conflict. However, this is an Aristotelian logic which is no longer our own. Our virtual has definitively overtaken the actual and we must be content with this extreme virtuality which, unlike the Aristotelian, deters any passage to action. We are no longer in a logic of the passage from virtual to actual but in a hyperrealist logic of the deterrence of the real by the virtual.

In this process, the hostages are once again revealing. Extracted like molecules in an experimental process, then distilled one by one in the exchange, it is their virtual death that is at issue, not their real death. Moreover, they never die: at best they disappear. There will never be a monument to the unknown hostage, everyone is too ashamed of him: the collective shame which attaches to the hostage reflects the absolute degradation of real hostility (war) into virtual hospitality (Saddam Hussein's "guests").

The passage to action suffers widespread infamy: it supposedly corresponds to a brutal lifting of repression, thus to a psychotic process. It seems that this obsession with the passage to action today governs all our behaviour: obsession with every real, with every real event, with every real violence, with every pleasure which is too real. Against this obsession with the real we have created a gigantic apparatus of simulation which allows us to pass to the act "in vitro" (this is true even of procreation). We prefer the exile of the virtual, of which television is the universal mirror, to the catastrophe of the real.

War has not escaped this virtualisation which is like a surgical operation, the aim of which is to present a face-lifted war, the cosmetically treated spectre of its death, and its even more deceptive televisual subterfuge (as we saw at Timisoara). Even the military has lost the privilege of use value, the privilege of real war. Deterrence has passed by that way and it spares no-one. No more than the politicians, the military personnel do not know what to make of their real function, their function of death and destruction. They are pledged to the decoy of war as the others are to the decoy of power.

PS To demonstrate the impossibility of war just at the moment when it must take place, when the signs of its occurrence are accumulating, is a stupid gamble. But it would have been even more stupid not to seize the opportunity.

The Gulf War: is it really taking place?

We may well ask. On the available evidence (absence of images and profusion of commentary), we could suppose an immense promotional exercise like that one which once advertised a brand-name (GARAP) whose product never became known. Pure promotion which enjoyed an immense success because it belonged to pure speculation.

The war is also pure and speculative, to the extent that we do not see the real event that it could be or that it would signify. It reminds us of that recent suspense advertisement: today I take off the top, tomorrow I take off the bottom; today I unleash virtual war, tomorrow I unleash real war. In the background, a third advertisement in which an avaricious and lubricious banker says: your money appeals to me. This sadly celebrated advertisement is reincarnated by Saddam Hussein saying to the West: your power appeals to me (as they rushed to palm off a good share of it to him); then to the Arabs, with the same hypocrisy: your religious war appeals to me (as they rushed to put all their money on him).

In this manner, the war makes its way by promotion and speculation, including the use of hostages transformed into marketing ploys, and in the absence of any clarification of plans, balance sheets, losses or operations. No enterprise would survive such uncertainty, except precisely speculative risk management, otherwise known as the strategy of turning a profit from the worst, in other words, war (= Highly Profitable Senseless Project or HPSP). War itself has taken this speculative turn: it is highly profitable but uncertain. It can collapse from one day to the next.

Nevertheless, from this point onwards the promotional advantages are fabulous. Defeated or not, Saddam is assured of an unforgettable and charismatic label. Victorious or not, American armaments will have acquired an unequalled technological label. And the sumptuary expenditure in material is already equivalent to that of a real war, even if it has not taken place.

We have still not left the virtual war, in other words a sophisticated although often laughable build-up against the backdrop of a global indeterminacy of will to make war, even in Saddam's case. Hence the absence of images – which is neither accidental nor due to censorship but to the impossibility of illustrating this indeterminacy of the war.

Promotional, speculative, virtual: this war no longer corresponds to Clausewitz's formula of politics pursued by other means, it rather amounts to *the absence of politics pursued by other means*. Non-war is a terrible test of the status and the uncertainty of politics, just as a stock market crash (the speculative universe) is a crucial test of the economy and of the uncertainty of economic aims, just as any event whatever is a terrible test of the uncertainty and the aims of information. Thus "real time" information loses itself in a completely unreal space, finally furnishing the images of pure, useless, instantaneous television where its primordial function irrupts, namely that of filling a vacuum, blocking up the screen hole through which escapes the substance of events.

Nor is promotion the pursuit of the economy by other means. On the contrary, it is the pure product of uncertainty with regard to the rational aims of production. This is why it has become a relentless function, the emptiness of which fills our screens to the extent of the absence of any economic finality or rationality. This is why it competes victoriously with the war on our screens, both alternating in the same virtual credit of the image.

The media promote the war, the war promotes the media, and advertising competes with the war. Promotion is the most thick-skinned parasite in our culture. It would undoubtedly survive a nuclear conflict. It is our Last Judgement. But it is also like a biological function: it devours our substance, but it also allows us to metabolise what we absorb, like a parasitic plant or intestinal flora, it allows us to turn the world and the violence of the world into a consumable substance. So, war or promotion?

The war, along with the fake and presumptive warriors, generals, experts and television presenters we see speculating about it all through the day, watches itself in a mirror: am I pretty enough, am I operational enough, am I spectacular enough, am I sophisticated enough to make an entry onto the historical stage? Of course, this anxious interrogation increases the uncertainty with respect to its possible irruption. And this uncertainty invades our screens like a real oil slick, in the image of that blind sea bird stranded on a beach in the Gulf, which will remain the symbol-image of what we all are in front of our screens, in front of that sticky and unintelligible event.

Unlike earlier wars, in which there were political aims either of conquest or domination, what is at stake in this one is war itself: its status, its meaning, its future. It is beholden not to have an objective but to prove its very existence (this crisis of identity affects the existence of us all). In effect, it has lost much of its credibility. Who, apart from the Arab masses, is still capable of believing in it and becoming inflamed by it? Nevertheless, the spectacular drive of war remains intact. In the absence of the (greatly diminished) will to power, and the (problematic) will to knowledge, there remains today the widespread will to spectacle, and with it the obstinate desire to preserve its spectre or fiction (this is the fate of religions: they are no longer believed, but the disincarnate practice remains). Can war still be saved?

Certainly, Iran and Iraq did as much as they could to save the fiction of murderous, fratricidal, sacrificial and interminable (1914 style) war. But they were savages and that war from another period proved nothing with regard to the status and the possibility of a modern war. WW III did not take place and yet we are already beyond it, as though in the utopian space of a post-war-which-did-not-take-place, and it is in the suspense created by this non-place that the present confrontations unfold and the question is posed: can a war still take place?

This one is perhaps only a test, a desperate attempt to see whether war is still possible.

Empty war: it brings to mind those games in World Cup football which often had to be decided by penalties (sorry spectacle), because of the impossibility of forcing a decision. As though the players punished themselves by means of "penalties" for not having been able to play and take the match in full battle. We might as well have begun with the penalties and dispensed with the game and its sterile stand-off. So with the war: it could have begun at the end and spared us the forced spectacle of this unreal war where nothing is extreme and which, whatever the outcome, will leave behind the smell of undigested programming, and the entire world irritated as though after an unsuccessful copulation.

It is a war of excesses (of means, of material, etc.), a war of shedding or purging stocks, of experimental deployment, of liquidation and firesale, along with the display of future ranges of weaponry. A war between excessive, superabundant and overequipped societies (Iraq included), committed both to waste (including human waste) and the necessity of getting rid of it. Just as the waste of time nourishes the hell of leisure, so technological wastes nourish the hell of war. Wastes which incarnate the secret violence of this society, uncoerced and non-degradable defecation. The renowned American stocks of WW II surplus, which appeared to us as luxury, have become a suffocating global burden, and war functions well within its possibilities in this role of purgative and expenditure.

If the critical intellectual is in the process of disappearing, it seems by contrast that his phobia of the real and of action has been distilled throughout the sanguineous and cerebral network of our institutions. In this sense, the entire world including the military is caught up in a process of intellectualisation.

See them become confused in explanations, outdo themselves in justifications and lose themselves in technical details (war drifts slowly into technological mannerism) or in the deontology of a pure electronic war without hitches: these are aesthetes speaking, postponing settlement dates into the interminable and decisions into the undecidable. Their war-processors, their radars, their lasers and their screens render the passage to war as futile and impossible as the use of a word-processor renders futile and impossible the passage to the act of writing, because it removes from it in advance any dramatic uncertainty.

The generals also exhaust their artificial intelligence in correcting their scenario, polishing their war script so much that they sometimes make errors of manipulation and lose the plot. The famous philosophical épochè has become universal, on the screens as much as on the field of battle.

Should we applaud the fact that all these techniques of war-processing culminate in the elision of the duration and the violence of war? Only eventually, for the indefinite delay of the war is itself heavy with deadly consequences in all domains.

By virtue of having been anticipated in all its details and exhausted by all the scenarios, this war ends up resembling the hero of *Italien des Roses* (Richard Bohringer in the film by Charles Matton), who hesitates to dive from the top of a building for an hour and a half, before a crowd at first hanging on his movements, then disappointed and overcome by the suspense, exactly as we are today by the media blackmail and the illusion of war. It is as though it had taken place ten times already: why would we want it to take place again? It is the same in *Italien des Roses*: we know that his imaginary credit is exhausted and that he will not jump, and in the end nobody gives a damn whether he jumps or not because the real event is already left behind.

This is the problem with anticipation. Is there still a chance that something which has been meticulously programmed will occur? Does a truth which has been meticulously demonstrated still have a chance of being true? When too many things point in the same direction, when the objective reasons pile up, the effect is reversed. Thus everything which points to war is ambiguous: the build-up of force, the play of tension, the concentration of weapons, even the green light from the UN. Far from reinforcing the probability of the conflict, these function as a preventative accumulation, as a substitution for and diversion from the transition to war.

Virtual for five months, the war will shortly enter its terminal phase, according to the rule which says that what never began ends without having taken place. The profound indeterminacy of this war stems from the fact of its being both terminated in advance and interminable. The virtual succeeds itself – accidents aside, which could only be the irruption of the other in the field. But no one wants to hear talk of the other. Ultimately, the undecidability of the war is grounded in the disappearance of alterity, of primitive hostility, and of the enemy. War has become a celibate machine.

Thanks to this war, the extraordinary confusion in the Arab world is in the process of infecting the West – just revenge. In return, we try desperately to unify and stabilise them in order to exercise better control. It is an historic arm-wrestle: who will stabilise the other before being destabilised themselves? Confronted by the virulent and ungraspable instability of the Arabs and of Islam, whose defence is that of the hysteric in all his versatility, the West is in the process of demonstrating that its values can no longer lay claim to any universality than that (extremely fragile) of the UN.

Faced with the Western logic of under-compensation (the West tends towards the euphemisation and even the inhibition of its power), the Oriental logic of Saddam responds with over-compensation. Although far from having proved himself against Iran, he attacks the West. He operates beyond the reach of his own forces, there where only God can help him. He undertakes an act of magical provocation and it is left to God, or some other predestined connection, to do the rest (this was in principle the role allotted to the Arab masses).

By contrast, through a kind of egocentric generosity or stupidity, the Americans can only imagine and combat an enemy in their own image. They are at once both missionaries and converts of their own way of life, which they triumphally project onto the world. They cannot imagine the Other, nor therefore personally make war upon it. What they make war upon is the alterity of the other, and what they want is to reduce that alterity, to convert it or failing that to annihilate it if it proves irreducible (the Indians). They cannot imagine that conversion and repentance, borne by their own good will, should have no echo in the other, and they are literally disturbed when they see Saddam playing with them and refusing to accede to their reasons. This is perhaps why they have decided to annihilate him, not out of hatred or calculation, but for the crime of felony, treachery, malevolent will and trickery (exactly as with the Indians).

For their part, the Israelis have no such tenderness. They see the Other in all its bare adversity without illusions or scruples. The Other, the Arab, is unconvertible, his alterity is without appeal; it must not be changed, it must be beaten down and subjugated. In doing so, however, while they may not understand they at least recognise it. The Americans, for their part, understand nothing and do not even recognise this fact. It is not an important match which is being played out in the Gulf, between Western hegemony and the challenge from the rest of the world. It is the West in conflict with itself, by means of an interposed mercenary, after having been in conflict with Islam (Iran), also by means of an interposed Saddam. Saddam remains the fake enemy. At first the champion of the West against Islam, then the champion of Islam against the West. In both cases he is a traitor to his own cause since, even more than the few thousand incidental Westerners, it is the Arab masses that he holds hostage, captures for his own profit and immobilises in their suicidal enthusiasm. It is moreover towards Christmas, at the very moment when he frees the hostages (thereby skilfully stroking the Westerners with the same demagogy that he strokes the children in front of the TV), that he launches his call to the Arab people on the holy war.

It is thus a mistake to think that he would contribute to the unification of the Arab world and to honour him for that. In fact, he only did it to hoodwink them, to make them work for him, to deceive them once again and to render them powerless. People like him are necessary from time to time in order to channel irruptive forces. They serve as a poultice or an artificial purgative. It is a form of deterrence, certainly a Western strategy, but one of which Saddam, in his pride and his stupidity, is a perfect executant. He who loves decoys so much is himself no more than a decoy and his elimination can only demystify this war by putting an end to that objective complicity which itself is no decoy.

But, for this very reason, is the West determined to eliminate him? The exhibition of American prisoners on Iraqi TV. Once more the politics of blackmail, of hostages, the humiliation of the USA by the spectacle of those "repentants" forced to avow symbolically American dishonour. Our own as well, we whom the screens submit to the same violence, that of the battered, manipulated and powerless prisoner, that of forced voyeurism in response to the forced exhibitionism of the images. Along with the spectacle of these prisoners or these hostages, the screens offer us the spectacle of our powerlessness. In a case such as this, information exactly fulfills its role which is to convince us of our own abjection by the obscenity of what is seen. The forced perversion of the look amounts to the avowal of our own dishonour, and makes repentants of us as well.

That the Americans should have allowed themselves to be ridiculed without departing from their own program and war indicates a weakness in their symbolic detonator. Humiliation remains the worst kind of test, arrogance (Saddam's) the worst kind of conduct, blackmail the worst kind of relationship and the acceptance of blackmail the worst kind of dishonour. The fact that this symbolic violence, worse than any sexual violence, should finally have been withstood without flinching testifies to the depth or the unconscious character of Western masochism. This is the rule of the American way of life: *nothing personal*! And they make war in the same manner: pragmatically and not symbolically. They thereby expose themselves to deadly situations which they are unable to confront. But perhaps they accept this in expiation of their power, in an equivalence which is after all symbolic?

Two intense images, two or perhaps three scenes which all concern disfigured forms or costumes which correspond to the masquerade of this war: the CNN journalists with their gas masks in the Jerusalem studios; the drugged and beaten prisoners repenting on the screen of Iraqi TV; and perhaps that seabird covered in oil and pointing its blind eyes towards the Gulf sky. It is a masquerade of information: branded faces delivered over to the prostitution of the image, the image of an unintelligible distress. No images of the field of battle, but images of masks, of blind or defeated faces, images of falsification. It is not war taking place over there but the disfiguration of the world.

There is a profound scorn in the kind of "clean" war which renders the other powerless without destroying its flesh, which makes it a point of honour to disarm and neutralise but not to kill. In a sense, it is worse than the other kind of war because it spares life. It is like humiliation: by taking less than life it is worse than taking life. There is undoubtedly a political error here, in so far as it is acceptable to be defeated but not to be put out of action. In this manner, the Americans inflict a particular insult by not making war on the other but simply eliminating him, the same as one would by not bargaining over the price of an object and thereby refusing any personal relationship with the vendor. The one whose price you accept without discussion despises you. The one whom you disarm without seeing is insulted and must be avenged. There is perhaps something of this in the presentation of those humiliated captives on television. It is in a sense to say to America: you who do not wish to see us, we will show you what you are like.

Just as the psychical or the screen of the psyche transforms every illness into a symptom (there is no organic illness which does not find its meaning elsewhere, in an interpretation of the ailment on another level: all the symptoms pass through a sort of black box in which the psychic images are jumbled and inverted, the illness becomes reversible, ungraspable, escaping any form of realistic medicine), so war, when it has been turned into information, ceases to be a realistic war and becomes a virtual war, in some way symptomatic. And just as everything psychical becomes the object of interminable speculation, so everything which is turned into information becomes the object of endless speculation, the site of total uncertainty. We are left with the symptomatic reading on our screens of the effects of the war, or the effects of discourse about the war, or completely speculative strategic evaluations which are analogous to those evaluations of opinion provided by polls. In this manner, we have gone in a week from 20% to 50% and then to 30% destruction of Iraqi military potential. The figure fluctuates exactly like the fortunes of the stock market. "The land offensive is anticipated today, tomorrow, in a few hours, in any case sometime this week... the climatic conditions are ideal for a confrontation, etc." Whom to believe? There is nothing to believe. We must learn to read symptoms as symptoms, and television as the hysterical symptom of a war which has nothing to do with its critical mass. Moreover, it does not seem to have to reach its critical mass but remains in its inertial phase, while the implosion of the apparatus of information along with the accompanying tendency of the rate of information to fall seems to reinforce the implosion of war itself, with its accompanying tendency of the rate of confrontation to fall.

Information is like an unintelligent missile which never finds its target (nor, unfortunately, its anti-missile!), and therefore crashes anywhere or gets lost in space on an unpredictable orbit in which it eternally revolves as junk.

Information is only ever an erratic missile with a fuzzy destination which seeks its target but is drawn to every decoy – it is itself a decoy, in fact it scatters all over the environs and the result is mostly nil. The utopia of a targetted promotion or targetted information is the same as that of the targetted missile: it knows not where it lands and perhaps its mission is not to land but, like the missile, essentially to have been launched (as its name indicates). In fact, the only impressive images of missiles, rockets or satellites are those of the launch. It is the same with promotions or five year plans: the campaign launch is what counts, the impact or the end results are so uncertain that one frequently hears no more about them. The entire effect is in the programming, the success is that of the virtual model. Consider the Scuds: their strategic effectiveness is nil and their only (psychological) effect lies in the fact that Saddam succeeded in launching them.

The fact that the production of decoys has become an important branch of the war industry, just as the production of placebos has become an important branch of the medical industry and forgery a flourishing branch of the art industry – not to mention the fact that information has become a privileged branch of industry as such – all of this is a sign that we have entered a deceptive world in which an entire culture labours assiduously at its counterfeit. This also means that it no longer harbours any illusion about itself.

It all began with the leitmotif of precision, of surgical, mathematical and punctual efficacy, which is another way of not recognising the enemy as such, just as lobotomy is a way of not recognising madness as such. And then all that technical virtuosity finished up in the most ridiculous uncertainty. The isolation of the enemy by all kinds of electronic interference creates a sort of barricade behind which he becomes invisible. He also becomes "stealthy," and his capacity for resistance becomes indeterminable. In annihilating him at a distance and as it were by transparency, it becomes impossible to discern whether or not he is dead.

The idea of a clean war, like that of a clean bomb or an intelligent missile, this whole war conceived as a technological extrapolation of the brain is a sure sign of madness. It is like those characters in Hieronymus Bosch with a glass bell or a soap bubble around their head as a sign of their mental debility. A war enclosed in a glass coffin, like Snow White, purged of any carnal contamination or warrior's passion. A clean war which ends up in an oil slick.

The French supplied the planes and the nuclear power stations, the Russians the tanks, the English the underground bunkers and runways, the Germans the gas, the Dutch the gas masks, while the

Italians supplied the decoy equivalents of everything – tanks, bunkers, inflatable bombers, missiles with artificial thermal emissions, etc. Before so many marvels, one is drawn to compete in diabolical imagination: why not false gas masks for the Palestinians? Why not put the hostages at decoy strategic sites, a fake chemical factory for example?

Has a French plane been downed? The question becomes burning, it is our honour which is at stake. That would constitute a proof of our involvement, and the Iraqis appear to take a malicious pleasure in denying it (perhaps they have a more accurate idea of our involvement?). Whatever the situation, it will be necessary here too to set up decoys, simulated losses and *trompe l'oeil* victims (as with the fake destruction of civic buildings in Timişoara or Baghdad).

A war of high technological concentration but poor definition. Perhaps it has gone beyond its critical mass by too strong a concentration?

Fine illustration of the communication schema in which emitter and receiver on opposite sides of the screen, never connect with each other. Instead of messages, it is missiles and bombs which fly from one side to the other, but any dual or personal relation is altogether absent. Thus an aerial attack on Iraq may be read in terms of coding, decoding and feedback (in this case, very bad: we cannot even know what we have destroyed). This explains the tolerance of the Israelis: they have only been hit by abstract projectiles, namely missiles. The least live bombing attack on Israel would have provoked immediate retaliation.

Communication is also a clean relation: in principle, it excludes any violent or personal affect. It is strange to see this disaffection, this profound indifference to one another, played out at the very heart of violence and war.

The fact that the undetectable Stealth bombers should have begun the war by aiming at decoys and undoubtedly destroying fake objectives, that the Secret Services (also "furtive") should have been so mistaken in so many ways about the realities of Iraqi weaponry, and the strategists so wrong about the effects of the intensive electronic war, all testifies to the illusionism of force once it is no longer measured against an adversary but against its abstract operation alone. All the generals, admirals and other meretricious experts should be sent to an inflatable strategic site, to see whether these decoys wouldn't in fact attract a real bomb on their heads.

Conversely, the Americans' innocence in admitting their mistake (declaring five months later that the Iraqi forces are almost intact while they themselves are not ready to attack) and all that counter-propaganda which adds to the confusion would be moving if it did not testify to the same strategic idiocy as the triumphal declarations at the outset, and did not further take us for complicit witnesses of this suspicious sincerity of the kind which says: you see, we tell you everything. We can always give credit to the Americans for knowing how to exploit their failures by means of a sort of *trompe l'oeil* candour.

A UN bedtime story: the UN awoke (or was awakened) from its glass coffin (the building in New York). As the coffin fell and was shattered (at the same time as the Eastern Bloc), she spat out the apple and revived, as fresh as a rose, only to find at once the waiting Prince Charming: the Gulf War, also fresh from the arms of the cold war after a long period of mourning. No doubt together they will give birth to a New World Order, or else end up like two ghosts locked in vampiric embrace.

Seeing how Saddam uses his cameras on the hostages, the caressed children, the (fake) strategic targets, on his own smiling face, on the ruins of the milk factory, one cannot help thinking that in the West we still have a hypocritical vision of television and information, to the extent that, despite all the evidence, we hope for their proper use. Saddam, for his part, knows what the media and information are: he makes a radical, unconditional, perfectly cynical and therefore per-fectly instrumental use of them. The Romanians too were able to make a perfectly immoral and mystificatory use of them (from our point of view). We may regret this, but given the principle of simula-tion which governs all information, even the most pious and object-ive, and given the structural unreality of images and their proud indifference to the truth, these cynics alone are right about informa-tion when they employ it as an unconditional simulacrum. We believe that they immorally pervert images. Not so. They alone are conscious of the profound immorality of images, just as the Bokassas and Amin Dadas reveal, through the parodic and Ubuesque use they make of them, the obscene truth of the Western political and democratic structures they borrowed. The secret of the underdeveloped is to parody their model and render it ridiculous by exaggeration. We alone retain the illusion of information and of a right to information. They are not so naive.

Never any acting out, or passage to action, but simply acting: roll cameras! But there is too much film, or none at all, or it was desensitised by remaining too long in the humidity of the cold war. In short, there is quite simply nothing to see. Later, there will be something to see for the viewers of archival cassettes and the generations of video-zombies who will never cease reconstituting the event, never having had the intuition of the non-event of this war.

The archive also belongs to virtual time; it is the complement of the event "in real time," of that instantaneity of the event and its diffusion. Moreover, rather than the "revolution" of real time of which Virilio speaks, we should speak of an involution in real time; of an involution of the event in the instantaneity of everything at once, and of its vanishing in information itself. If we take note of the speed of light and the temporal short-circuit of pure war (the nanosecond), we see that this involution precipitates us precisely into the virtuality of war and not into its reality, it precipitates us into the absence of war. Must we denounce the speed of light?

Utopia of real time which renders the event simultaneous at all points on the globe. In fact, what we live in real time is not the event, but rather in larger than life (in other words, in the virtual size of the image) the spectacle of the degradation of the event and its spectral evocation (the "spiritualism of information": event, are you there? Gulf War, are you there?) in the commentary, gloss, and verbose *mise en scène* of talking heads which only underlines the impossibility of the image and the correlative unreality of the war. It is the same aporia as that of *cinéma vérité* which seeks to short-circuit the unreality of the image in order to present us the truth of the object. In this manner, CNN seeks to be a stethoscope attached to the hypothetical heart of the war, and to present us with its hypothetical pulse. But this auscultation only provides a confused ultrasound, undecidable symptoms, and an assortment of vague and contradictory diagnoses. All that we can hope for is to see them die live (metaphorically of course), in other words that some event or other should overwhelm the information instead of the information inventing the event and commenting artificially upon it. The only real information revolution would be this one, but it is not likely to occur in the near future: it would presuppose a reversal of the idea we have of information. In the meantime, we will continue with the involution and encrustation of the event in and by information, and the closer we approach the live and real time, the further we will go in this direction.

The same illusion of progress occurred with the appearance of speech and then colour on screen: at each stage of this progress we moved further away from the imaginary intensity of the image. The closer we supposedly approach the real or the truth, the further we draw away from them both, since neither one nor the other exists. The closer we approach the real time of the event, the more we fall into the illusion of the virtual. God save us from the illusion of war.

At a certain speed, the speed of light, you lose even your shadow. At a certain speed, the speed of information, things lose their sense. There is a great risk of announcing (or denouncing) the Apocalypse of real time, when it is precisely at this point that the event volatilises and becomes a black hole from which light no longer escapes. War implodes in real time, history implodes in real time, all communication and all signification implode in real time. The Apocalypse itself, understood as the arrival of catastrophe, is unlikely. It falls prey to the prophetic illusion. The world is not sufficiently coherent to lead to the Apocalypse.

Nevertheless, in confronting our opinions on the war with the diametrically opposed opinions of Paul Virilio, one of us betting on apocalyptic escalation and the other on deterrence and the indefinite virtuality of war, we concluded that this decidedly strange war went in both directions at once. The war's programmed escalation is relentless and its non-occurrence no less inevitable: the war proceeds at once towards the two extremes of intensification and deterrence. The war and the non-war take place at the same time, with the same period of deployment and suspense and the same possibilities of de-escalation or maximal increase.

What is most extraordinary is that the two hypotheses, the apocalypse of real time and pure war along with the triumph of the virtual over the real, are realised at the same time, in the same space-time, each in implacable pursuit of the other. It is a sign that the space of the event has become a hyperspace with multiple refractivity, and that *the space of war has become definitively non-Euclidean*. And that there will undoubtedly be no resolution of this situation: we will remain in the undecidability of war, which is the undecidability created by the unleashing of the two opposed principles.

Soft war and pure war go boating.

There is a degree of popular good will in the micro-panic distilled by
the airwaves. The public ultimately consents to be frightened, and to
be gently terrorised by the bacteriological scenarios, on the basis of a
kind of affective patriotism, even while it preserves a fairly profound
indifference to the war. But it censors this indifference, on the grounds
that we must not cut ourselves off from the world scene, that we must
be mobilised at least as extras in order to rescue war: we have no
other passion with which to replace it. It is the same with political
participation under normal circumstances: this is largely second hand,
taking place against a backdrop of spontaneous indifference. It is the
same with God: even when we no longer believe, we continue to
believe that we believe. In this hysterical replacement function, we
identify at once those who are superfluous and they are many. By
contrast, the few who advance the hypothesis of this profound indifference will be received as traitors.

By the force of the media, this war liberates an exponential mass of
stupidity, not the particular stupidity of war, which is considerable,
but the professional and functional stupidity of those who pontific-
ate in perpetual commentary on the event: all the Bouvards
and Pécuchets for hire, the would-be raiders of the lost image, the
CNN types and all the master singers of strategy and information
who make us experience the emptiness of television as never
before. This war, it must be said, constitutes a merciless test. Fortunately, no one will hold this expert or general or that intellectual for
hire to account for the idiocies or absurdities proffered the day before,
since these will be erased by those of the following day. In this
manner, everyone is amnestied by the ultra-rapid succession of
phony events and phony discourses. The laundering of stupidity
by the escalation of stupidity which reconstitutes a sort of total
innocence, namely the innocence of washed and bleached brains,
stupefied not by the violence but by the sinister insignificance of the
images.

Chevènement in the desert: *Morituri te salutant!* Ridiculous. France
with its old Jaguars and its presidential slippers.
    Capillon on television: the benefit of this war will have been to
recycle our military leaders on television. One shudders at the thought

that in another time, in a real war, they were operational on the battlefield.

Imbroglio: that pacifist demonstration in Paris, thus indirectly for Saddam Hussein, who does want war, and against the French Government which does not want it, and which from the outset gives all the signs of refusing to take part, or of doing so reluctantly.

Deserted shops, suspended vacations, the slowdown of activity, the city turned over to the absent masses: it may well be that, behind the alibi of panic, this war should be the dreamed-for opportunity to soft-pedal, the opportunity to slow down, to ease off the pace. The crazed particles calm down, the war erases the guerrilla warfare of everyday life. Catharsis? No: renovation. Or perhaps, with everyone glued at home, TV plays out fully its role of social control by collective stupefaction: turning uselessly upon itself like a dervish, it affixes populations all the better for deceiving them, as with a bad detective novel which we cannot believe could be so pointless.

Iraq is being rebuilt even before it has been destroyed. Aftersales service. Such anticipation reduces even further the credibility of the war, which did not need this to discourage those who wanted to believe in it.

Sometimes a glimmer of black humour: the twelve thousand coffins sent along with the arms and ammunition. Here too, the Americans demonstrate their presumption: their projections and their losses are without common measure. But Saddam challenged them with being incapable of sacrificing ten thousand men in a war: they replied by sending twelve thousand coffins.

The overestimation of losses is part of the same megalomaniac light show as the publicised deployment of "Desert Shield" and the orgy of bombardment. The pilots no longer even have any targets. The Iraqis no longer even have enough decoys to cater for the incessant raids. The same target must be bombed five times. Mockery.

The British artillery unleashed for twenty four hours. Long since there was nothing left to destroy. Why then? In order "to cover the noise of the armoured columns advancing towards the front by the noise of the bombardment." Of course, the effect of surprise must be maintained (it is February 21). The best part is that there was no longer anyone there, the Iraqis had already left. Absurdity.

Saddam is a mercenary, the Americans are missionaries. But once the mercenary is beaten, the missionaries become *de facto* the mercenaries of the entire world. But the price for becoming a perfect mercenary is to be stripped of all political intelligence and all will. The Americans cannot escape it: if they want to be the police of the world and the New World Order, they must lose all political authority in favour of their operational capacity alone. They will become pure executants and everyone else pure extras in the consensual and policed New World Order.

Whoever the dictator to be destroyed, any punitive force sure of itself is even more frightening. Having assumed the Israeli style, the Americans will henceforth export it everywhere and, just as the Israelis did, lock themselves into the spiral of unconditional repression.

For the Americans, the enemy does not exist as such. *Nothing personal.* Your war is of no interest to me, your resistance is of no interest to me. I will destroy you when I am ready. Refusal to bargain, whereas Saddam Hussein, for his part, bargains his war by overbidding in order to fall back, attempting to force the hand by pressure and blackmail, like a hustler trying to sell his goods. The Americans understand nothing in this whole psychodrama of bargaining, they are had every time until, with the wounded pride of the Westerner, they stiffen and impose their conditions. They understand nothing of this floating duel, this passage of arms in which, for a brief moment, the honour and dishonour of each is in play. They know only their virtue, and they are proud of their virtue. If the other wants to play, to trick and to challenge, they will virtuously employ their force. They will oppose the other's traps with their character armour and their armoured tanks. For them, the time of exchange does not exist. But the other, even if he knows that he will concede, cannot do so without another form of procedure. He must be recognised as interlocutor: this is the goal of the exchange. He must be recognised as an enemy: this is the whole aim of the war. For the Americans, bargaining is cheap whereas for the others it is a matter of honour, (mutual) personal recognition, linguistic strategy (language exists, it must be honoured) and respect for time (altercation demands a rhythm, it is the price of there being an Other). The Americans take no account of these primitive subtleties. They have much to learn about symbolic exchange.

By contrast, they are winners from an economic point of view. No time lost in discussion, no psychological risk in any duel with the other: it is a way of proving that time does not exist, that the other does not exist, and that all that matters is the model and mastery of the model.

From a military point of view, to allow this war to endure in the way they have (instead of applying an Israeli solution and immediately exploiting the imbalance of force while short-circuiting all retaliatory effects), is a clumsy solution lacking in glory and full of perverse effects (Saddam's aura among the Arab masses). Nevertheless, in doing this, they impose a suspense, a temporal vacuum in which they present to themselves and to the entire world the spectacle of their virtual power. They will have allowed the war to endure as long as it takes, not to win but to persuade the whole world of the infallibility of their machine.

The victory of the model is more important than victory on the ground. Military success consecrates the triumph of arms, but the programming success consecrates the defeat of time. War-processing, the transparency of the model in the unfolding of the war, the strategy of relentless execution of a program, the electrocution of all reaction and any live initiative, including their own: these are more important from the point of view of general deterrence (of friends and foes alike) than the final result on the ground. Clean war, white war, programmed war: more lethal than the war which sacrifices human lives.

We are a long way from annihilation, holocaust and atomic apocalypse, the total war which functions as the archaic imaginary of media hysteria. On the contrary, this kind of preventative, deterrent and punitive war is a warning to everyone not to take extreme measures and inflict upon themselves what they inflict on others (the missionary complex): the rule of the game that says everyone must remain within the limits of their power and not make war by any means whatever. Power must remain virtual and exemplary, in other words, virtuous. The decisive test is the planetary apprenticeship in this regulation. Just as wealth is no longer measured by the ostentation of wealth but by the secret circulation of speculative capital, so war is not measured by being waged but by its speculative unfolding in an abstract, electronic and informational space, the same space in which capital moves.

While this conjuncture does not exclude all accident (disorder in the virtual), it is nevertheless true that the probability of the irruption of those extreme measures and mutual violence which we call war is increasingly low.

Saddam the hysteric. Interminable shit kicker. The hysteric cannot be crushed: he is reborn from his symptoms as though from his ashes. Confronted by a hysteric, the other becomes paranoid, he deploys a massive apparatus of protection and mistrust. He suspects the hysteric of bad faith, of ruse and dissimulation. He wants to constrain him to the truth and to transparency. The hysteric is irreducible. His means are decoys and the overturning of alliances. Confronted with this lubricity, this duplicity, the paranoid can only become more rigid, more obsessional. The most violent reproach addressed to Saddam Hussein by Bush is that of being a liar, a traitor, a bad player, a trickster. *Lying son of a bitch!* Saddam, like a good hysteric, has never given birth to his own war: for him, it is only a phantom pregnancy. By contrast, he has until now succeeded in preventing Bush from giving birth to his. And, with the complicity of Gorbachev, he almost succeeded in fucking him up the ass. But the hysteric is not suicidal, this is the advantageous other side to Saddam. He is neither mad nor suicidal. Perhaps he should be treated by hypnosis?

The Iraqis and the Americans have at least one thing in common, a heinous crime which they (and with them the West) share. Many things about this war are explained by this anterior crime from which both sides sought to profit with impunity. The secret expiation of this crime feeds the Gulf War in its confusion and its allure of the settling of accounts. Such is the shared agreement to forget it that little is spoken about this prior episode (even by the Iranians), namely the war against Iran. Saddam must avenge his failure to win, even though he was the aggressor and sure of his impunity. He must avenge himself against the West which trained him for it, while the Americans, for their part, must suppress him as the embarrassing accomplice in that criminal act.

For any government official or despot, power over his own people takes precedence over everything else. In the case of the Gulf War, this provides the only chance of a solution or a de-escalation. Saddam will prefer to concede rather than destroy his internal hegemony or sacrifice his army, etc. In this sense, sheltering his planes in Iran is a good sign: rather than an offensive sign, it is the ploy of a burglar who stashes his haul in order to retrieve it when he comes out of prison, thus an argument against any heroic or suicidal intention.

While one fraction of the intellectuals and politicians, specialists in the reserve army of mental labour, are whole-heartedly in favour of the war, and another fraction are against it from the bottom of their hearts, but for reasons no less disturbing, all are agreed on one point: this war exists, we have seen it. There is no interrogation into the event itself or its reality; or into the fraudulence of this war, the programmed and always delayed illusion of battle; or into the machination of this war and its amplification by information, not to mention the improbable orgy of material, the systematic manipulation of data, the artificial dramatisation . . . If we do not have practical intelligence about the war (and none among us has), at least let us have a sceptical intelligence towards it, without renouncing the pathetic feeling of its absurdity.

But there is more than one kind of absurdity: that of the massacre and that of being caught up in the illusion of massacre. It is just as in La Fontaine's fable: the day there is a real war you will not even be able to tell the difference. The real victory of the simulators of war is to have drawn everyone into this rotten simulation.

12

The Illusion of the End

The ascent of the vacuum towards the periphery

On the eve of the 1990s, in the midst of some unexpected events and
with an eye to others just as unpredictable, there formed, among a
number of friends, the idea of an agency which would itself be
invisible, anonymous and clandestine: the Stealth Agency. This
could equally well be called:

> ANATHEMATIC ILLIMITED
> TRANSFATAL EXPRESS
> VIRAL INCORPORATED
> INTERNATIONAL EPIDEMICS[1]

As an agency for gathering news of unreal events in order to disin-
form the public of them, it remained, itself, unreal. It thus fulfilled its
role perfectly, eluding all radar screens – a formula unique and forever
virtual.

Implied in this Agency was the point that there are no longer
any ideas grappling with facts – that was the 'Utopia' of the 1960s
and 1970s – no longer really any actors grappling with events,
nor intellectuals grappling with their meaning, but a storm of
events of no importance, without either real actors or author-
ized interpreters: *actio* has disappeared at the same moment as
auctoritas. All that remains is *actualité*, 'action' in the cinematographic sense, and 'auction', the selling-off of the event on the over-
heated news market. The event captured not, as it used to be, in
action, but in speculation and chain reactions spinning off towards

the extremes of a facticity with which interpretation can no longer keep pace.

Simulation is precisely this irresistible unfolding, this sequencing of things as though they had a meaning, when they are governed only by artificial *montage* and non-meaning. Putting the event up for auction by radical disinformation. Setting a price on the event, as against setting it in play, setting it in history. If there are any historical stakes, they remain secret, enigmatic; they are resolved in events which do not really take place. And I am not referring here to ordinary events, but to the events of Eastern Europe, the Gulf War, etc. Now, the aim of the Agency was precisely to set up against this simulation a radical desimulation or, in other words, *to lift the veil on the fact of events not taking place*. And thus to make itself secret and enigmatic in their image, to get through to a certain void, a certain non-meaning, by contrast with the media, which are frantic to plug up all the gaps. To move within the void of events like Chuang Tzu's butcher in the interstitial void of the body.[2] Admittedly, this kind of sly, surreptitious intervention on the side of the void against the grotesque, Ubuesque infatuation with news and the political scene was merely a dream and, by dint of being secret and enigmatic, no more came into being, in the end, than did the events themselves. It fell into the same black hole, the same virtual space, as the non-events of which it was to speak (secretly, unbeknown to everyone, while remaining operational, exactly like these new-style events which are only events to the extent that they are media events). An apparently irresolvable paradox. But the idea is not dead.

The Stealth Agency chimed in with events being on strike, with history being on strike. Like history, it was a consumer of absent events, attempting to give the most precise non-information about that absence of events, that indefinite sit-in strike in which history – the empty space over which the spectres of Power still hover – was occupied, just as workers might occupy a factory – that empty space of Labour, over which the spectre of Capital still hovers.

It is as though events passed on the strike call to each other. One after the other they deserted their time, transforming it into an empty *actualité* where only the visual psychodrama of news was left to unfold. And this event strike led to history being locked out. The fact that it is no longer the event that generates news, but the reverse, has incalculable consequences, as the whole *travail du négatif* disappears on the horizon of the media, exactly as work disappears on the horizon of capital. Here again, the relations are inverted: it is no longer work that serves the reproduction of capital, but capital which produces and reproduces work. A gigantic parody of the relations of production.

This disruption of cause and effect is not now the work of the critical consciousness, but of objective irony alone. Thus it was the Agency's duty not only to avoid the temptation of providing information on the events which had 'downed tools', but also to avoid appending a critical commentary to them, in order to capture the originality of this non-event, which is the originality of an objective irony. For the radical irony of our history is that things no longer really take place, while nonetheless seeming to. This is the opposite of the traditional ruse of history which brought about changes that were crucial but did not appear to be so.

When you think that we took the events in Eastern Europe at face value, with their good, sound coin of freedom and 'democratic values', and the Gulf War, with its Human Rights and New World Order! These events were auctioned off well above their value. The historical scene today is like the art market. Against this speculative inflation, which leaves everyone on edge – that is, both overexcited and indifferent, riveted and apathetic – against these *gidouille* events, worthy of the *Grande Gidouille* of History,[3] we had to find an ironic form of the disruption of information, a casual form of writing to match the casual *événementialité* of our age, together with a subtly catastrophic form which fits with the coming of the end of the century. We had to find, in this event strike, the thread running through, which is that of deterrence, the baleful form which presides over the nullity of our age.

Deterrence is a very peculiar form of action: it is *what causes something not to take place*. It dominates the whole of our contemporary period, which tends not so much to produce events as to cause something not to occur, while looking as though it is a historical event. Or else events do take place in the stead of some other event which did not. War, history, reality and passion – deterrence plays its part in all these. It causes strange events to take place(!), events which do not in any way advance history, but rather run it backwards, back along the opposite slope, unintelligible to our historical sense (only things which move in the direction of history [*le sens de l'histoire*] have historical meaning [*sens historique*]), events which no longer have a negative (progressive, critical or revolutionary) potency since *their only negativity is in the fact of their not taking place*. Disturbing.

The hold deterrence has on us even extends to the past. It can remove all certainty about facts and evidence. It can destabilize memory just as it destabilizes prediction. It is a diabolical force which wrecks the actual acting out of events or, if they still take place – if they have taken place – destroys their credibility.

Perhaps this curvature of things which deprives them of meaning or linear end is merely a depression in the meteorological sense of the term – the emptiness we feel being the effect not of a failing of meaning or memory, but of a strange attraction coming from elsewhere. Perhaps the atony, the catatonia we are experiencing is to be interpreted in the opposite sense, not as a void left by the ebbing of past events, but a void due to the suction effect of a future event, to the anticipatory sucking up by a nearby mass of all the oxygen we breathe, creating a violent depressurizing of the social, political, cultural and mental sphere.

A pataphysical hypothesis, that of anti-gravity, anti-density – of a science of imaginary solutions rising above physics and metaphysics. In his *Exploits and Opinions of Dr Faustroll*, Jarry sketches the contours of this strange attraction, brought about by overturning the principles of physics: 'Current science is based on the principle of induction: most people have seen a certain phenomenon most often precede or follow some other phenomenon and conclude therefrom that this will always be the case . . . But, instead of formulating the law of the fall of a body towards a centre, why not give preference to that of the ascent of a vacuum towards a periphery, the vacuum being considered a unit of non-density, a hypothesis far less arbitrary than the choice of a concrete unit of positive density.'

Inverse attraction by the void, rather than attraction of solids by other solids. Perhaps it is this which gives our events this particular coloration, this flavour (or, rather, insipidity) of emptiness, this inanity. Even as they occur, they might already be 'vanishing events' – of little meaning because already heading towards the void. Running counter to the old physics of meaning would be a new gravitation – the true, the only gravitation: attraction by the void. Doubtless the most basic of natural laws.

This would explain quite a number of anomalies, including those in the realms of the mind and the 'psychological' field. So, our forms of action and mobility are not so much a matter of positive drives as of expulsion and repulsion. The centrifugal mobility of particles seeking to escape from density and join up with what? A mysterious periphery of space, an anti-gravity. Thus it would be possible to escape from the heavy form, the gravity of 'desire', conceived as positive attraction, by the much more subtle eccentricity of seduction, which would be, to take up again some old cosmogonies that were not without their charm, the last-gasp escape from the body of molecules that are much too light and know only one line of flight – towards the void (so it is with poetic language, where each particle finds its resolution in anagrammatical resonance).

We may say of the new events that they hollow out before them the void into which they plunge. They are intent, it seems, on one thing alone – being forgotten. They leave hardly any scope for interpretation, except for all interpretations at once, by which they evade any desire to give them meaning and elude the heavy attraction of a continuous history to enter upon the light orbit of a discontinous one. They arrive – mostly unforeseen – more quickly than their shadows, but they have no sequel. Meteoric events, of the same chaotic inconsequence as cloud formations. So, with the events of Eastern Europe, for example, we have the impression of a long negative accumulation and a sudden resolution, like the obvious, instant conclusion to operations which elude our understanding. In these conditions, such events, which are nonetheless important, have the strange aftertaste of something that has already happened before, something unfolding retrospectively – an aftertaste which does not bode well for a meaningful future. Our only surprise is that we were not able to foresee them and our only regret that we do not know how to draw any consequences from them. The screen of history fluctuates at the same irregular rhythm as natural phenomena.

One has the impression that events form all on their own and drift unpredictably towards their vanishing point – the peripheral void of the media. Just as physicists now see their particles only as a trajectory on a screen, we no longer have the pulsing of events, but only the cardiogram, have neither representation nor recollection of them, but merely the (flat) encephalogram, neither desire nor enjoyment of them, but only the psychodrama and the TV image.

It is a bit like *in vitro* procreation: the embryo of the real event is transferred into the artificial womb of the news media, there to give birth to many orphaned foetuses which have neither fathers nor mothers. The event is entitled to the same procreative practices as birth and the same euthanasian practices as death.

It is to this perhaps that we owe this 'fun physics' effect: the impression that events, collective or individual, have been bundled into a memory hole. This blackout is due, no doubt, to this movement of reversal, this parabolic curvature of historical space. For the past can only be represented and reflected if it pushes us in the other direction, towards a future of some kind. Retrospection is dependent on a prospection which enables us to refer to something as past and gone, and thus as having really taken place. If, by some strange revolution, we set off in the opposite direction and turn inwards into this dimension of the past, then we can no longer represent that something to ourselves. The beam of memory bends, and makes every event a black hole. We experience this subjectively too, in the sudden loss of our memories, the break in the continuity of names, faces and familiar forms. In this kind of catastrophic memory failure, there is neither natural forgetting nor unconscious repression. It is the inversion of the temporal field of gravity which means that the signs of the past no longer have sufficient specific mass, sufficient nuclear mass to hold them, nor the mirror of the present enough to reflect them. The memory gaps are a little bit like the holes in the ozone layer, the holes into which our protective screen is breaking up. But perhaps they are not big enough for what falls into them to begin to spin, releasing the light particles from the heavy, widening and deepening the black hole through which the dead bodies will release their ethereal substance, as in Dante or Giordano Bruno. It is in the absolute void that the absolute event occurs. So the void must only have been relative, since death has remained virtual.

The event strike

What has been lost is the glory of the event, what Benjamin would term its aura. For centuries, the keynote of history was glory, a very powerful illusion and one which played on the everlasting nature of time, in that it was inherited from one's ancestors and would be handed on to one's descendants. That passion seems laughable today. Whereas, in the past, the aim was to lose oneself in something prodigious, to achieve the 'immortality' Hannah Arendt speaks of, which had a transcendence equal to that of God (glory and salvation long contended for the souls of men, like passion and compassion, those rivals before the Eternal), what we seek now is not glory but identity, not an illusion but, on the contrary, an accumulation of proofs – anything that can serve as evidence of a historical existence.

The prodigious event, the event which is measured neither by its causes nor its consequences but creates its own stage and its own dramatic effect, no longer exists. History has gradually narrowed down to the field of its probable causes and effects, and, even more recently, to the field of current events – its effects 'in real time'. Events now have no more significance than their anticipated meaning, their programming and their broadcasting. Only *this event strike* constitutes a true historical phenomenon – this refusal to signify anything whatever, or this capacity to signify anything at all. This is the true end of history, the end of historical Reason.

But it would be too much to hope that we had finished with history. For it is possible not only that history has disappeared (the *travail du négatif*, political reason, the prestige of the event have all gone), but also that we still have to *fuel its end*. It is entirely as though we were still continuing to manufacture history, whereas, in accumulating the signs of the social, the signs of the political, the signs of progress and change, we are merely feeding the end of history. While history, cannibalistic and necrophagous, constantly calls for new victims, for new events, so as to be done with them a little bit more. Socialism is a fine example of this. It is to socialism that it will have fallen, by the collapse of the historical reason it claimed to embody, to manage the end of history, to fuel the end.

We used to ask what might come after the orgy – mourning or melancholia? Doubtless neither, but an interminable clean-up of all the vicissitudes of modern history and its processes of liberation (of peoples, sex, dreams, art and the unconscious – in short, of all that makes up the orgy of our times), in an atmosphere dominated by the apocalyptic presentiment that all this is coming to an end. Rather than pressing forward and taking flight into the future, we prefer the retrospective apocalypse, and a blanket revisionism. Our societies have all become revisionistic: they are quietly rethinking everything, laundering their political crimes, their scandals, licking their wounds, fuelling their ends. Celebration and commemoration are themselves merely the soft form of necrophagous cannibalism, the homeopathic form of murder by easy stages. This is the work of the heirs, whose *ressentiment* towards the deceased is boundless. Museums, jubilees, festivals, complete works, the publication of the tiniest of unpublished fragments – all this shows that we are entering an active age of *ressentiment* and repentance.

Acts of glorification and commemoration clearly form part of this collective flagellation. We are particularly well served in France: our public life has been overtaken by a veritable ritual of mourning and condolence. And all our monuments are mausoleums: the Pyramid, the Arch at La Défense, the Musée d'Orsay, that fine Pharaonic chamber, the new National Library, cenotaph of culture. Not counting the Revolution, which is a monument in itself, the bicentenary of which was the finest simulation of an event to be seen at the end of the century.

There are two forms of forgetting: on the one hand, the slow or violent extermination of memory, on the other, the spectacular promotion of a phenomenon, shifting it from historical space into the sphere of advertising, the media becoming the site of a temporal strategy of prestige... This is how we have manufactured for ourselves, with great swathes of promotional images, a synthetic memory which serves as our primal reference, our founding myth, and which, most importantly, absolves us of the real event of Revolution.

'Revolution is not on the agenda in France because the Great Revolution occurred and has served as an example for all others over two centuries... Our entire aim in present-day France is to ensure that there will be no revolution' (Louis Mermaz). This is how it is: it happened, it is finished, it will never happen again. The whole of our system is based on this negative anticipation. Not only are we no longer able to produce a new history, we are not even able to ensure its symbolic reproduction. We build an opera house at the Bastille. A laughable rehabilitation: royal music is to be served up there to the people. Yet it is not the people who will benefit. It is the cultural elite who will go there, confirming the rule that the privileged are happy to hallow with art and pleasure the places where others died.

Might one suggest to the people that they storm the opera house and tear it down on the symbolic date of 14 July? Might one suggest that they parade the bloody heads of our modern cultural governors on the end of pikestaffs?

But we no longer make history. We have become reconciled with it and protect it like an endangered masterpiece. Times have changed. We have today a perfectly pious *vision* of the Revolution, cast in terms of the Rights of Man. Not even a nostalgic vision, but one recycled in the terms of post-modern intellectual comfort. A vision which allows us to eliminate Saint-Just from the *Dictionnaire de la Révolution*. 'Overrated rhetoric', says François Furet, perfect historian of the repentance of the Terror and of glory.

There are those who let the dead bury their dead, and there are those who are forever digging them up to finish them off. Having failed both in their symbolic murder and their work of mourning, it is not enough for them that others should be dead; they have to disinter them once again to impale them – this is the Carpentras complex (after the Timişoara complex: the faking of corpses for TV), the desecration complex.

Nothing lends itself so well to this operation as the centenary of a death. With Rimbaud, Van Gogh and Nietzsche, 1991 will have been exceptional in terms of vile acts of desecration.

One can see a kind of suicidal behaviour in this compulsion on the part of the cultural and intellectual elite to exalt thinkers who have only scorn for that elite and are its living condemnation: Céline, Artaud, Bataille, Nietzsche. Might this be a product of one of those failures of instinct which the last-mentioned diagnosed more than a century ago – a failure which characterizes a species doomed by its inability to judge what is good for it? If the left were a species, and culture obeyed the laws of natural selection, it would have disappeared long ago. Flirting with what is implacably opposed to it, dying from a total contradiction between its critical thinking and its action, attempting to reconcile its critical subconscious and its presence in power by turning culture into a mode of government. These things are all part and parcel, already, of the forms of repentance.

It isn't just terrorists who repent. Intellectuals showed them the way, the Sartreans and others having been in the van of repentance from the 1950s onwards. Today, the whole century is repenting, class (or race) repentance everywhere predominating over class pride and consciousness. It is the sign that the century is becoming intellectualized. It is becoming intellectual today just as it became bourgeois a century ago. And the term 'intellectual' will one day disappear, just as the word 'bourgeois' – which now exposes only the person who uses it to ridicule – has disappeared.

The auto-dissolution common to both West and East is visible in the deterioration of the structures of power and representation (thus, the more the political sphere becomes intellectualized, the more it secretly denies its own will to govern, and this *ressentiment* towards itself is the source of all corruption). But it can also be seen in the multiple strategies for re-enchanting values, cultures and differences. We expend all the energy of that dissolution in resisting our own end, which we can then neither enjoy nor be engulfed by. A gigantic night of the fourth of August[4] would be preferable, a great night of the Rights of Man, on which the whole of humanity would renounce those rights as the aristocrats once renounced their privileges, and the renunciation would take on excessive dimensions. What can occur to rescue us from endlessly trawling over our own culture?

It seems we are condemned to the infinite retrospective of all that has preceded us. What is true of politics and morality seems true of art also. The whole drift of painting has withdrawn from the future and shifted towards the past. Present-day art is currently reappropriating the works of the – distant, recent or even contemporary – past. This is what Russell Connor calls the 'abduction of modern art'.[5] Now, admittedly, this reappropriation is supposed to be ironic. But the humour here is merely the transparent invocation of humour. Like the worn threads of a piece of fabric, it is an irony produced only by the disillusion of things, a fossilized irony. The little trick of placing the nude from Manet's *Déjeuner sur l'herbe* opposite Cézanne's *Card Players*, as one might put an admiral's hat on a monkey, is nothing more than the advertising-style irony currently engulfing the world of art. It is the irony of repentance and *ressentiment* towards one's own culture. No doubt repentance and *ressentiment* constitute the last stage of the history of art, just as, according to Nietzsche, they constitute the last stage of the genealogy of morals. It is a parody, or rather a palinode, of art and the history of art (a development reflecting that of history *tout court*) – a parody of culture by culture itself as an act of vengeance, characteristic of radical disillusionment. It is as though history were rifling through its own dustbins and looking for redemption in the rubbish.

The end of history is, alas, also the end of the dustbins of history. There are no longer any dustbins even for disposing of old ideologies, old regimes, old values. Where are we going to throw Marxism, which actually invented the dustbins of history? (Yet, there is some justice here since the very people who invented them have fallen in.) Conclusion: if there are no more dustbins of history, *this is because History itself has become a dustbin*. It has become its own dustbin. Just as the planet itself is becoming its own dustbin.

When ice freezes, all the excrement rises to the surface. And so, when the dialectic was frozen, all the sacred excrement of the dialectic came to the surface. When the future is deep-frozen – and, indeed, even the present – we see all the excrement come up from the past.

The problem then becomes one of waste. It is not just material substances, including nuclear ones, which pose a waste problem but also the defunct ideologies, bygone utopias, dead concepts and fossilized ideas which continue to pollute our mental space. Historical and intellectual refuse pose an even more serious problem than industrial waste. Who will rid us of the sedimentation of centuries of stupidity? As for history – that living lump of waste, that dying monster which, like the corpse in Ionesco,[6] continues to swell after it has died – how are we to be rid of it?

The ecological imperative is that all wastes must be recycled. Otherwise, they will circle endlessly like satellites around the earth, which has itself returned to the state of a lump of cosmic waste. What is happening with history is the foreshadowing of this dilemma: we can either perish under the weight of the non-degradable waste of the great empires, the grand narratives, the great systems made obsolete by their own gigantism, or else recycle all this waste in the synthetic form of a heteroclite history, as we are doing today in the name of Democracy and Human Rights, which are never anything but the confused end-product of the reprocessing of all the residues of history – crusher residues in which all the ethnic, linguistic, feudal and ideological phantoms of earlier societies float. Amnesia, anamnesis, the anachronistic revival of all the figures of the past – royalty, feudalism. Though did they ever really disappear? Democracy itself (a proliferating form, the lowest common denominator of all our liberal societies), this planetary democracy of the Rights of Man, is to real freedom what Disneyland is to the imaginary. In relation to the modern demand for freedom, it offers the same characteristics as recycled paper.

There is in fact no insoluble waste problem. The problem is resolved by the post-modern invention of recycling and the incinerator. The Great Incinerators of history, from whose ashes the Phoenix of post-modernity is resuscitated! We have to come to terms with the idea that everything that was not degradable or exterminable is today recyclable, and hence that there is no final solution. We shall not be spared the worst – that is, *History will not come to an end* – since the leftovers, all the leftovers – the Church, communism, ethnic groups, conflicts, ideologies – are indefinitely recyclable. What is stupendous is that nothing one thought superseded by history has really disappeared. All the archaic, anachronistic forms are there ready to re-emerge, intact and timeless, like the viruses deep in the body. History has only wrenched itself from cyclical time to fall into the order of the recyclable.

NOTES

1   All the terms in capitals are in English in the original.
2   In English translations of Chuang Tzu (Zhuang Zi), this figure is often identified as a 'cook'. Thomas Merton's translation contains the following lines: 'Guided by natural line,/By the secret opening, the hidden

space,/My cleaver finds its own way./I cut through no joint, chop no bone' (*The Way of Chuang Tzu*, London: Unwin, 1970, p. 46).

3   The *gidouille* here is the great belly or paunch of Jarry's Père Ubu, which has acquired a broader sense in French 'pataphysical' usage. On its origins and signification, see, for example, Keith Beaumont, *Alfred Jarry: A Critical and Biographical Study*, Leicester: Leicester University Press, 1984.

4   A reference to the date in 1789 on which the nobles gave up their feudal rights. Not only was this in itself, as Simon Schama remarks, 'a bonfire of particularisms', it also ushered in what he describes as 'a cult of self-dispossession' (*Citizens*, London, 1989, p. 439).

5   This expression has been retranslated from the French exhibition catalogue in which the author encountered it.

6   A reference to Ionesco's *Amédée, ou comment s'en débarrasser*.

13

The Perfect Crime

Radical thought

The novel, which is a work of art, exists, not by its resemblances to life, which are forced and material... but by its immeasurable difference from life...

(R.L. Stevenson)

So, too, the value of thought lies not so much in its inevitable convergences with truth as in the immeasurable divergences which separate it from truth.

It is not true that, in order to live, one has to believe in one's own existence. Indeed, our consciousness is never the echo of our existence in real time but the 'recorded' echo, the screen for the dispersal of the subject and its identity (only in sleep, unconsciousness and death do we exist in real time, are we identical to ourselves). That consciousness results much more spontaneously from a challenging of reality, from a bias towards the objective illusoriness of the world rather than its reality. This challenging is more vital for our survival and the survival of the species than the belief in reality and existence, which is of the order of otherworldly spiritual consolation. Our world is as it is, and it is no more real for that. 'Man's most powerful instinct is to come into conflict with the truth and, therefore, with the real.'

Belief in reality is one of the elementary forms of religious life. It is a failing of the understanding, a failing of common sense, as well as the last refuge of moral zealots and the apostles of rationality.

Fortunately, no one lives by this principle – not even those who profess it. And with good reason. No one believes fundamentally in the real, nor in the self-evidence of their real lives. That would be too sad.

But surely, say these good apostles, you aren't going to discredit reality in the eyes of those who already find it difficult enough to get by, and who surely have a right to reality and the fact that they exist? The same objection for the Third World: surely you aren't going to discredit affluence in the eyes of those dying of starvation? Or: surely you aren't going to run down the class struggle in the eyes of those who haven't even had their bourgeois revolution? Or again: you aren't going to discredit feminist and egalitarian demands in the eyes of all those who haven't even heard of women's rights, etc.? You may not like reality, but don't put others off it! It's a question of democratic morality: you must not demoralize the masses. You must never demoralize anyone.

Underlying these charitable intentions is a profound contempt. First, in the fact of instating reality as a kind of life insurance or a burial plot held in perpetuity, as a kind of human right or consumer good. But, above all, in crediting people with placing their hope only in the visible proofs of their existence: by imputing this plaster-saint realism to them, one takes them for naive and feeble-minded. In their defence, it has to be said that the propagandists of reality vent that contempt on themselves first of all, reducing their own lives to an accumulation of facts and evidence, causes and effects. Well-ordered resentment always begins at home.

Say: This is real, the world is real, the real exists (I have met it) – no one laughs. Say: This is a simulacrum, you are merely a simulacrum, this war is a simulacrum – everyone bursts out laughing. With forced, condescending laughter, or uncontrollable mirth, as though at a child-ish joke or an obscene proposition. Everything to do with the simu-lacrum is taboo or obscene, as is everything relating to sex or death. Yet it is much rather reality and obviousness which are obscene. It is the truth we should laugh at. You can imagine a culture where every-one laughs spontaneously when someone says: 'This is true', 'This is real'.

All this defines the irresolvable relationship between thought and reality. A certain form of thought is bound to the real. It starts out from the hypothesis that ideas have referents and that there is a possible ideation of reality. A comforting polarity, which is that of tailor-made dialectical and philosophical solutions. The other form of thought is eccentric to the real, a stranger to dialectics, a stranger even to critical thought. It is not even a disavowal of the concept of reality. It is illusion, power of illusion, or, in other words, a playing with reality, as seduction is a playing with desire, as metaphor is a playing with truth. This radical thought does not stem from a philosophical doubt, a utopian transference, or an ideal transcendence. It is the material illusion, immanent in this so-called 'real' world. And thus it seems to come from elsewhere. It seems to be the extrapolation of this world into another world.

At all events, there is incompatibility between thought and the real. There is no sort of necessary or natural transition from the one to the other. Neither alternation, nor alternative: only otherness and distance keep them charged up. This is what ensures the singularity of thought, the singularity by which it constitutes an event, just like the singularity of the world, the singularity by which it too constitutes an event.

It has doubtless not always been so. One may dream of a happy conjunction of idea and reality, cradled by the Enlightenment and modernity, in the heroic age of critical thought. Yet critical thought, the butt of which was a certain illusion – superstitious, religious or ideological – is in substance ended. Even if it had survived its catastrophic secularization in all the political movements of the twentieth century, this ideal and seemingly necessary relationship between the concept and reality would, at all events, be destroyed today. It has broken down under pressure from a gigantic technical and mental simulation, to be replaced by an autonomy of the virtual, henceforth liberated from the real, and a simultaneous autonomy of the real which we see functioning on its own account in a demented – that is, infinitely self-referential – perspective. Having been expelled, so to speak, from its own principle, extraneized, the real has itself become an extreme phenomenon. In other words, one can no longer think it as real, but as exorbitated, as though seen from another world – in short, as illusion. Imagine the stupefying experience which the discovery of a real world other than our own would represent. The objectivity of our world is a discovery we made, like America – and at almost the same time. Now what one has discovered, one can never then invent. And so we discovered reality, which remains to be invented (or: so we invented reality, which remains to be discovered).

Why might there not be as many real worlds as imaginary ones? Why a single real world? Why such an exception? Truth to tell, the real world, among all the other possible ones, is unthinkable, except as dangerous superstition. We must break with it as critical thought once broke (in the name of the real!) with religious superstition. Thinkers, one more effort![1]

In any case, the two orders of thought are irreconcilable. They each follow their course without merging; at best they slide over each other like tectonic plates, and occasionally their collision or subduction creates fault lines into which reality crashes. Fate is always at the intersection of these two lines of force. Similarly, radical thought is at the violent intersection of meaning and non-meaning, of truth and non-truth, of the continuity of the world and the continuity of the nothing.

Unlike the discourse of the real, which gambles on the fact of there being something rather than nothing, and aspires to being founded on the guarantee of an objective and decipherable world, radical thought, for its part, wagers on the illusion of the world. It aspires to the status of illusion, restoring the non-veracity of facts, the non-signification of the world, proposing the opposite hypothesis that there is nothing rather than something, and going in pursuit of that nothing which runs beneath the apparent continuity of meaning.

The radical prediction is always the prediction of the non-reality of facts, of the illusoriness of the state of fact. It begins only with the presentiment of that illusoriness, and is never confused with the objective state of things. Every confusion of that kind is of the order of the confusion of the messenger and the message, which leads to the elimination of the messenger bearing bad news (for example, the news of the uncertainty of the real, of the non-occurrence of certain events, of the nullity of our values).

Every confusion of thought with the order of the real – that alleged 'faithfulness' to the real of a thought which has cooked it up out of nothing – is hallucinatory. It arises, moreover, from a total misunderstanding about language, which is illusion in its very movement, since it is the bearer of that continuity of the void, that continuity of the nothing at the very heart of what it says, since it is, in its very materiality, deconstruction of what it signifies. Just as photography connotes the effacing, the death of what it represents – which lends it its intensity – so what lends writing, fictional or theoretical, its intensity is the void, the nothingness running beneath the surface, the illusion of meaning, the ironic dimension of language, correlative with that of the facts themselves, which are never anything but what they are [*ne sont jamais que ce qu'ils sont*]. That is to say, they are never more than what they are and they are, literally, never only what they are [*jamais que ce qu'ils sont*]. The irony of the facts, in their wretched reality, is precisely that they are only what they are but that, by that very fact, they are necessarily beyond. For *de facto* existence is impossible – nothing is wholly obvious without becoming enigmatic. Reality itself is too obvious to be true.

It is this ironic transfiguration which constitutes the event of language. And it is to restoring this fundamental illusion of the world and language that thought must apply itself, if it is not stupidly to take concepts in their literalness – messenger confused with the message, language confused with its meaning and therefore sacrificed in advance.

There is a twofold, contradictory exigency in thought. It is not to analyse the world in order to extract from it an improbable truth, not to adapt to the facts in order to abstract some logical construction from them, but to set in place a form, a matrix of illusion and disillusion, which seduced reality will spontaneously feed and which will, consequently, be verified remorselessly (the only need is to shift the camera angle from time to time). For reality asks nothing other than to submit itself to hypotheses. And it confirms them all. That, indeed, is its ruse and its vengeance.

The theoretical ideal would be to set in place propositions in such a way that they could be disconfirmed by reality, in such a way that reality could only oppose them violently, and thereby unmask itself. For reality is an illusion, and all thought must seek first of all to unmask it. To do that, it must itself advance behind a mask and constitute itself as a decoy, without regard for its own truth. It must pride itself on not being an instrument of analysis, not being a critical tool. For it is the world which must analyse itself. It is the world itself which must reveal itself not as truth, but as illusion. The derealization of the world will be the work of the world itself.[2]

Reality must be caught in the trap, we must move quicker than reality. Ideas, too, have to move faster than their shadows. But if they go too quickly, they lose even their shadows. No longer having even the shadow of an idea.... Words move quicker than meaning, but if they go too quickly, we have madness: the ellipsis of meaning can make us lose even the taste for the sign. What are we to exchange this portion of shadow and labour against – this saving of intellectual activity and patience? What can we sell it to the devil for? It is very difficult to say. We are, in fact, the orphans of a reality come too late, a reality which is itself, like truth, something registered only after the event.

The ultimate is for an idea to disappear as idea to become a thing among things. That is where it finds its accomplishment. Once it has become consubstantial with the surrounding world, there is no call for it to appear, nor to be defended as such. Evanescence of the idea by silent dissemination. An idea is never destined to burst upon the world, but to be extinguished into it, into its showing-through in the world, the world's showing-through in it. A book ends only with the disappearance of its object. Its substance must leave no trace. This is the equivalent of a perfect crime. Whatever its object, writing must make the illusion of that object shine forth, must make it an impenetrable enigma – unacceptable to the *Realpolitiker* of the concept. The objective of writing is to alter its object, to seduce it, to make it disappear for itself. Writing aims at a total resolution – a poetic resolution, as Saussure would have it, that resolution indeed of the rigorous dispersal of the name of God.

Contrary to what is said about it (the real is what resists, what all hypotheses run up against), reality is not very solid and seems predisposed, rather, to retreat in disorder. Whole swathes of reality are collapsing, as in the collapse of Baliverna (Buzzati), where the slightest flaw produces a chain reaction. We find decomposed remnants of it everywhere, as in Borges's 'Of Exactitude in Science'.[3]

Not only does it no longer put up any resistance against those who denounce it, but it even eludes those who take its side. This is perhaps a way of exacting vengeance on its partisans: by throwing them back on their own desire. In the end, it is perhaps more a sphinx than a bitch.

More subtly, it wreaks vengeance on those who deny it by paradoxically proving them right. When the most cynical, most provocative hypothesis is verified, the trick really is a low one; you are disarmed by the lamentable confirmation of your words by an unscrupulous reality.

So, for example, you put forward the idea of simulacrum, without really believing in it, even hoping that the real will refute it (the guarantee of scientificity for Popper).

Alas, only the fanatical supporters of reality react; reality, for its part, does not seem to wish to prove you wrong. Quite to the contrary, every kind of simulacrum parades around in it. And reality, filching the idea, henceforth adorns itself with all the rhetoric of simulation. It is the simulacrum which ensures the continuity of the real today, the simulacrum which now conceals not the truth, but the fact that there isn't any – that is to say, the continuity of the nothing.

Such is the paradox of all thought which disputes the validity of the real: when it sees itself robbed of its own concept. Events, bereft of meaning in themselves, steal meaning from us. They adapt to the most fantastical hypotheses, just as natural species and viruses adapt to the most hostile environments. They have an extraordinary mimetic capacity: no longer is it theories which adapt to events, but the reverse. And, in so doing, they mystify us, for a theory which is verified is no longer a theory. It's terrifying to see the idea coincide with the reality. These are the death-throes of the concept. The epiphany of the real is the twilight of its concept.

We have lost that lead which ideas had over the world, that distance which meant that an idea remained an idea. Thought has to be exceptional, anticipatory and at the margin – has to be the projected shadow of future events. Today, we are lagging behind events. They may sometimes give the impression of receding; in fact, they passed us long ago. The simulated disorder of things has moved faster than we have. The reality effect has succumbed to acceleration – anamorphosis of speed. Events, in their being, are never behind themselves, are always out ahead of their meaning. Hence the delay of interpretation, which is now merely the retrospective form of the unforeseeable event.

What are we to do, then? What becomes of the heterogeneity of thought in a world won over to the craziest hypotheses? When everything conforms, beyond even our wildest hopes, to the ironic, critical, alternative, catastrophic model?

Well, that is paradise: we are beyond the Last Judgement, in immortality. The only problem is to survive there. For there the irony, the challenging, the anticipation, the maleficence come to an end, as inexorably as hope dies at the gates of hell. And it is indeed there that hell begins, the hell of the unconditional realization of all ideas, the hell of the real. You can see why, as Adorno says, concepts prefer to scupper themselves rather than reach that point.

Something else has been stolen from us: indifference. The power of indifference, which is the quality of the mind, as opposed to the play of differences, which is the characteristic of the world. Now, this has been stolen from us by a world grown indifferent, as the extravagance of thought has been stolen from us by an extravagant world. When things, events, refer one to another and to their undifferentiated concept, then the equivalence of the world meets and cancels out the indifference of thought – and we have boredom. No more altercations; nothing at stake. It is the parting of the dead sea.

How fine indifference was in a world that was not indifferent – in a different, convulsive, contradictory world, a world with issues and passions! That being the case, indifference immediately became an issue and a passion itself. It could pre-empt the indifference of the world, and turn that pre-emption into an event. Today, it is difficult to be more indifferent to their reality than the facts themselves, more indifferent to their meaning than images. Our operational world is an apathetic world. Now, what good is it being passionless in a world without passion, or detached in a world without desire?

It is not a question of defending radical thought. Every idea one defends is presumed guilty, and every idea that cannot defend itself deserves to disappear. On the other hand, one must fight all charges of irresponsibility, nihilism or despair. Radical thought is never depressive. On this point, there is total misunderstanding. Ideological and moralistic critique, obsessed with meaning and content, obsessed with the political finality of discourse, never takes into account writing, the act of writing, the poetic, ironic, allusive force of language, of the juggling with meaning. It does not see that the resolution of meaning is to be found there – in the form itself, the formal materiality of expression.

Meaning, for its part, is always unhappy. Analysis is, by definition, unhappy, since it is born of critical disillusionment. But language, for its part, is happy, even when referring to a world without illusion and without hope. That might even be the definition of a radical thinking: a happy form and an intelligence without hope.

Critics, being unhappy by nature, always choose ideas as their battleground. They do not see that if discourse always tends to produce meaning, language and writing, for their part, always create illusion – they are the living illusion of meaning, the resolution of the infelicity of meaning by the felicity of language. And this is surely the only political – or transpolitical – act that can be accomplished by the person who writes.

As for ideas, everyone has them. More than they need. What counts is the poetic singularity of the analysis. That alone can justify writing, not the wretched critical objectivity of ideas. There never will be any resolving the contradictoriness of ideas, except in the energy and felicity of language. 'I do not paint sadness and loneliness,' says Hopper. 'What I wanted to do was to paint sunlight on the side of a house.'

At any rate, better a despairing analysis in felicitous language than an optimistic analysis in an infelicitous language that is maddeningly tedious and demoralizingly platitudinous, as is most often the case. The absolute tediousness secreted by that idealistic, voluntaristic thought is the secret sign of its despair – as regards both the world and its own discourse. That is where true depressive thought is to be found, among those who speak only of the transcending and transforming of the world, when they are incapable of transfiguring their own language.

Radical thought is a stranger to all resolving of the world in the direction of an objective reality and its deciphering. It does not decipher. It anagrammatizes, it disperses concepts and ideas and, by its reversible sequencing, takes account both of meaning and of the fundamental illusoriness of meaning. Language takes account of the very illusion of language as definitive stratagem and, through it, of the illusion of the world as infinite trap, as seduction of the mind, as spiriting away of all our mental faculties. While it is a vehicle of meaning, it is at the same time a superconductor of illusion and non-meaning. Language is merely the involuntary accomplice of communication – by its very form it appeals to the spiritual and material imagination of sounds and rhythm, to the dispersal of meaning in the event of language. This passion for artifice, for illusion, is the passion for undoing that too-beauteous constellation of meaning. And for letting the imposture of the world show through, which is its enigmatic function, and the mystification of the world, which is its secret. While at the same time letting its own imposture show through – the impostor, not the *composteur* [composing stick] of meaning. This passion has the upper hand in the free and witty use of language, in the witty play of writing. Where that artifice is not taken into account, not only is its charm lost, but the meaning itself cannot be resolved.

Cipher, do not decipher. Work over the illusion. Create illusion to create an event. Make enigmatic what is clear, render unintelligible what is only too intelligible, make the event itself unreadable. Accentuate the false transparency of the world to spread a terroristic confusion about it, or the germs or viruses of a radical illusion – in other words, a radical disillusioning of the real. Viral, pernicious thought, corrosive of meaning, generative of an erotic perception of reality's turmoil.

Promote a clandestine trade in ideas, of all inadmissible ideas, of unassailable ideas, as the liquor trade had to be promoted in the 1930s. For we are already in a state of full-scale prohibition. Thought has become an extremely rare commodity, prohibited and prohibitive, which has to be cultivated in secret places following esoteric rules.

Everything must take place in secret. We shall take the view that the official thought market is universally corrupt and implicated in the prohibition of thought by the dominant clerisy. Every intervention by critical, enlightened and right-thinking intellectuals, all of them politically correct even when they do not know it, will be considered vacuous and shameful.

Eradicate within oneself every trace of the intellectual conspiracy. Spirit away the reality file to wipe out all its conclusions. It is, in fact, reality which is fomenting its own disavowal, preparing its own ruin by way of our lack of reality. Hence the feeling that this whole affair – the world, thought and language – has come from elsewhere, and might disappear as though by magic. For the world does not seek to exist more, nor to persist in existing. It seeks, rather, the wittiest way to escape reality. It seeks, by way of thought, what can lead it to its doom.

The absolute rule is to give back more than you were given. Never less, always more. The absolute rule of thought is to give back the world as it was given to us – unintelligible. And, if possible, to render it a little more unintelligible.

NOTES

1   A reference to the famous section of Sade's *La philosophie dans le boudoir* entitled 'Français, encore un effort si vous voulez être républicains'.
2   This phrase echoes the socialist dictum that the workers themselves will bring about their own emancipation.
3   The references here are to Dino Buzzati's *Il crollo della Baliverna* and to Jorge Luis Borges, 'Of Exactitude in Science', in *A Universal History of Infamy*, Allen Lane, London 1973, p. 141.

14

Paroxysm: Interviews with Philippe Petit

Endgame

Philippe Petit: At the beginning of your book *The Illusion of the End* (1992/94), you give the impression of having taken leave of history once and for all. You speak of the disappearance of history, of the idea that 'history, meaning and progress are no longer able to reach their escape velocity', and that the event, as a result of being driven out of its original sphere by information and the media, no longer circulates in memories, but in computer memory banks. 'History', you also write, 'is no longer able to transcend itself...; it is...imploding into current events.'

Doesn't diagnosis of this kind mean that all hope of political change is condemned from the outset? How does it allow us to escape from the world of those who believe in nothing and seem fated to ruminate on that nothing? Has history taken its leave of you, or is this you signing its death certificate?

Jean Baudrillard: Neither of those things. In that chapter, which I called 'Pataphysics of the Year 2000', I set out from the idea that we shall not get back to history as it was before information and the media, that the excess of history or the excess of eventfulness cancelled out the very possibility of historical action. It isn't that there are more events, but the event in itself is multiplied by its dissemination, by news and information. I'd say that it's because everything has become history that it's no longer possible to believe in history. Mentalities, daily life, sexuality – everything has been historicalized. It is, then, rather by excess than by rarefaction that we have gradually lost the concept and meaning of history. This is not the end of history in Fukuyama's sense, by the resolution of all the contradictions to which it had given rise, but the dilution of history as event: its media *mise en scène*, its excess of visibility. The continuity of time, which is a way of defining history (for there to be a possible recurrence of a sequence of meaning there has necessarily to be a past, a present and a future, with a continuity between them), is less and less certain. With instant information, there's no longer any time for history itself. In a sense, it doesn't have time to take place. It's short-circuited. To point this out isn't to believe in nothing any more, as you put it, but to register this curving back of history and try to thwart its lethal effects.

PP: Why put so much stress, then, on the idea that 'imagining the future is beyond us'? This suggests that we must always expect the worst. And then the fall of communism was no small event! European history well and truly awoke from its dogmatic slumbers. Even if the landscape after the battle in the Balkans is, to say the least, damaged....

JB: With the end of communism, we told ourselves: 'History is beginning again'. This is a form of the incantation or hallucination of a new perspective. The history of Central and Eastern Europe had been frozen and, once unfrozen, it took on a new look. It isn't the reappearance of a history in progress, with a future in its kitbag, that has emerged. It's the revival of a history that has already taken place. It's a phantom history that's coming back to haunt the post-communist societies. 'A reverse rewriting of the whole twentieth century.' A collage of the residues of history. In the homeostatic space of the new world order, the two systems are exchanging their residues by a perverse contamination. Unfrozen liberty in the East and magnified, museified liberty in the West are the two sides of a single coin. And the parallel events, such as nationalism, which we see re-emerging, no longer have the same meaning in a history in the making and a history being unmade, in an ascending history or a repentant history.

PP: They no longer have the same meaning, but they do have meaning, none the less....

JB: Events collide and succeed one another, but they don't engender new relations of force. They are, as it were, stuck in the past, in past problems. Yesterday's problems are there, but we no longer know how to solve them and there is no means of making way for some new event. There was, admittedly, an illusion of a perspective in 1989, but we very quickly saw that the protagonists of that 'happy ending' had no more cards up their sleeve. So as the recycling of history began, we began to live out the film backwards....

Today we look solely to the symbolic term of the millennium to set us off again. The year 2000 as sole fatidical non-event. A magical waiting, itself millenarian, for non-parousia. In the meanwhile, everyone's lying low – creeping catalepsy, collective catatonia, eyes riveted on the countdown. But this is an empty suspense: it's as though the whole of the twentieth century were emptying itself of its substance in these few years, as though it were scaling down all its demands to the point of wiping out the very traces of its history.

PP: Perhaps. But you can't deny that communism has failed and the collapse of the Soviet system has actually occurred!

JB: The communist system and the Berlin Wall didn't fall outwards, as a mark of openness and freedom, but inwards, as a mark of disintegration and of a dismantling that was violent, but had no liberatory consequences. They self-destructed, leaving behind an empty space, as when buildings implode. The only thing that collapse released was the contagious germs of collapse. And this, in fact, is what happened with the USSR: what immediately gravitated, or radiated, out from there were ferments of deliquescence and disappearance, or of blackmail by threat of disappearance, which the East European countries have joyously exported to the West, in exchange for which they have, in the guise of freedom, earned themselves irradiation by free-market capitalism and a system of values much more efficient than their own, but one that is equally deliquescent. An exchange of courtesies in which we can see that the Wall protected the West from the East as much as the opposite. In which we can see that communism at least preserved the fiction of Western values. Which might make one hope for its rehabilitation, or its return, or something equivalent – as a last-ditch measure for re-polarizing the world.

PP: In the meantime, what is happening?

JB: The two systems are contaminating each other. The one sends the other its technologies and markets; the other sends back its pollution, viruses and angst. Things aren't finally settled, but I think what has triumphed isn't capitalism but the global, so to speak, and the price paid has been the disappearance of the universal in terms of a value system. We are, admittedly, seeing a kind of excrescence of human rights and democracy, but only in so far as their efficacy has long since disappeared. We're no longer in a power struggle between two systems, but in a kind of negative competition to see who'll be first to get their hands on their own values and sell them off – it's a liquidation race.

Communism and its marvellous, life-size collapse – that is to say, its collapse on a grand historical scale – is the liquidation of the social, of the political as idea, as value, as utopian ideal, in the disaster of achieved utopia. But isn't it the same in the West: the life-size failure of the achieved utopia of happiness? The collapse of the Western value system is precisely correlative with the collapse of communism in Eastern Europe. Western stupefaction, that of a happiness fuelled by hormones and animal feed, this flabby, technological ecstasy, this interactive virus we pass over to Eastern Europe in exchange for its opening-up to democracy, is even worse than the opposite contagion of totalitarianism, of rigid control and bureaucratic inertia. It's the corruption of the visible, as against the corruption of the hidden, the secret, the repressed. The year 1989 can be seen to have marked the beginning of the immense reciprocal contamination of the two worlds. And perhaps the deliquescence, the distintegration of the capitalist world, of its principles and values, even preceded that of socialism in the East? Perhaps this latter fell into line with the Western world's indifference to its own values – no longer having before it any ideology, any political will worthy of the name? All that's different is today forced to capitulate before the undifferen-tiated universe. Entropy has won, the entropy of the market and democracy, pulling irresistibly towards a generalized exchangism of all values. Hence the wave of revisionism sweeping across a Western world conscious of this irresistible degradation, and tempted finally to restore some good old values (including that of communism) to rescue its own identity. Here we have communism at last become a humanism!

PP: What is capitalism for you today?

JB: I really don't know. It's a sort of dilution of the universal in a global state of affairs. It's a sort of purely operational general equivalent. It no longer even invovles any opposing or negative values, such as revolution or the indignity of labour. For a long time the communists proposed an antagonistic system. There's no antagonistic system today simply because the system itself no longer has any values or gravity. All that remains is an automatic transcription of the world into the global.

PP: What distinction do you draw between the universal and the global?

JB: In the global, all differences fade and de-intensify, giving way to a pure and simple circulation of exchanges. All liberties fade before the mere liberation of exchange. Globalization and universality don't go together; they might be said, rather, to be mutually exclusive. Globalization is the globalization of technologies, the market, tourism, information. Universality is the universality of values, human rights, freedoms, culture, democracy. Globalization seems irreversible; the universal might be said, rather, to be on its way out. At least as it has constituted itself as a system of values on the scale of Western modernity, which is something that has no equivalent in any other culture. Even a living, contemporary culture like the Japanese has no term for it. No word to refer to a system of values which regards itself as attuned to all cultures and their difference but which, paradoxically, does not conceive itself as relative, and aspires, in all ingenuousness, to be the ideal transcendence of all the others. We don't imagine for a moment that the universal might merely be the particular style of thinking of the West, its specific product – an original one, admittedly, but in the end no more exportable than any other local product. Yet this is how the Japanese see it – as a specific, Western feature – and, far from signing up to an abstract concept, they, by a strange twist, relativize our universal and incorporate it into their singularity.

PP: Why are you so absolutely intent on the universal dissolving into the particular culture of a people? I don't mind admitting with you that rationalist moralism has had a chequered history, and that the betrayal of the universal denounced by Benda in 1927 is no longer the issue today, but I can't see why the reconstruction of the Enlightenment ideal would be such an impossible task? After Adorno, there is Habermas. . . .

JB: Every culture worthy of the name meets its ruin in the universal. Every culture which universalizes itself loses its singularity and dies away. This is how it is with those we've destroyed by their enforced assimilation, but it's also how it is with ours in its pretension to universality. The difference is that the others died of their singularity, which is a noble death, whereas we're dying from the loss of all singularity, from the extermination of all our values, which is a senseless death. We believe that the fate of every value is to be elevated to universality, without gauging the mortal danger that promotion represents: far from being an elevation, it is a reduction or, alternatively, an elevation to the degree zero of value. In Enlightenment times, universalization occurred at the top, by an upward progression. Today, it happens at the bottom, by a neutralization of values due to their proliferation and indefinite extension. This is how it is with human rights, democracy, etc.: their expansion corresponds to their weakest definition, their maximum entropy. Degree Xerox of value. It's the triumph of *la pensée unique*[1] over universal thought. What becomes globalized is, first of all, the market, the promiscuity of all exchanges and all products, the perpetual flow of money. In cultural terms, it's the promiscuity of all signs and all values – or, in other words, pornography. For the worldwide broadcasting and parading of everything and anything over the networks is pornography. There's no need for sexual obscenity; this interactive copulation suffices. At the end of this process, there's no longer any difference between the global and the universal. The universal itself is globalized: democracy, human rights, circulate precisely like any global product, like oil or capital. Given all this, we may ask ourselves whether the universal hasn't already succumbed to its own critical mass, and if it has ever had anything but lip-service paid to it, or found a place anywhere but in official moralities. At any rate, for us the mirror of the universal is broken (we can, in fact, see in this something like the mirror-stage of humanity). But perhaps this represents an opportunity, for, in the fragments of this broken mirror, all the singularities re-emerge. The ones we thought threatened survive; the ones we thought had disappeared revive. The increasingly intense resistances to globalization – social and political resistances, which may seem like an archaic rejection of modernity at all costs – have to be seen as harbouring an original defiant reaction to the sway of the universal. Something which goes beyond the economic and the political. A kind of agonizing revisionism in respect of the established positions of modernity, in respect of the idea of progress and history – a kind of rejection not only of the famous global technostructure, but of the mental structure of the identification of all cultures and all continents in the concept of the universal. This resurgence – or even insurrection – of singularity may assume violent, anomalous, irrational aspects from the viewpoint of 'enlightened' thought – it may take ethnic, religious or linguistic forms but also, at the individual level, temperamental and neurotic ones. But it would be a basic error (the very error one sees emerging in the moral orchestration of the politically correct discourse common to all the powers that be, and to many 'intellectuals') to condemn all these upsurges out of hand as populist, archaic or even terroristic. Everything which constitutes an event today is done against the universal, against that abstract universality (including the frantic antagonism of Islam to Western values – it's because it's the most vehement protest against this Western globalization that Islam is the number one enemy today). If we will not understand this, we'll be caught up in an endless and pointless wrestling match between a universal thought assured of its power and good conscience and an ever greater number of implacable singularities. Even in our societies, which are acculturated to the universal, you can see that none of what has been sacrificed to this concept has really disappeared. It has simply gone underground. And what is now running backwards is a whole self-styled progressive history, a whole evolutionism crystallized on its end point – an end point which has, in fact, in the meantime been lost sight of. That utopia has fallen apart today, and its deep-level dislocation is advancing even more quickly than its consolidation by force.

PP: That dislocated utopia is not entirely unlike Nietzsche's last man. It's a standard democratic utopia reduced to its simplest expression. . . .

JB: Its congenital illusion is precisely the democratic illusion. We have before us a complex three-term arrangement: there is the globalization of exchanges, the universality of values and the singularity of forms (languages, cultures, individuals and characters, but also chance, accident, etc. – all that the universal, in keeping with its law, impugns as an exception or an anomaly). Now, as universal values lose some of their authority and legitimacy, the situation changes and becomes more radical. So long as they could assert themselves as mediating values, they were (more or less well) able to integrate the singularities as differences, in a universal culture of difference. They can no longer do this, however, as triumphant globalization sweeps away all differences and values, ushering in a perfectly in-different (un)culture. And once the universal has disappeared, once the universal is out of the equation, all that remains is the all-powerful global technostructure standing over against the singularities which have gone back to the wild state and been thrown back on their own devices.

The universal has had its historical chance. But today, confronted with a new world order to which there is no alternative, with an irrevocable globalization on the one hand and the waywardness or tenacious insurrection of singularities on the other, the concepts of liberty, democracy and human rights cut a very pale figure indeed, being merely the phantoms of a vanished universal. And it's hard to imagine that universal rising from its ashes, or to believe things can be sorted out by the mere play of politics – this latter being caught up in the same deregulation, and having barely any more substance to it than intellectual or moral power. Matters are not, however, finally settled, even if it's now all up with universal values. In the void left by the universal, the stakes have risen, and globalization isn't certain to be the winner. In the face of its homogenizing, solvent power, we can see heterogeneous forces springing up all over, forces which are not only different, but antagonistic and irreducible.

PP: Are you wholly intent on demoralizing the West?

JB: The demoralization of the West is constitutive of its history. I didn't invent it. 'The new sentimental order', the order of disaffection, repentance and the 'victim society', is the extension of a crisis of meaning which began in the nineteenth century with the fallout from the Industrial Revolution and colonization, and has continued throughout our long twentieth century. For thirty years we've been living in the last phase of it – or rather, the penultimate one – that is to say, the paroxystic phase. Other people's misery and humanitarian catastrophes have become our last stamping ground for adventurers.

What's called 'the new world order' has nothing of a historical field about it any more. It's a kind of horizontal field in which everyone must find their mark. If they don't, or won't, they will be forced to. From this point of view, the 'new world order' is a fundamentalist concept. It's the fundamentalism of the void, but all the fiercer for that. The essential fault line today runs through Islam, but it also runs through the heart of every so-called civilized, democratic country – and certainly even through each of us.

PP: Let's desert the West!

JB: At all events, we have to look to other worlds than the Western. The underdeveloped or developing societies are no longer what they were, since the very concept of development has been a damp squib. Precisely in their inability to achieve a coherent democratic (economic and political) principle, these societies are perhaps the foreshadowing of a later state of events, in which all societies, including our own, will have to confront the collapse of all these fine rational principles (but the 'advanced' societies have hardly achieved such a coherent demo-cratic principle themselves, and what they have handed on to the rest of the world has been the failed, caricatured version of the model). This fateful situation is perhaps an opportunity, then. And in this sense, it is *those* societies, in their very confusion, which are in the van, not *our* Western societies, which are so proud of their technological lead and so full also of a fierce and *bien-pensant* evolutionism which prevents them from thinking anything but the world supremacy of their model. That supremacy is merely virtual – and today, moreover, it employs virtual technologies (now, technology, in common with every other medium, is double-edged, and the power of the virtual is a virtual power).

Furthermore, this model is itself going to the dogs; it's on its last legs, and is merely the ruin, the shadow, of itself. Or, more exactly, it could be said to be like the man who has lost his shadow, and has become transparent, irradiated by his own energy and infected at a deep level by his own viruses. Even from the standpoint of the evolutionism to which they adhere, the pole position of these societies is, then, problematic and imperilled. They are seeing the resurgence of all the singularities and anomalies they claimed to have abolished, and we can see them, like the societies of the Third World (which will also have served to prefigure our situation), breaking down economically and politically. Even the most solidly established nations are beginning to break up (Corsica, the Basque Country, Lombardy, Russia, Canada. Once the mirror of deterrence has been shattered, the end of the twofold division of the world is making way for general dissemination, for fractality). The future lies with the adolescent societies which will not have taken the route through economics and politics, but can cope very well with the technological without burdening themselves with all these – humanist and rational – historical categories; or, in other words, with values which are in any case turning round against themselves today, and revealing their impotence.

PP: When you say that 'in most current conflicts, all that is involved is a police-style "homeopathic violence" internal to the system', I find that hard to follow. How can you speak of homeopathic violence with regard to Iraq or the former Yugoslavia?

JB: With these conflicts, we're no longer in historical violence of the kind that might give birth, dialectically, to a history. What is dominant is an absolute model of order and peace – homeostatic, if you like, rather than homeopathic. We no longer wish to wage war, but we act in the name of a duty to contain all possible disorder. The Americans parachuted peace into Bosnia in exactly the same way as they parachuted war into Iraq. What we have here is a model in which peace and war are concertina-ed, the two being indistinct today, as Orwell accurately foresaw. From the standpoint of this parachuting operation, whether or not there are thousands of deaths is immaterial. The Gulf operation could have been carried out without a single fatality: this was in fact the case on the American side. That was a war that was clean from the technological and conceptual points of view. But this is no longer a war. It is the same police-style violence in peace and war.

PP: Both history and war are losing their substance. 'The West is militarily impotent to react to Serbian aggression to the precise degree that it finds it impossible to risk the life of a single soldier,' you wrote in your column in *Libération* while Sarajevo was being bombed. Perhaps war has no future in Western Europe, but doesn't it still have one in Eastern Europe?

JB: Violence is a relation of otherness. Between the Pentagon and the Iraqis, the whole space was taken up by technology. There was no room for the violence of war properly so-called. In Bosnia, the violence is real, terrible, ambiguous. And it isn't just an old quarrel between *frères ennemis*. It's also, taken all in all, a form of revolt against the world order. The violence of war is not a mere resurgence of the past; it can express a sort of surge of vital energy, like hatred, against a 'cleansing' in all fields at the global level.

PP: Wouldn't it be more accurate to speak of emergence rather than resurgence?

JB: I entirely agree that we should view the war in the Balkans in its radical contemporary setting: that of globalization and the identity-based reactions it provokes. Seen that way, the exacerbation of national, linguistic and religious sentiment, or of a sense of identity, is a form of singular resistance. It doesn't arise in the name of any universal. It doesn't seek to organize itself. Singularities don't organize among themselves; they confront one another. They have no mission to discover a universal ascent of humanity. I even believe they are the product of the universal's disappearing beneath the global order. Every community fights for a kind of exceptionality and singularity. From this it makes a set of rules – and possibly a murderous, destructive one.

PP: Isn't citizenship a form of historical goal?

JB: The problem is one of knowing what might give it form. Where would the new balance be between the universal and the particular? Where would the system of representation be which is capable of giving form to an identity that respected the universal?

PP: Why do you think global time is the only time there can be?

JB: I don't know if it's the only time there can be, but I see it is coming. It's succeeded in creating a monopoly out of a balanced plurality. So these fine ideas of citizenship, which may be shared by individuals on the ground, have already been kidnapped, taken hostage. Moreover, the global system speaks a universalistic, pluralistic language very well. That's its official language, and that's what it operates behind. All the pious values of citizenship are being liquidated. To these old values and that distant utopia of the universal I prefer values which are their own justification in a kind of existential 'acting-out': 'I exist. I'm so-and-so, I exist.' That is to say, an assertion of identity, not as a desperate acknowledgement, but as a challenge.

PP: But identity isn't singularity?

JB: Indeed it isn't. These reactions are the desperate search for a mirror in which to find a self-image. Today, whether it be groups, nations or individuals, people are no longer fighting alienation but a kind of total dispossession.

PP: When small nations fight for their existence, how is that a dispossession?

JB: Because they are already virtually condemned. They are in the ebbing of identity. They are no longer in a battle for an ascending identity, for a sovereignty. They are fighting with their backs to the wall and for a cause which is not glorious, because identity is a weak value, a neutral value. They are simply fighting to prove they exist, or sometimes even, like the Armenians, to prove they no longer exist, that they have been massacred.

PP: On identity I can agree. But history! On page 23 of *The Illusion of the End*, you write:

[W]e no longer make history. We have become reconciled with it and protect it like an endangered masterpiece. Times have changed. We have today a perfectly pious 'vision' of the Revolution, cast in terms of the Rights of Man. Not even a nostalgic vision, but one recycled in the terms of postmodern intellectual comfort. A vision which allows us to eliminate Saint-Just from the *Dictionnaire de la Révolution*. 'Overrated rhetoric', says François Furet, perfect historian of the repentance of the Terror and of glory.

Does this pious vision of the Revolution apply to contemporary historical consciousness?

JB: It's on the way to becoming our common consciousness. The cleaning-up of the French Revolution, the assertion that the Revolution failed because it ended in terror – this kind of repentance and retrospective cleansing is merely revisionism.

But it's no exception. It's incredible how everything today is of the order of cleansing. The museification of events, the rehabilitations and commemorations, are all aimed at this laundering of events. That the powers that be should do such work is their affair, but that intellectuals and those who were actors in history should afford themselves the cynical luxury of carrying out this cleansing is scandalous. Do you know a country which isn't a product of the ravages of history? History isn't made by historical rationality alone. The societies which haven't allowed themselves violent, extravagant events have remained in a cataleptic state. What is it with these fine souls rectifying history? I find historical Pharisaism repugnant....

PP: Yet you were an '*intellectuel engagé*'.

JB: More *dégagé*. The so-called committed intellectuals have had so little influence on politics, in spite of their reflections on the matter. The concept of history, such as comes into general use in the nineteenth century, corresponds to the moment when we were beginning to leave history. It's always the same. It's at the moment when we begin to intellectualize a phenomenon that in reality it disappears. With Sartre we managed to maintain a kind of nostalgia, but it was already over. 'Committed' theory is always a desperate attempt to reconstruct what's on the point of vanishing.

PP: Foucault thought it was possible to make a diagnosis of the present.

JB: Diagnosis no longer has the objective meaning it had in Foucault. I don't believe this diagnosis is still possible. Is it possible today to record things objectively? I doubt it. Scientists hardly make diagnoses of objects – which are ungraspable – any longer, but they build up all kinds of hypotheses. Can we do any more than that? I'm not sure we can. One may analyse situations with the same intelligence as Sartre. But that's a level of intellectual gratification. And yet the other level remains, the level of hypotheses. Is it an interesting hypothesis to reconsider history in the light of a generic concept? I don't think so.

PP: Let's concede that. You no longer believe in history as a rational concept, you no longer believe in the promises of history. But what about the criticism of the world in the name of its own promises, as Adorno put it? Do you still believe in that? Do you still, with Gilles Deleuze, believe 'not in another world, but in the bond between man and the world, in love or in life'?[2]

JB: The world, if we take it as we find it, has no history. It has, at best, a destiny, but how are we to know what that is? How are we to know if what's in play is the destination of the *genre humain* as it was born at the beginning of its history, a humanity whose genealogy we can trace out, a humanity that is perpetually ascending? What has changed is that the stakes have shifted to the level of the species, not the historico-cultural entity. It's the destiny of the species that's in play. Now, it's much more difficult to believe in a project of the species. Even in our own day, nine-tenths of humanity is outside history, outside a system of interpretation and recording which was born with modern times and will disappear. History is a kind of luxury Western societies have afforded themselves. It's 'their' history. The fact that it seems to be disappearing is unfortunate for us, but it allows destiny, which has always been the lot of other cultures, to take over. The other cultures have never lacked destiny, whereas we, in our Western societies, are bereft of it.

PP: Bergson didn't have to deal with unemployment and the crisis of work. There are social syndromes, such as the disintegration of work and of wage-based society, which are of the order of unprecedented changes. Isn't this a new historico-political task?

JB: Don't capital and labour have the same destiny? Can we describe work today as a productive force and as the basis of wealth? So long as labour was experienced by the majority of human beings as an alienation, it was possible to allot it a subversive role. Man faced up to the machines as best he could. It was said that they were alienating, and man tried to free himself from them. But in our new logistics of man-machine interaction, we're no longer dealing with labour. Man and the machine are interfaced. There's no longer any subject of labour. There's an operation. We're no longer in a situation of transcendent, vertical confrontation. We are, rather, in a horizontal situation of functioning and networks. Nowadays, someone who works is pretty much a corpse they can't manage to get rid of. The System would quite like to get rid of it, but it can't quite manage the trick, and the suffering workers don't want to lose their *raison d'être* either. This is paradoxical. But in the overall picture now, labour no longer figures as a ruptural energy, nor even as a source of wealth: it's merely a form of identity claim. Modern technologies, all this high-tech equipment, are no longer so much extensions of man, as McLuhan used to say, but human beings are now becoming, rather, a kind of extension of the logistical system – and then what comeback can there be? How can they refer to their own labour, since this no longer has any true definition? There's no longer really a price, or value, of labour. Labour is caught up so much in multiplying interconnected networks, like information, that it can't even really be evaluated. It's caught in that speculative form of work that is employment, which is no longer part of a social contract, but quoted now as an economic indicator. And it isn't just workers who are in this position. There are no more Sartre-style group-subjects. Even the capitalists, the bosses, the strategists are no longer in the position of subjects, any more than intellectuals are. They're just playing extra time....

PP: Paul Virilio, who is more Christian than you, thinks intellectuals have a duty to resist the global forms of domination. They are, he says, in the position of the painters who resisted photography in the last century. Aren't you, in your way, a resistance fighter waiting to go over to the offensive?

JB: We worked together for a long time with Virilio, very closely and without any problems. At the time I didn't see his Christianity surface. It surprises me, because his books deny the very possibility of a morality of resistance. His analysis of the cyberworld is intransigent, inexorable and, if I may venture the term, *fatale*. I find it remarkable and very fine. But I don't believe in what he sets against that world. I hope he believes in it. He puts himself in an apocalyptic position, in the position of an anti-apocalyptic prophet, while remaining convinced that the worst may occur. In the end we diverged on this point, as I don't believe in this real apocalypse. I don't believe in realism, at any event, nor in a linear maturing of the apocalypse. Ultimately, if we could hope for this total accident, then the only thing would be to precipitate it; we shouldn't resist it.

The coming of the virtual itself is our apocalypse, and it deprives us of the real event of the apocalypse. Such is our paradoxical situation, but we have to push the paradox to the limit. And Virilio in fact does this, while reserving a fallback argument for himself.

PP: What do you mean by saying 'we have to push the paradox to the limit'?

JB: Recognizing that the movement of the system itself is irreversible, that there's no possible get-out within the logic of the system. That logic really is global in the sense that it has absorbed all negativities, including the humanist, universalist resistance, etc. Pushing to the limit means acknowledging this irreversibility and pushing it to the limit of its possibilities, to the point of collapse. Bringing it to saturation point, to the point where the system itself creates the accident. Thought contributes to this acceleration. It anticipates its end. This is the provocative function of thought: having no illusions as to its critical function or to its 'commitment', but giving all it's got to imagining the end.

PP: Why are you so keen on this notion of irreversibility? It's odd. The globalization of the economy doesn't lead irrevocably to the homogenization of the world; it doesn't prevent us from reconstructing politics either, does it?

JB: You can always fight the global in the name of the universal. I prefer the direct confrontation between globalization and all the antagonistic singularities. To maintain the humanist mediations at all costs is to put an obstacle in the way of that confrontation in its radicality.

PP: To what extent is your theory a justifiable response to the ordeal of globalization?

JB: I don't claim that. I claim that theory must anticipate.
We have to recognize the clear-out being effected by the system. There's no redeeming of history. I believe it's better to focus on the radical originality of a situation. The thought which flows from this has a chance of being itself more original. This is the opposite of repentance. The judgement of the intellectual world is too often the judgement of repentance.

PP: Your obsession would have pleased Witkiewicz!

JB: It's true there's no longer any history 'in progress'. But we have to distinguish between the event and history. History assumes a continuity, an explanatory principle. By contrast, what happens may run against history, against politics. 'Sixty-eight seemed to me to be a discontinuity of that type and, in this sense, a harbinger. Since then, all that has really constituted an event has been done against politics and history. I've been accused of being on the side of the system on the pretext that I describe the perverse effects of these things. That's wrong. Underlying what I write is … not hope, but events irreducible to the involutive logic of global systems. The only nihilistic analysis of events is the pious one. Every radical analysis is stunningly optimistic!

NOTES

1   *'La pensée unique'* has in recent years been one of the watchwords of French political discussion. It implies a single-track thinking of the kind once referred to in Britain by the acronym TINA ('There is no alternative'). The editor of *Le Monde diplomatique* defined it as 'the translation into ideological terms, with universalist pretensions, of the interests of a set of economic forces, in particular those of international capital', and identified its major sources as the great economic and monetary institutions: the World Bank, the IMF, the OECD, GATT, the European Commission, etc. (Ignacio Ramonet, 'La pensée unique', *Le Monde diplomatique*, 490, January 1995, p. 1). [*Trans.*]
2   Gilles Deleuze, *Cinéma 2: L'Image-temps*, Paris: Minuit, 1985.

Index